PRAISE FOR NIKKI STARCAT SHIELDS

The Elements of Creativity: The Sacred Path to Writing Your Book

"Nikki has done a most brilliant job here of showing writers & authors-to-be how to implement necessary intention and structure, while increasing deep inspiration. This is the genius of earth meeting heaven, of commitment making room for awe, of 'doing the work' while being divinely assisted along the way. As an author of three books, I was delighted at how much I learned here! I already know my next writing project will be smoother and easier as a result. This book is for newbies and experts alike. Discovering how to flow with life makes everything so much more straightforward, including accomplishing creative endeavors. Let *The Elements of Creativity* do exactly this for you. Let it be your companion, experienced teacher and friend for the journey. Let it bring your book from percolating idea into glorious form."

-Kris Ferraro, International Energy Coach, speaker, and author of *Your Difference Is Your Strength, Manifesting,* and the #1 Amazon bestseller *Energy Healing*

The Heart of the Goddess: A Handbook for Living Soulfully

"The material is both challenging and accessible while the read is truly beautiful ... graceful, elegant writing. I don't recall the last time I read something I couldn't put down for the joy of reading the next beautifully crafted sentence. Nikki Starcat Shields provides a level of transparency that is brave, honest, and relatable. Easily digestible as a single entity, yet entirely useful as a sort of workbook, I find myself referring to individual chapters as I encounter real life parallels. I highly recommend this beautiful book for anyone on, or seeking to start, an intentional spiritual journey." – Debra J.

"Nikki Starcat Shields has written a book that can be a powerful tool for everyone, including beginners, interested in discovering more about the Feminine Divine. The work that she has created is very beautiful and written in a unique style that is highly readable and b ˙ ˙
Shannon P.

Cultivating Self-Love: Your Path to Wholeness

"This is a beautiful book about what it means to real
amazing tools to help on the journey to self-love and is written in a way that makes it hard to put down until the very end. Once I finished it, I was

excited to go back and read it again, more slowly so that I could truly absorb all of the amazing wisdom and start putting the concepts and ideas into practice. I am sure it will be an amazing resource to use over and over as I travel this journey of self-discovery and self-love." – D. Ford

"It's such a warm and refreshing book about self-discovery and appreciation. I love to read it when I need to tap into my inner core. It really helps ground me. I love that there are personal growth exercises that you can use as a practice to observe yourself and figure out your path. We don't give ourselves enough attention and time in a positive way. This book allows you to recognize yourself as your greatest ally." – A. Birkeland

"A particularly excellent book, with many gems and thought-provoking moments... Nikki's writing style is like those moments where your best friend sits you down and tells you the truths you need to hear. Each chapter had pearls of wisdom I held onto and mulled around before going into the next chapter. If you're looking for some simple but effective ways to cut through your own inner monologue and reprogram your brain with love and gratitude, this is a simple, loving book that points you in the right direction without preaching." – Keri Alley

Centered In Spirit: Crafting Your Daily Practice

"I couldn't have picked this book up at a more perfect time – I had been needing some inspiration for my on-again, off-again daily spiritual practice, and *Centered in Spirit: Crafting Your Daily Practice* was exactly what I was looking for. While this book would be perfect for someone interested in developing a daily practice, it's also incredibly useful for those of us who have an existing routine that needs a little fine-tuning. The suggestions presented in this book are very concrete and real-life, which I also appreciated. I would recommend this book to anyone, and I definitely think it should be a part of any spiritual development must-read book list." – C. Moore

"The author's writing style is easy to read and this book is chock full of content. I feel like actually carving out time for myself is possible with these techniques! Loved it!" – V. Frautten

"Very helpful guide for setting up and staying with daily spiritual practices. Information and practices I had never thought of as spiritual. A good read." – A. Coppertree

The Elements of Creativity
The Sacred Path to Writing Your Book

INSPIRED LIVING SERIES: CHAKRA 5

NIKKI STARCAT SHIELDS

DEDICATION

I dedicate this book to two of my favorite creations: Tristan and Bridget.

CONTENTS

ACKNOWLEDGEMENTS

Many thanks to my beloved Brent BlackLion Nelson for the editing, cover design, and formatting. He is also my Tech Guru and cheers me on, always.

I appreciate my friend Katie Gall for her help improving the fictional portions of the book. I also love our weekly accountability sessions and how we continue to encourage one another on our creative journeys. Thank you.

I'm so thankful to Jennifer Elizabeth Moore for her friendship and mentorship. She has given generously of her time and energy in so many ways, from unexpected gifts to readings on the backstory of each fictional character to hosting book launch events, and more. Jen, you are a blessing.

Thank you to my coach Britt Bolnick for helping me release my visibility fears and learn to shine.

Thanks to Trina Ward of Trina's Proofreading for her great work proofreading the manuscript.

I'm grateful to my friend Shan Jeniah Burton for her assistance during the final stages of publication.

I wish to deeply thank the attendees of my 2023 summer retreat, Writing From the Heart, for all their feedback and cheerleading.

A big shout-out of gratitude to all the Thriving Artists and aspiring authors in my community. You inspire me daily and make it all possible.

As always, I appreciate my family and friends for all their support and love. You're the best.

MY STORY: AN INTRODUCTION

Greetings beautiful being! I'm Nikki Starcat Shields. I'm in my 50s and am happily thriving in my second career, which is made up entirely of the things I love most — creativity, words, and stories. I'm an author, a writing coach, and the leader of transformational writing retreats. In my work, I also draw heavily on three-plus decades as a Pagan priestess and witch.

Why am I writing about creativity? Who am I to advise you on how to access your creative flow?

It's story time.

I was born into this life addicted to stories. I credit my mom for reading to me from a very early age, though I suspect I'd also come in fresh from a past life as a scribe or scholar somewhere. I was reading on my own by the time I was 3 years old. From that time on, I didn't go anywhere without a book. I devoured the written word like it was candy. Throughout childhood, I filled little pocket notebooks with words I was learning, story ideas, and quotes I liked. I spent my free time reading, daydreaming, conversing with an array of imaginary friends, and visiting the faeries in the woods near my home. When adults asked what I wanted to be when I grew up, the answer was always "a writer," with an unspoken "duh" added for emphasis.

As is true for most of us, the mainstream culture soon messed with those plans. I was a shy and sensitive child, and I began to fall into the role of a people-pleaser. Academics were easy for me, and teachers liked it when I reflected back the answers they'd just fed me. Getting straight-As became my way to fit into the system.

I'm not trying to brag when I say I'm smart, as well as creative. I was slotted into the "gifted and talented" program, and it was assumed from the get-go that I'd eventually be bound for college, even though it wasn't common in my lower-class rural family.

Although a high I.Q. comes with its perks, there are also drawbacks. I'm talking about the expectations and beliefs that got put on me (and perhaps you, too). Beginning in junior high, I learned that artists starve, and that you couldn't "make a living" as a writer. This mysterious "making a living" was infused with images of big fancy homes, trendy clothes, and sports cars. These were things my family and I didn't have, and they sounded pretty great. I pored over *The Preppy Handbook* and aspired to Izod shirts and Ivy League schools. What can I say? This was the mid-80s.

In high school, I pointed my writing aspirations toward journalism. It seemed like a reasonable compromise. I could be an anchorwoman on TV, or a correspondent for a big newspaper. I wrote term papers, poems, and articles for the school paper, and mostly gave up my childhood imagination games. I continued to devour books, and in Advanced Placement English we dissected the classics, guided by our hip young teacher.

While I applied to (among others) Emerson College in Boston, known for an excellent journalism program, and was accepted, I ended up going to the University of Maine because it was far more affordable. This was probably for the best. As it turned out, the stress of deadlines was anathema to my highly sensitive system. Instead of journalism, I turned my focus to broadcasting. Radio announcing? I could do that. While there wasn't much creativity involved, at least compared to writing, it looked like a decent way to "make a living." I graduated with a B.A. in Broadcasting, a minor in English, and a whole lot of doubt about my ability to write well.

With the exception of keeping a personal journal, I stopped writing. For *years*. I got a decent job in my field working in public radio. The people were great. I had a caring mentor and kept getting promoted. Public radio was an ethical gig, which became more important in the 90s, as some of us shifted from material girls to hippie chicks. Public radio was morally acceptable, and I did "make a living." I met my husband (who I'll call Quester, in these pages) in college, and after I graduated, we got married.

I did well in my public radio gig. But it wasn't my calling. The Muses got sick of me not returning their calls, and began sticking their heads through the door, uninvited.

I started writing in little bits and pieces, reflecting on my tentative steps onto a spiritual path, which had begun in college. I'd been raised by agnostics but discovered that my strong affinity with nature and those conversations with the fae weren't just my imagination. I remember reading Margot Adler's *Drawing Down the Moon*, which was her survey of Earth-based spirituality, also known as neo-Paganism, a growing religious movement then and since. I was thrilled that there was a name for the beliefs Mom and I had taken for granted. I was a Pagan, and the Goddess was real! I wrote about my experiences in the Maine-based EarthTides Pagan Network newsletter. Yes, one of those stapled-together paper deals. This was before the internet was a thing.

When I think about the ways I gradually tiptoed away from the mainstream, I laugh to remember my high school years, longing to be a "preppie" from a rich family. Because of my mom, I was already a feminist. I became a vegetarian, a Deadhead, a witchy priestess, polyamorous, then a homeschooling Mom, and the solo breadwinner while my husband did the "Mr. Mom" thing, raising our two kids.

When the Muses started aggressively rearranging the furniture in my head – which coincided with the hubby being ready to take a break from full-time parenting – I decided I was done with ignoring them.

In 2008, to the surprise of most everyone in my life, I quit my radio job (mostly). I was inspired by a new relationship (I did mention the polyamory thing, right?) with a man who sparked my creativity.

What did I do with my newfound free time? I hung out with my kids and got involved in some cool homeschooling organizations. My new beau, BlackLion, and I started tossing around ideas for a business we could create. At my longtime public radio mentor's request, I still did a little bit of radio work here and there. I took time to learn and study things that interested me.

I still didn't write. Not at first.

Other than the Pagan newsletter articles, of course, plus blogging and journaling. Which, for the record, totally counts as writing. But I didn't see it that way at the time. I felt stuck.

The details of what had me stuck don't really matter. Though if I were you, reading this book, I'd be curious. Long story short, we got into a serious financial crunch. I still had all that doubt about my abilities as a writer; I had closed and locked some mental doors to my formerly thriving world of the imagination. I was also raising young teens, which if you've done it, you know takes a lot of energy.

The reason that I say the details don't matter, though, is because *everyone* I talk to who wants to write a book but isn't yet doing it has a complicated life. The very real things that keep people from writing their books range from an intense day job to ailing parents to relationship troubles to trying to run a business to chronic pain – and that's just a small sampling. Your reasons are yours, and mine were mine. One important thing to notice is that you obviously care enough about your book idea and your creativity to take the time to read this book.

Another key is that, since I've lived it and come out the other side – and helped my clients do the same – you can learn from my own journey. Mistakes included.

What did I do, exactly, to get unstuck? When I was preparing to write this book, I did some research. As a lifelong journal keeper, my shelf of old journals is a resource that I turn to fairly often (partly because I have a terrible memory). I read what I'd written there leading up to the publication of my first book. Here are some of the things I did that helped the most – along with some of the mistakes I made along the way.

The one action that made the most difference in my journey was that I continued to show up. I would lament in my journal that I sucked as a writer, I'd never make it, and I'd surely be

14

stuck working for other people for the rest of my life – or we'd get thrown out of our house and die on the streets. Yeah, I can be pretty melodramatic when I'm unhappy. But a few days later, I'd be right back up there on the horse, talking about an article I'd submitted or a new series of posts for my blog that I was excited about.

The only way to become a good writer is to write. Practice is the key to success at any endeavor. I learned that from my kids. They both played soccer for many years, and their dedication to practicing and improving was impressive. They must have gotten it from their dad. Remember how I said having academic smarts can be a liability? For years, since schoolwork came easy to me, with anything I tried that didn't go well, I assumed that I was just always going to be bad at it. Not knowing about the power of practice, I missed out on a lot of fun things. I'm thankful to my kiddos for setting me straight on that.

Anyway, by continuing to write – in my journal, on my blog, in newsletters and magazine articles, and anywhere else I could – I was gradually building my writing skills.

One mistake I made, though, was to try and spread myself too thin. I wrote for too many different outlets, on too many topics. If I were to do it again, I'd probably rein myself in a bit. Yes, it's important to show up and start getting your work out there. But at the same time, you need to have enough energy to devote to your Big Book Project. It took me longer to finish that first full-length manuscript than it probably had to – although as they say, hindsight is 20/20.

Another thing that helped me immensely on my journey was my spiritual path. That's why I've organized this book the way I have, walking you through the writer's journey along the spiral path of the five elements. My quest to reclaim my innate creativity goes hand in hand with my exploration as a spiritual seeker.

I started doing a daily spiritual practice in 1997 and have kept it up ever since – even during the most difficult life crises. It's been an anchor, a foundation which I've relied on over and over. That's not to say that you need to be a witch or a Pagan to benefit from the techniques I'll share in this book. I firmly believe that each person has their own unique flavor of spirituality. Even so, using the elements as a series of touchpoints for the journey will help you along the way. I'll talk more about the connection between spirituality and creativity in Chapter 1.

The third useful lesson is about dealing with your old baggage. I've had a lot of my own to unpack before I would allow myself to do the things I most wanted to do in the world. We all have old beliefs, patterns, and traumas that weigh us down. My biggest ones had to do with self-worth, insecurity, people-pleasing, and a "lack" mentality. Once again, the benefit of hindsight allows me to say that quite clearly now. At the time, a lot of my baggage was still hidden in the shadows. I had a lot of stress, self-criticism, and fear that just felt like normal everyday life.

My mistake here was that my exploration of shadow work was, for a long time, very tentative. I didn't know what I was doing, and at first I didn't reach out for help. This made for a lot of "one step forward, three steps back" scenarios. I also let other peoples' opinions keep me from fully exploring my own needs, especially when it came to unpacking my baggage. Let's just say that shadow work and being a people-pleaser don't go very well together. You have to be willing to set some firm boundaries and stop playing some of the interpersonal drama games that we humans are so attached to — and for a long time I was unwilling to go there.

Before I've entirely scared you away with all this talk of shadow work, let me just tell you about the fourth lesson: play. Yes, you heard that right. Playfulness is an essential part of the writer's journey. We'll talk about why that's so a bit later. But even when I was struggling most, there were plenty of times when I was able to let go and have a terrific time.

Because I was unschooling the kids and wanted them to have lots of opportunities to try different things, I went along for the ride with them. That allowed me to play with art, music, performance, poetry, and other forms of creative expression. I once made and decorated a fancy cake every month for a year — and blogged about it. I joined a modern vaudeville troupe, playing in the band and performing in silly skits. I led vision board workshops at homeschooling conferences. And of course, I played with kids – a lot. Doing all of these things (and more) helped me to regain full access to my imagination.

The fifth useful tactic was that I stayed open to opportunities that came my way. One of the most profound experiences I had during that time of struggle was when I said yes to an offer of a free session with a woman who channeled a non-physical entity. I got to get on the phone with her and talk directly with the being she channeled, which was so empowering. I'd been reading the Seth books since college, but to get advice directly from the other side – wow. They gave me a personalized list of affirmations to work with for a month, and it made a major difference in my attitude and thus my results.

Let me give you a less woo-woo example, too. In the process of putting myself out there on the web, I regularly posted in groups and on pages, mostly on blogs and Facebook. After I'd liked a post on a Pagan book page, I got a private message from someone urging me to check out the books by a small Pagan press in Britain, Moon Books. It turned out that he was the editor, and during our conversation I told him I was thinking of putting together a book based on my writings for the EarthTides Pagan Network over the previous ten years. He was very supportive and encouraged me to submit a book proposal. That's how my first book, *Starcat's Corner: Essays on Pagan Living*, came to be! Keeping an eye out for aligned opportunities means sometimes you can skip the traditional route.

As you can probably tell by now, my path to becoming a published author wasn't direct. The same is true for my work as a writing coach, which along with my own writing, is now my full-time second career. I don't have a MFA degree in writing, or even a coaching certificate. I used to let this lack of official papers sap my confidence, but I don't any longer – we'll talk more about that later. What I do have, at this point, is experience.

This book is my sixth, and I have several others underway – including fiction. I have clients who have published books, who are writing their manuscripts, and who are just getting started. I use this journey of the elements with the writers in my signature group coaching program. By grounding the work of writing a book in the ancient system of the elements, you'll be able to not only finish that book manuscript, but become open to new avenues of creativity and success in all areas of life. Creativity really is your birthright as a human being. Let's step onto this path together, and see where it leads.

How to Use This Book

Before we talk about the elements themselves, I'll say a few words about how to use this book. Obviously you can binge-read this book straight through if that's your style. You're in charge of how you take it in.

As we make our way along the path, though, I'm going to act as if you're reading this book while following the advice and beginning to write your book manuscript. Maybe you don't feel quite ready to do that right now, but I encourage you to make a start. You won't know whether or not you can do it until you try. The only way to figure out which of my ideas and suggestions work for you is to give them a chance. As we move through the chapters, I'll unveil new lessons and techniques for each step of the journey of writing a book draft. Some of it will resonate with you, while other parts might not. Take what you need and leave the rest.

You'll also find, perhaps not surprisingly after reading the introduction, stories. I've sprinkled in vignettes that provide a glimpse into the life of three aspiring authors on the creative journey. These are fictional people, and their stories come partly from my imagination, but I've created them as an amalgam of some of my clients, friends, and colleagues. My wish is that you'll resonate with one or more of them, and will let their struggles and celebrations inspire you.

I encourage you to dedicate a notebook or journal (or Google doc, if you're all-digital) to making notes about your writing process. Throughout the book, I'll be giving you writing prompts and questions to answer. Note the answers in your writing notebook. I know all too well that doing that is going to be a challenge. It's not as easy as just reading the book. But trust me – doing the work when you encounter it will go a long way toward easing the process of writing your manuscript. Try it. That said, if you choose to answer the prompts in your mind and not bother with writing them down, that's completely fine. Please don't let the presence of a prompt or exercise cause you to put down the book. There are plenty of gems here for everyone, even those of us who don't want to pick up a pen when we're reading in bed. I've been there and done that many times myself. No judgment!

Even if you don't start writing your book right away, and you find that I'm talking to you about a place along the trail that you haven't quite reached yet, you can still gain wisdom from reading the whole book. Again, don't set it down because you don't have time to answer the journaling prompts or put my suggestions into play. Maybe the most important thing you'll gain from reading The Elements of Creativity is the notion that writing a book is actually possible for you. You might just need some more direct hand-holding, and perhaps reading this book gives you permission to reach out for the support of a writing coach, take a writing class, sign up for a writing retreat, or find an accountability partner. Contrary to popular belief, writing a book doesn't have to be a do-it-all-by-yourself project.

My aim is to encourage you, in whatever ways you'll allow. My vision is a vast network of empowered, creative people who are embracing the rise of the Feminine Divine (no matter one's sex, gender, and/or orientation - see page 32 for more on gender) and the awakening of human consciousness by sharing their deepest wisdom and most inspiring passions. Together, we Thriving Artists are changing the world by collaboratively building a more conscious society, in all aspects of human life and beyond.

In order to get this empowering wisdom into the world, I help people give birth to their heart-centered books. I assist them in finding the topics that sing from their soul and putting their wisdom into writing that will reach seekers who are ready to learn. I encourage them as they become Thriving Artists themselves.

Ready to join the Thriving Artist revolution? Awesome! Let's start with the basics – the five sacred things. But first, it's storytime.

Kelly's Creative Journey

For those who never bother to read the How to Use This Book portion - I see you, and no judgment. I just wanted you to know that the stories found sprinkled throughout the text (in italics) are fiction. I made them up as examples of situations new writers encounter, using experiences from my own life as well as those of clients and colleagues, and adding my own imaginative details. There, now you know.

Kelly didn't exactly wake up one day and decide to write a book. It was more of a slow burn. She lay in bed on a bright spring morning, looking out the window and thinking about when she was a little kid. Her parents would drop her off at her grandmother Zayde's house on Saturday, wanting to get their errands done and grab a workout without her tagging along. Kelly didn't mind that at all. Zayde's house was a paradise to her. She sat at the big oak table with crayons and paper and wrote stories, while Zayde bustled around the kitchen, cooking and baking and cleaning. Kelly loved to write. She'd draw pictures to accompany the stories, and her grandmother would stop to look and listen while she sipped coffee. The memories of those early years, before the divorce and a job opportunity sent Kelly and her mother across the country, were tinged with fondness and a sort of rosy filter.

The only writing she'd done since then, aside from the required papers back in high school and college, was rather recent. After a back injury, she'd taken up yoga for the first time, and that had led to all kinds of other things. She'd attended retreats and workshops that encouraged her to journal. She'd resisted at first - she remembered thinking Really?! What does this have to do with my back pain? *- but* then had discovered the relief of writing about the struggles in her life. It was better than a session with her therapist, honestly.

She now had a fairly regular journaling practice. She wrote most days. That had led to a new thought, or, she supposed, an inspiration. What if she wrote a book about her experiences as a hospice worker, back before the kids were born?

She wouldn't want it to be a boring, trite, how-to sort of thing, though, and she definitely didn't want to get all sappy about the end of life. Somehow she'd have to make it interesting to readers, and those were the type of skills she didn't have. There were already tons of books about working with the dying, and some of them were actually good. How would her own ideas add to the conversation?

Kelly sighed and snuggled into the comforter. She was learning to love Saturdays, when she could sleep in and do whatever she wanted. Whatever she wanted! That made it a little easier that her kids were hardly ever around these days. What a cliche she'd become. The suburban Pinterest mother whose two teens were now, respectively, the gorgeous and brainy valedictorian-to-be whose entire world was college prep, and the emo-goth girl with an extra side of attitude. Neither one wanted anything to do with Kelly, but at least it was for normal teen reasons, and not because Kelly was an awful mother, like her own had been. Or at least, she fervently hoped not.

She was gradually getting better at not being needed. The perimenopause was helping - it made the idea of extra rest more attractive, since her sleep cycle was peppered with hot flashes. Her husband Darren had taken the dogs out for a walk an hour ago, and she'd been lying here daydreaming ever since. She hadn't even gotten up to grab a cup of the coffee she could smell.

A few moments later, she heard the kitchen door bang shut and braced herself for the enthusiastic greetings of Winnie and Joy, their golden retrievers. After a lot of face-licking and tail-wagging, and a quick kiss from Darren, Kelly *hauled herself out of bed and headed for that cup of coffee, then a shower. She'd think about the book idea later.*

***

It was Monday morning, edging toward noontime. Kelly sat in her home office - she was an administrator at the hospice house now, and worked from home three days a week. The dogs were sleeping on the floor under her feet, ignoring the fancy dog beds in order to be closer to her. Darren was at the architectural firm where he worked. The girls were at school. The neighborhood was quiet. The only sounds Kelly heard were the dogs snoring softly, the humming of the furnace, and the inevitable creaks of the old house as it settled. Her thoughts drifted away from her quarterly financial report, landing on her book idea. She kept returning to a memory of Maggie, the first patient she'd gotten to know well before they died, and the strange, almost magical circumstances of Maggie's passing.

Kelly wasn't religious, and she wasn't even sure she'd call herself spiritual, but that experience had made her positive that there was more to life than we normally knew about. Maggie had described things that she couldn't have known about, including the exact arrival time of her estranged daughter, and even details of Kelly's own life that she'd never shared with anyone. It had creeped her out a bit at the time, but gradually, over the years, Kelly had become accustomed to the unusual stories that surrounded death and the end of life.

She missed working directly with the patients and families. Her admin job was fine - her coworkers were great, the hours had been better than shift work while the girls were little, and the money was good - but she wanted more. She had the itch to pick up her journal and write about Maggie and the insights the passing of this amazing elder had brought. She glanced at the clock on her laptop. It was almost lunchtime. She'd take her journal with her to the dog park and jot some notes down then. She had to wrap up this report today and get it ready for the board meeting on Thursday.

Kelly sighed and returned her focus to the columns of numbers.

***

Kelly put down her phone and leaned her head into her hands.

"What's wrong?" Darren asked, looking up from his iPad.

"Oh, nothing really. I'm just wishing I'd never told Sophia about my book idea."

"Why? She's usually pretty positive," Darren answered, refilling his wine glass and tilting the bottle toward her with an eyebrow raised.

"No more for me, thanks," she said. "That's just the thing, there's a fine line between "encouraging" and "pushy." She's so encouraging that it's starting to get annoying. She's pushing me to write it, but I'm just not sure."

"I thought you'd already started," Darren said.

"I wrote some notes about what I wanted to include, but that's all. I don't even know why. I want to write it, but it's low-priority. There's so much other stuff I need to be doing."

"Aw, come on, babe," he said, inching his chair closer to hers and pushing away their empty plates. "You've been talking about this for months now, since that Vermont retreat. Sophie's just trying to be helpful."

"I know, I know." She leaned over toward him, putting her head on his chest. His familiar smell was comforting; aftershave and spices. "It just feels so overwhelming. I'm not a writer. These stories - I don't think I can do them justice."

"Maybe you should take some writing classes," he suggested. "You know, get some guidance, learn some new skills?"

"I guess," she said. She didn't know if she had the bandwidth for it, but it wasn't a terrible idea. "I'll do some research on it later. Let's clear up and go watch some shows."

Darren grabbed the dishes and headed for the kitchen. He was easygoing about most things, and wouldn't push her. Her half-sister Sophia, though, was a go-getter, and wanted everyone else to follow their dreams, too. She'd never relent until Kelly was hip-deep into her first draft - no, she'd never relent until the book was published, which seemed to Kelly like a pipedream.

Right now she wanted that second glass of wine after all, and to curl up on the couch with Darren and the doggos and forget the whole thing.

CHAPTER 1:
WHAT ARE THE ELEMENTS OF CREATIVITY?

An Overview of the Elements

Earth, Air, Fire, Water, and Spirit – these five basic elements, represented by the points on the pentagram or five-pointed star, are common to many Pagan traditions. They are the powerful energies which surround us, that which we call upon to witness and guide our sacred rituals.

I've been working with the five sacred elements of the neo-Pagan tradition for many years now. The elements are my companions in daily life. As I've learned and practiced my spirituality, my magick has become fully entwined with my own creative process.

It occurred to me at some point over the past few years that creative expression also contains certain basic elements. These elements have helped me to build a creative life which not only feels fun, but allows me to bring projects to completion and usher them into the world. In pairing these writing basics with the five sacred things, a clear system has emerged that I now use to help my clients write their books.

In this book, I'll be sharing how each of the five elements can help support you in your creative endeavors — from writing a book, to creating a course for your business, to painting your masterpiece.

First, here's a brief overview of the qualities of each element. We'll go more in depth later, but this is a good place to start if these concepts are brand new to you, or if you'd like a little refresher:

EARTH: The element of Earth reveals our connection with the land. Giant mountains, mighty trees, and burrowing creatures sing to us the slow, patient song of Earth. Earth is composed of rocks, sand, dirt, composted plant material, and ancient bones.

We live in our physical bodies here on the Earth plane. We are rooted to the Earth through our cells, our ancestors, and the land we inhabit. As we observe the land where we live, watching as the seasons change, we connect ourselves deeply to the energies of our sacred spaces. We notice the slow changes, the dance of time.

AIR: The element of Air swirls around us, unseen but essential to life. Air's essence is expressed by capricious winds, the flight of birds, and music of all types. Air forms the whooshing motion of the bellows that are our lungs, powering our daily life.

We need Air to exist. We can live for a time without sunlight or food or even water, but when we cease breathing for mere moments, that is the end of this lifetime. The physical process of breathing is complex, yet we do it all the time, unconsciously. Deliberate focus on the breath is an ideal way to calm our thoughts and emotions when we are in turmoil. Air brings us back to ourselves.

FIRE: The element of Fire lights the darkness of our outer and inner landscapes. It is in the faraway light of the stars, the life-giving warmth of our Sun, the Moon's mystical reflection, the sudden flash of lightning, the friction of flint on steel, and the spark of passion in the belly.

We wouldn't be here without Fire. The Sun brings us the warmth our bodies need and feeds the plants that provide us with air to breathe and food to eat. The inner Fires of our amazing bodies allow us to digest and metabolize our food so we can fuel our physical existence. Since ancient times, Fire has been acknowledged in our myths as a sacred gift.

WATER: The element of Water nourishes us, body and soul. Life on this planet began in and emerged from the deep, mysterious waters of Mother Ocean. Our bodies are made up largely of Water and our consciousness flows like a stream.

Our emotions ebb and flow each day like the ever-changing waves of the sea. Yet we can also plumb the depths of our souls, the place where our dreams connect us to the collective unconscious. When we dive deep into those mysterious waters, we receive messages from our intuition, from our divine connection to the source of life.

SPIRIT: Spirit, in the Center, is the fifth element. It is the place where the others meet, the time outside of time, the eternal merging of all things. Spirit is felt in the tingling sensation of energy rising, unseen but present. Spirit is our connection to the holy Mysteries of the non-physical realm. It is where we access the deepest wellspring of our creativity.

Witches and Pagans (as well as clergy in other cultures) call on the five elements at the beginning of their ritual work. The weaving of the energies of the elements creates a sacred container, often visualized as a sphere or a circle, for the spiritual work being done.

Triple Self Alignment

What does doing a magickal ritual have to do with writing a book? I'm so glad you asked.

My ideas about accessing creativity on a regular basis have their roots in neo-Paganism. One of my favorite Pagan authors is Starhawk, who was a founder of the Reclaiming tradition in the late 1970s. Her book *The Spiral Dance* was life-changing for me.

In that book she talks about The Triple Self. In this useful metaphor, Starhawk divides the psyche into three parts (sort of like Freud did, but better). Other authors have also written about The Triple Self, using their own terminology. I've included works by T. Thorn Coyle and Scott Cunningham in the Resources section. In this book, I'm using the terms that Starhawk wrote about.

Talking Self is the waking consciousness — the voice you hear in your head. It's that left-brain, analytical side of your mind. This is the part of you that worries, and loves to fix things and solve problems. For me, it feels like it's located in the head, behind the third eye, between your eyebrows.

Younger Self is the right-brained, wild, messy part of the psyche. Like a young child, she adores play, bright colors, and everything sparkly. Younger Self is all about the sensual pleasures of life. In my experience, she's centered in the heart.

Deep Self is your connection to the non-physical, to the collective unconscious. This is your intuition, your wisdom and the knowledge that comes from something beyond your physical self. I feel this in the gut, the solar plexus area. You might also feel this connection in your heart center, or perhaps lower in your abdomen, around the sacral chakra. I see Deep Self as the powerful wellspring of our creativity.

You know those timeless moments when you're fully immersed in creating, and everything seems to flow smoothly? That's when your Triple Self is fully aligned, and you're able to tap into that wellspring.

So, here's the key piece to understand in this model of the self: Talking Self and Deep Self are *not* able to communicate directly. They are just too different. They don't speak the same language.

You *need* your Younger Self (or Jung-er self, if you prefer) to be the translator between the two.

That's where having a Writing Ritual comes in. When you engage Younger Self in what you're doing, she'll happily (and playfully) serve as that intermediary.

Rather than force your creativity to flow — and we all know how well *that* works — you can access Younger Self and play yourself into the groove.

What does she love most? All the sensory things that make up a magickal ritual: candles, crystals, flowers, a delicious warm beverage, inspiring music, meditation, yoga stretches, chocolate or fruit, incense, clothing that feels comfortable against the skin, sparkly pens, mantras...

You get the idea. When you set up your writing habit with (some of) these elements, Younger Self comes to the party all set to play. Getting her on board automatically puts you in full communication with the creative wellspring of your Deep Self.

From there, your writing will flow.

Creating a Writing Ritual that includes your favorite sensory elements is a powerful way to get yourself into that state of flow, quickly and easily. It's a shortcut — one that you can custom-design to appeal to *your* inner wild child.

As we move through the elements, you'll have opportunities to try it for yourself. I'll encourage you to do some experimenting, to see what your Younger Self loves most. Once you discover what those things are, you'll make sure you have those things at hand each time you sit down to write. You'll learn to set yourself up for success: build a music playlist just for writing, stock up on your favorite tea or coffee, and beautify your writing space.

One of my clients asked, "So essentially you're romancing yourself?" Yes. That's exactly what I'm talking about. You'll court your Triple Self by appealing to Younger Self, and then watch your writing flourish! Before we delve into the specifics of creating your Writing Rituals, let's take care of some more of the basics.

Overview of the Borderlands

When you imagine the elements visually, what comes to mind? They've often been placed around the edges of a circle or mapped to the points of a pentagram. You might see the elements like a compass, sitting at the directions that are traditionally associated with them – Earth in the North, Air in the East, Fire in the South, and Water in the West (Spirit is, of course, set solidly in the Center, touching each of the others).

No matter which map you choose to use, when you visualize or draw them, you'll see that there are points where the elements come in contact with one another. Let's use our compass as an example.

When you move clockwise from Earth and North, you'll run up against Air and East. Of course, if you reversed the direction counterclockwise, you'd find yourself in Water and West. For the purposes of this book, we're going to use a clockwise motion, also known as moving deosil. In most Pagan traditions, you move deosil when you're creating, welcoming, or encouraging a particular energy. Counterclockwise, or widdershins, is reserved for when you wish to release or banish an energy. Since we're dedicated to increasing your creativity, we'll proceed clockwise.

The place where one element meets another is a transition point that is referred to as a Borderland. Borderlands are, by definition, neither one thing nor the other. They are a liminal space, which means that the energy of that space is in the process of transforming. It's where one energy meets another, moving toward some kind of integration. This chaotic energy can be incredibly inspiring.

Think about going to the beach. It's a liminal space, the Borderland where the sea and land meet. It feels magickal when you're there. Or perhaps it feels uncomfortable to you – the Borderlands can be like that, too, especially when you're dealing with an element that's particularly tricky for you. But don't worry. I'm going to share ways to work with the intermingling energy of the Borderlands between the elements.

Actually, at this point, I want to say that it might be helpful to you to have your astrology chart available. You can get your chart done by a professional, or just use one of those free online sites if that's easiest. You'll need to know your birth date, time, and place. I realize that not everyone has all of these details – Quester doesn't know what time he was born, and has been unable to find out, so some of the details of his chart remain mysterious. But if you're able to acquire a birth chart, you can get some details on your own relationship to the elements.

The most important things to know are your Sun sign (this is the most commonly known, and those mainstream horoscopes in the newspaper are based on them), your Moon sign, and your rising sign (this is the sign that appears in the

9 o'clock position on your astrology chart). You can also see where the other planets fall, though they are not as key as these big three.

Each of the 12 astrological signs has a corresponding element associated with it. Taurus, Virgo, and Capricorn are Earth signs. Gemini, Libra, and Aquarius are Air (I know, Aquarius is the water-bearer for heaven's sake, but it's still an Air sign, for whatever occult reason). Aries, Leo, and Sagittarius are connected with Fire. Cancer, Scorpio, and Pisces are Water.

I'll use my own chart as an example. My Sun sign is Virgo, which is Earth. My rising sign is Cancer, a Water sign. My Moon sign is Libra, connected with Air. I also have a bunch of other planets clustered in Libra, which is probably why I'm drawn to the field of communication. What's missing, or not as prevalent? Yup, Fire.

The element that has posed a challenge for me at various times in my life? You guessed it – Fire. For that very reason, the lack of Fire in my chart, I often get inspired by people who do have a lot of Fire in theirs.

Playing with astrology and the elements isn't essential to your creative process, but it can provide an enlightening window into why certain things are hard – or easy – for you.

Back to the Borderlands. When you enter into one of those spaces where the elements mingle – say for example, from Fire to Water – you can lean on your own particular strengths and/or find ways to shore up those gaps. In my case, the Borderland going from the passion and momentum of Fire, where I look to people and energies outside myself for motivation, to the flow and mystery of Water, which is prevalent in my chart via my rising sign, can be a bumpy ride sometimes. As you'll see later on in the book, Fire has to do with finding one's voice as a writer (and/or for a particular project), while the Water realms can be associated with finding nurturing from one's chosen community. If this sounds like a bit of a balancing act, it can be. As the old saying goes, "fire and water don't mix." Yet by being aware of the Borderlands where these two very different energies touch, it's possible to find that balance. The image I have in my head is like a yin-yang symbol, where Water and Fire dance around one another, each containing a bit of the other's essence.

Since we're moving clockwise (deosil, remember?) around the spiral, we'll encounter transitions between Earth and Air, Air and Fire, Fire and Water, and Water and Earth. As you move through the book and encounter the various borderlands, you'll get a sense of how to allow them to work for you in your creative life. You might even discover or create your own symbols and images for each one. This will help guide you as you move through the process of creating your book – and living life as a Thriving Artist. Around the circle we go!

What About the Other Two Elemental Combinations?

Have you noticed that in discussing our journey around the elemental spiral, I haven't yet mentioned the other two combinations of elements? Let's talk about those next.

Before we do that, let's talk about gender for a moment (don't worry, this will become relevant soon). The notion of gender is undergoing a revolution in our society as of this writing. I'm very much in favor of it. It's an exploration that's been going on for a long time, but largely under the radar, thanks to judgmental religions that wanted to keep it all controlled.

I'm very much still learning the new language of gender, even as things change rapidly. I've discovered that some of the existing language in the magickal community can be a barrier to inclusiveness. Before I go into talking about the meetings of the elements which dwell across from one another on the circle, I wanted to be clear about what I mean when I talk about "masculine" and "feminine."

Western occult magick is full of polarities. The ultimate goal is to accept the paradoxical notion that all of the expressions of consciousness – whether people, things, or events – contain all polarities. It's akin to the uniting of the divided will (more about that later). In order to be whole, holy, wholly complete, we realize that we are a drop in the ocean that is the All.

At the same time, we are manifest here on the physical plane, where the polarities are quite evident. The cool thing that the gender revolution is doing is showing the difference between three different spectrums that were once considered one polarity. There is your biological sex, which describes the reproductive parts you were born with. There is your gender identity, which is how you think about yourself. You might identify as woman, non-binary, genderqueer, genderfluid, man, or something else. Finally, there is your gender expression, which is concerned with how you demonstrate your gender to the world around you. You might variously express yourself as feminine, androgynous, or masculine (and it might change from day to day or week to week).

This third category is what I refer to when I talk about, for instance, the Feminine Divine. I want to acknowledge that the way we categorize certain gender expressions (wearing the color pink, or dressing in combat boots, to name two obvious examples) are highly influenced by history and culture.

The elements – or the deities, for that matter – don't have physical bodies. They dwell beyond the constraints of the world of polarity. However, a discussion of their gender expression is a convenient way to explore the qualities of these elements. It's a useful shortcut, so yes, I'm gonna go there.

You might also consider the Chinese symbol of the yin-yang, where wholeness is expressed as a circle or sphere, in which each type of energy contains a bit of the other, even here on the physical plane. I don't think I need to list the traditional associations, although they'll come up as we consider the elements which sit opposite one another on the circle. They're well ingrained in the modern psyche.

In most systems of the elements, Earth and Water are considered to have feminine qualities. They are receptive in nature. Earth represents the body, which has long been associated with the feminine, from the sacredness of the ability to give birth to our often-denigrated animal instincts. Water harkens to the womb, the dreamlands, emotional depths, and the power of intuition. Water flows around obstacles, and although it appears gentle, it has an enduring strength.

Fire and Air have more traditionally masculine qualities. They are both quite active energies. Fire is fast-moving, associated with passion and adventure. These were things that were denied to women in many cultures in much of Earth's recorded history, just as men were not supposed to cry or show their vulnerability. Air is tied to logic and scientific objectivity, which are specific ways of thinking and communicating about our experiences. If anything, Air seems to me to be the most androgynous element, aside from Spirit. But it's considered masculine in our dance of polarities.

The place of meeting between the opposites can be powerfully charged. In our creative journey, when the qualities of Earth and Fire connect, our projects can be powerfully propelled forward. We bring our newfound voice and the passion we have for it to the steadiness of a customized writing habit, and it can make for writing sessions where time flies by and the prose is inspired. This is when you get really hot and heavy with the Muse, and creative new ideas are forged in the crucible of your Writing Ritual. In my experience, you can't predict when this will happen, but when it does, it's best to clear your schedule and go along for the ride. This is when your most impassioned scenes and wildest wisdom are born onto the page. You'll know it when it happens.

Are there ways to encourage the energies of Earth and Fire to meet you in the creation of your manuscript? Of course. One of them, for me and many others, is National Novel-Writing Month (fondly known as NaNoWriMo). Every November, thousands of people pledge to write 50,000 words in 30 days. This means that your target goal is to write 1,667 words every day for an entire month. That kind of ramped-up writing habit is the perfect Earthy cauldron in which your writing can catch Fire! You have a lot of intense focus in a relatively short period of time. Few among us can sustain that kind of writing pace all year round, but NaNoWriMo provides a community experience of a pouring of one's passions onto the page, manifesting a huge chunk of a first draft. It's also, believe it or not, a whole lot of fun.

The other meeting of opposites is, of course, Air and Water. They are, if you'll forgive the awful pun, a perfect storm. Combining the solid skills of Air with the dreamy imagination of Water brings on a deluge of ideas. The Watery energy on its own touches the mystical realms, but it's often at rest within us. It's those liminal spaces we talked about earlier, such as the moments between sleep and waking or places like the seashore, that trigger our connections with the myths of the collective unconscious. When Air blows through, though, we can tap into our visionary ability to transform these tenuous imaginings into a more concrete form: words on the page. We're inspired to communicate our deepest thoughts and most fanciful visions to others in the form of writing. This meetup with Air also brings in the community ethic of the realm of Water. Ideas and stories are more powerful when they're shared, and it is the mental realm of Air that moves us forward into sharing our creations.

How can we encourage this meeting of Air and Water? I feel like one of the best ways is to spend time with other creative people. Hang out and talk about your creations with people who are interested, and who are also expressing their creativity. It was at a lunch date with my husband Quester, who is a musician and also a longtime Pagan, that this section was inspired. I was telling him about the book and what types of things I was writing recently for it, which included the Borderlands. "But you haven't talked about *all* the places where the elements touch," he pointed out, "if you're just going around the circle." I hadn't considered this oversight, although the cross-quarter days are a part of the Pagan Wheel of the Year, and their polarities are known to have both similarities and opposite qualities. I started to think about what I knew about these opposites, which sent me off on a (hopefully useful) tangent about gender and using it to describe elements. That's just one example of how sharing your ideas with other Thriving Artists will further your projects and bring fresh new inspiration to life.

Let's circle back around to the gender revolution. There's a whole lot of division right now based on our varying human beliefs about this topic. I feel like that division pulls apart communities that otherwise might do well to work together. Let's use feminism as an example.

I was raised as a feminist, and still consider myself one. But there are a lot of misconceptions about what that even means. I concede that humanist might be a better term. To me, the definition of feminist is honoring all the various spectrums of biological sex, gender identity, and gender expression, and holding them all as equally valuable. The reason that I don't have a problem with the term feminist is that there seems to be a pendulum that swings back and forth, throughout the tides of history, in relation to the values we put on the various qualities.

Long ago, there were matriarchal cultures where women and others who held the yin-type qualities were honored as wise and worthy of leading our societies. The magick of birth was revered. Women tended to live longer than men and were thus the keepers of wisdom and knowledge in cultures that were mainly oral traditions.

Then the pendulum swung back the other way, and women or those with yin qualities were seen as inferior at best, and evil sinners at worst. It was the yang energies that were viewed as fit for leadership, and physical strength was seen as the epitome of power. A lot of harm was done during these many centuries of patriarchy.

These days, between the gender revolution and the feminist movement, things are shifting once again. The pendulum is swinging, and I think that many of us hope that we'll end up in a place of balance, where all gender expressions, identities, and sexes are honored. Yet there is a backlash, which can be quite easily seen in the right-wing politics of the current era. There is still a lot of fear of and anger at the feminine, yin powers in our modern culture. I stand as a feminist in the face of those abusive attitudes.

The same is true for the current divisions over race. When things have been so extremely unfair for so long, a swing back to the other side of the pendulum's arc is actually a good thing.

36

I'm a white person with mainly Celtic ancestry, and I'd love to see people of color and indigenous people take the reins of leadership in our societies. I'd also like to see women and non-binary people running the show for a while. I don't condone prejudice against white men, though; I know too many wonderful people who fit those categories. But power is complicated, and in my opinion should be shared. If there are reparations needed, let's make them.

How does this connect with creativity and writing your book? Those who fit into categories of people who have been oppressed for millennia have perspectives that have been suppressed and reviled. There is much wisdom that needs to be heard. These stories need to be told. When you begin to dance with the elements and polarities, you are learning to become whole. The journey of a Thriving Artist is to unite your will, share your perspectives, and to encourage others to tell their stories as well. Our diversity is our strength. Creative people are the ones who, by definition, think well outside the boxes of mainstream culture. Together we can encourage the changes and the peaceful revolutions that are underway. It makes more sense to work together than to argue over who uses which terms correctly. Respect should be the basis of our communication.

Thriving Artists can lead the way in this realm. Many of us are already doing so. By harnessing the powers of the polarities, and uniting them within your own psyche, you're contributing to the healing of these ancient rifts. Use the intense energies of the Earth-Fire, Air-Water combinations to help propel your own work forward and to support your fellow artists on their own journey along the sacred path.

Kelly's Creative Journey

Kelly sat at her desk, looking out at the backyard and the pink and orange clouds of sunset. She'd finished her work day and showered, put a chicken and some veggies in the crockpot, and now she sat at her desk in front of a blank laptop screen. She'd decided it was past time to work on her book, but her brain wasn't cooperating. The blank page stubbornly stayed blank.

Still, she wasn't giving up. She was going to sit here at least until dinner time. Darren was picking up the girls from debate club and field hockey practice after his meeting. So all Kelly had to do right now was write.

Why wasn't anything working? She thought about the writing craft books she'd been devouring on her Kindle. "Just start," most of them said. "Write anything that comes to mind. Writing, like anything, is a practice."

She sighed and looked away from the window. This shouldn't be so hard. She had tons of stories from her years doing hospice care. Maybe she should try the advice and just start at the beginning. Kelly heard Julie Andrews from The Sound of Music, singing in her head.

"Let's start at the very beginning, a very good place to start..."

Shut up, Julie, she thought with a grin, and put her hands on the keys.

"My first day as a hospice nurse began badly, with me spilling a whole tray of pudding cups..."

Kelly released her worries about how she'd craft the story, and just let the words flow forth onto the page, describing the scene from memory.

***

Kelly closed the browser window and went to her email, attaching the book file to a message to herself. She wasn't going to take any chances of losing her work, so she saved to three different places after each session.

It was probably superstitious, like some of the other little ritual things she did in connection with each writing session — but it was working — and she wasn't going to question it.

She had no idea if her memoir was any good, and she had refused to show her writing to anyone yet, even Darren. But she had close to eighteen thousand words in the document, *and was proud of herself for writing on a semi-consistent basis.*

One of her little tricks, gleaned from one of her favorite books on writing, was to not read back what she'd written. Not yet. Kelly had adhered to this like it was a golden rule. Part of it was fear. She knew that. That critical voice in her head, the one that sounded exactly like her mother, told her that her writing had to be crap. She was just starting, she hadn't written for years, so what else could it be? Kelly did her best to ignore the voice and keep telling her favorite nursing stories.

Still, the very act of writing, however inexpert she felt, was rippling outward into other parts of her life. It was helping her adjust to the girls not needing her as much. Darren kept pointing out how far behind they were on two of their favorite TV series, but she liked how her evenings were filled up with fun creative things. She'd felt sort of guilty about it at first, but the girls were so busy with their own stuff that they hadn't seemed to notice. They were both out tonight until late, and Darren was at his poker game. Kelly got up and stretched, disturbing the dogs, who both looked suddenly alert. She reached down and petted their silky heads. She just had time to heat up some leftovers and eat before her online photography class.

CHAPTER 2:
MAKING THE MAP

About the Three Containers

In my own writing process and in working with clients, I've discovered that there are three essential containers that you need in order to write a book or do any kind of big creative project. These are: intention, habit, and outline.

Within these sacred containers, you'll do the work of writing your book. You'll also be set up to deal with the inevitable resistance that comes up when you've taken on a Big Project like this. We'll get to that later.

But for now, this is where we start our journey, looking out over an uncharted territory. Don't worry. I've traversed it before, and I have some signposts to guide us. Since the journey is somewhat different for each person, you'll be making the map as you explore the territory.

I could have also called this chapter "gathering the tools." We'll be using the five elements as a framework as we travel through the process of writing your book. First, there are a few basic tools you'll need as we move forward.

The first container is your intention for writing your book. This will include your *Big Why*, the reason you want to write your book in the first place. The effect you want your book to have on the readers and the world is part of this too. So are the results that you want to see in your own life and career by sharing your wisdom and stories with a wider audience. It will also include your target audience (known in the entrepreneur world as your "ideal client") and, eventually, your logline. The logline is a summary of the book's contents. Think of it like your book's elevator speech. It will eventually result in the blurb on the back cover. But you don't need to know those details right away.

The second container is your writing habit. We touched on that in the section on The Triple Self, and I'll lead you through the creation of your own customized writing habit when we reach the element of Earth in Chapter 4.

The third key container is a Flexible Outline. I'll share more about that in a bit.

Each of these containers will be fully customized to your needs. Each writer approaches the process in a slightly – or perhaps significantly – different way. The best way to discover what works for you is to experiment, so I'll be offering you a bunch of different suggestions as we proceed. Grab your notebook and pen, or get to your laptop. Let's get started!

First, a word about starting with these containers. There's a common and old belief that many creative people hold, which is that planning will kill your creativity. As my beloved business coach, Britt Bolnick of In Arms Coaching, puts it, "There's a fear that you can't make a date with the Muses, because they only show up when they want to."

Happily, that's not exactly true. In my experience, planning can create *more* time for creativity, and can help you be more efficient and productive. Setting up these containers and having a plan serves to hold space for your creativity and keeps you from the tyranny of the blank page. The Muses will roll with it.

Look, I'll admit it right off the bat – writing a whole book isn't easy. It's a big job. Most of the time, we're not doing it just for the pleasure of writing (although that will become part of the journey). There will be times when you'll struggle with it and won't want to sit down and write. Having a solid intention for your book project will serve as an anchor when the going gets rough, which it most likely will. It also helps you feel a bit less alone as you begin the writing process.

When your book is anchored in your community and the wider world, it will begin to feel more real. It becomes an entity of its own. Crafting a writing habit with ritual elements – which will engage your Younger Self and enable you to access your Deep Self – helps you show up for your book and allows you to be in the flow when you're writing. Having a Flexible Outline helps you keep all the details written down so you don't have to hold them in your mind, thus making more space for that alignment and free flow of creativity.

Why Are You Writing This Book?

Let's begin by crafting your intention. One of the hardest things when beginning a book project can be writing a logline or summary. I always wonder: if I could summarize it in 100 or 200 words, would I really need to write the whole book?

However, having a summary (aka premise) and an intention for your book helps to establish your motivation and reclaim your momentum when it flees.

I like to start with something a bit easier than the summary – your *Big Why*. There's a reason why you want to write a book. It might be that, like me, you wanted to be an author from an early age, and now you're ready to reclaim that dream. Maybe you're one of those people who has lived such a powerful story that people keep telling you "you should write a book about that!" Perhaps you have an innovative technique that you teach or coach people in and want to establish your expertise with a book. The Muses might be tapping you on the shoulder, or even breaking down the door. Or it could be something else entirely. Your reasons are yours.

The way I begin the process of working with clients is to ask them to write about their intentions. Below are some prompts that will lead you through the process of writing what is essentially a Vision and Mission Statement for your book project.

The vision part is all about what your book will do for its readers. As you move through the prompts, think about the wisdom and stories you want to share. You want to hone in on the actual results your book will deliver to those who read it. This can range from laughter and entertainment to a profound transformation in their health or relationships. Your book might teach them a skill, tell them a story, or use your own story to inspire them to move forward in some area of their life. Once you've pondered that, allow yourself to think even bigger. Your book has the power to change the world. Even if you don't fully believe that yet, you can hold it as a possibility. The idea here is to dream big.

The mission part of your intention is a bit more targeted. It's concerned with what the book will do for you, its creator. Your book can establish you as an expert in your field, serve as a calling card for the work that you do in the world, or fulfill your lifelong dream of becoming a published author. Or all of this and more. Get creative. Think about how your book fits with the big picture of your life's purpose.

Diving into the Big Why behind your book will help ground you in what matters most. Ready? Let's go.

I suggest that you set a timer for two or three minutes for each question, and free write until the timer goes off.

- *Why are you feeling called to write this particular book right now?*
- *What impact, ideally, do you want your book to have in the world?*
- *What impact do you wish the completion and publication of your book to have on your own life?*
- *Picture your ideal reader. Who are they? Why are they drawn to your book? What questions are they asking that you are answering?*
- *How would you describe the essence of your book? If you struggle with this question, think about it in a whimsical way. Some examples using pop culture references: What are your book's superpowers? What kind of animal would it be? What's your book's daemon? What is your book's "away mission?"*

44

Now pause and read over what you've just written. Circle or highlight words and phrases that stand out as being especially important.

Your next task is to take a few minutes to begin shaping a draft version of a Vision and Mission Statement for your book project. I give clients just five or ten minutes to do this at the start. It's all a work in progress. None of this is set in stone, and it doesn't have to be perfect right out of the gate (I'm talking to you if you're a fellow recovering straight-A student!).

After you've completed your draft intention, let it sit for a few days. In the meantime, you can get started on writing your logline or summary.

I'm not going to give you prompts for this part, because your book project's genre will inform how you approach it. My advice is to look at the back covers (or the description field for digital versions) of books you enjoy that are in the same general category. If you're writing fiction, note how the summary doesn't give away the ending. Its purpose is to intrigue and invite the reader to dive in. Your logline should ideally be 100-250 words or so. It needs to fit on the back of the book, right? If your draft version is longer, that's fine. Again, we're not aiming for perfection just yet. This is a starting point, the beginning of the map that will lead to your completed manuscript.

Crafting Your Flexible Outline

Next we'll be crafting your book's outline together. When you hear the word "outline," you might groan or roll your eyes, thinking of the outlines you were forced to create before writing an academic paper. You know, with all the Roman numerals? Or is that just me? Rest assured that this is not the type of outline I'm talking about here, unless that's your jam.

Before we actually start making the outline, I have an important question for you. Are you a pantser or a plotter? Or do you have no idea what I'm talking about? If you aren't familiar with these terms, allow me to explain...

In the world of fiction writing, being a "plotter" means that you plan your story and all its details before you actually sit down to write it. A "pantser" is someone who writes a novel "by the seat of their pants," making it up as they go along.

I encountered these terms in the NaNoWriMo community. Even if you're not planning to write fiction, please bear with me. What I'm sharing here applies to nonfiction works as well.

Personally, I fall somewhere in between plotter and pantser. Whether I'm writing contemporary fantasy or books on spiritual practice or creativity, I like to start by outlining the bare bones first. Having the skeleton of the book mapped out, with chapter and section titles for nonfiction, or a basic story arc for fiction, helps guide my way as I dive in and begin the process of drafting a whole book.

Being a pantser, for me, would feel like too much pressure. Remembering all the details, the things I wanted to address, the direction I want the book to go — that clutters up my brain and makes me feel less creative. Holding the trajectory of the whole book in my head isn't for me.

Equally, having every detail drawn in fine detail feels constrictive. What if things change as I do the actual writing? (Spoiler alert: they inevitably do!) What if I get an inspired idea? I don't want to have to rework the whole thing or ignore something cool that just occurred to me. Walking the middle road allows me both creative freedom in the moment of writing and a useful bird's eye overview of the whole book.

When I sit down to write, I have a starting point — or can choose a topic from the outline that I feel like writing about at that moment (yup, most of my books are written out of order!). My outline is flexible, and I can add or change elements of it as the project progresses. While I encourage my writing clients to use mind maps and Flexible Outlines, I always emphasize that each person's process is different.

Like accomplished jazz musicians at the top of their game, some writers can improvise a whole book, doing so well and joyfully. Other "pantsers" prefer to rework their draft during the editing stage, so even if some details get lost along the way, any inconsistencies will be fixed in revisions.

There are writers who like to have every detail created in advance, so their creativity can follow the stream of the story. For them, improvisation is what might freeze them in their tracks.

What does this mean for you? If you're just starting to write, or maybe just thinking about writing, it means that you get to experiment. You get to try various approaches, and then follow the ones that feel best.

A good starting point is a mind map. Google "mind mapping" and you'll find it explained in basic terms. When you create a mind map, you write your story idea or book topic in the middle of the page, and then brainstorm freely, adding ideas as they appear. Notice how this process works for you — or if it doesn't. Be playful with it.

Figuring out how much or how little to plan your book in advance, plus capturing your ideas on paper or electronically, is an essential first step toward actually writing your book. The very first thing you have when you decide you want to write a book is an idea. You get inspiration for your book, or someone says, "You should write a book!" — about this cool thing you do, or your unique biz offering, or your amazing life story.

Before you start to actually write your book draft, it's time to take that Big Idea and break it down into smaller chunks. These will eventually become the sections and chapters of your book.

We're going to do a brain dump, to capture all the thoughts and ideas you have about your book. This part can be such fun! Let's get started.

Before you start to brainstorm, do something that will allow you to get into creative mode. You may not yet know what that is, which is fine. Here are some ideas: take a walk in nature, have a bubble bath, or take some deep breaths. Guided meditations are a terrific way to get into that deeply connected state; I like to find them on Insight Timer or YouTube.

When you feel ready, take your Big Book Idea and write it at the top of a page or in the center of a mind map. Using sparkly colorful pens is highly encouraged. It'll beckon your

Younger Self to get involved, and as you now know, when she's willing to play along, she'll often get Deep Self to join her, which will bring intuition and further inspiration to the table.

Now, brainstorm about all the anecdotes, pieces of wisdom, stories, how-tos, people, case studies, funny tidbits, deep thoughts, past events, etc. that might find their way into your book. The sky's the limit! This is your chance to brain dump all possible ideas related to your topic.

This brainstorming will eventually become your book's Flexible Outline. Have fun with this process. No idea is too silly. They may not all end up in the book — but they could spark new ideas that will. Enjoy your brainstorming session!

Your next step is to put all of these wild, wonderful ideas into the form of a Flexible Outline. The most basic way to do this is to type them up, in list form, in a Google, Pages, or Word document. But there are many ways to organize your outline.

I do suggest that you keep your outline in a separate document, not in the same one with the text of the book itself. This makes it much easier to go back and forth from one to another.

Here are some other forms your outline might take. As I mentioned before, I never use the traditional academic outline form from high school, because it feels too constraining for me. But you might like to use that type of form to keep your thoughts in order. You could use a spreadsheet. My partner BlackLion swears by them. If spreadsheets feel icky to you, don't do them. You can also use Scrivener or similar software for writers, index cards, sticky notes on the wall, a map, a flow chart, or a notebook that you keep just for this particular book project.

I want to emphasize that your Flexible Outline is a *mutable* container. It's a living document. It can — and should — change as you write the book. This is the map that you are making as you explore new territory and journey with the elements. The point is to customize it to your needs and allow it to change as you write.

My favorite thing about outlines? You don't have to write your book in order. When you sit down to work on your book, you can pick and choose depending on what feels inspiring in that moment.

When you create your book's Flexible Outline, just as you did when you started brainstorming, get yourself into creative mode. Start by putting your book's new draft Vision and Mission Statement at the top of a blank page. Take a moment to envision how you want to organize your book at this moment in time, knowing it will shift and change. Make some notes on what you're picturing.

Your next step is to copy your mind map or brainstorming notes into your new Flexible Outline. You might want to play with your ideas, moving them around and combining them in new ways. That's why it's helpful to have them in typed form, so you can freely cut and paste. Once you're reasonably happy with how the outline flows, put it away for a few days. Remember, this is a process that will take some time, and your outline won't be "done" until you finish the manuscript and make it into your book's Table of Contents.

That said, many aspiring authors never make it past the outline phase. Don't spend months or years refining your outline. The best way to update it is to do it on the fly, while you're writing the draft itself. Organizing your book's contents is not the same as writing it. I don't mean to sound harsh, here. But I want you to be different. I want you to be one of the Thriving Artists who isn't afraid to take on your Big Book Project.

I'll be with you every step of the way — and so will the elements.

We step onto the sacred path, mystically enough, in the center, with Spirit. After checking in with Kelly on her journey, that is...

Kelly's Creative Journey

Kelly's half-sister Sophia was coming to visit, arriving this evening, and Kelly was feeling super annoyed. She usually loved spending time with Sophia. Kelly's friends were mostly moms from the neighborhood, and wives of the couples she and Darren hung out with, but her relationship with her half-sister was different. She and Sophia loved doing all the girly things together, from pedicures to shopping to spa days. These weren't things Kelly did on her own, but Sophia's enthusiasm and sparkly personality always made it fun. They used to bring the kids when they were younger, but neither Sarah nor Amelia were interested these days, even though they loved Aunt Sophie. Lately Kelly had started looking forward to having Sophia all to herself.

This visit, though, Kelly knew, would interrupt her writing and her creative classes. She had stubbornly not told Sophia she was writing the book. Kelly knew how Sophia's presence, even for a long weekend, would take over every nook and cranny, every moment of each day. Kelly couldn't just excuse herself to her office to write, even if she said it was a work thing she had to do. Sophia was a thorough planner, and had made sure Kelly took time off so they could explore museums, get lunch out, and of course shop for bargains.

She knew she'd get off track with her writing, and it was already wearing on her. But what could she do? She'd just take the time off, and focus on doing stuff with her closest extended family member. It was only for a few days. Maybe it was a good sign that she'd gotten so attached to her writing routines. Kelly was writing four times a week now, for at least an hour each time. The book document was expanding, and she still hadn't given in to the urge to read back through her draft.

***

Kelly's heart was beating like the woodpeckers she and Darren had heard on their last hike. No, it was more like a jackhammer in the heart of the city. It was silly, she knew. It wasn't like she was in any actual danger.

She wished she hadn't let Sophia talk her into reading the book manuscript. They'd had a fun visit, despite Kelly's misgivings about taking time away from her writing. Sophia had been supportive, as always - something that Kelly continually marveled about. After growing up with her bitter, controlling mother, she didn't associate her side of the family with encouragement. But as adults, she and her half-sister (from her Dad's side, of course - her mother hadn't remarried or even dated, probably because she was such a bitch to everyone) had become each other's biggest cheerleaders. During Sophia's visit, they'd even gone to a coffee shop twice, so Kelly could write and Soph could work on her new website. They hadn't gotten much done because they kept stopping to talk, but it was a lovely gesture on Sophia's part.

Maybe that's why Kelly had given in eventually to Sophia's persuasive efforts to read what she'd written. Now that Sophia had returned home, Kelly had agreed to send her the partially-completed manuscript. She'd taken a leap of faith, sending it without having looked at it herself.

But now she was on the verge of a panic attack, because Sophia had told her that she'd be reading it this evening. All of Kelly's doubts and misgivings about her ability to write compelling - or even readable - stories of her life as a hospice nurse were activated. She paced her tiny office, chewing the inside of her cheek.

Darren poked his head in, startling her. "Pizza's ready. I made spinach salad, too."

"Okay," Kelly said hesitantly, not sure she could eat.

"What's wrong, hon?" Darren said, his brow furrowing.

"Sophia's reading my manuscript right now," she mumbled, burying her head in his sweatshirt, seeking that comforting smell. "It's freaking me out."

"Aww, Kell." He put his arm around her shoulders. "Come on. You love homemade pizza night. Let's go eat, and I'll put on some Grey's Anatomy. That'll distract you."

Kelly let herself be led to the living room. How bad could it be? If Sophia hated the book, she'd still give Kelly encouraging feedback - though not sugar-coated. All her craft books said that revisions were where the writing began to shine, anyway.

***

51

Kelly's fingers flew over the keys. Her "music to write by" playlist, so familiar now after many months, was coming to an end, but she wasn't done writing yet. Winnie was nudging her knee politely with her wet nose, wanting a walk. Kelly petted the dog's head absently.

"Be right with you, love. I'm finishing up this section." Kelly bit her lip and focused on capturing the scene in her mind's eye.

Writing the last sentence with a little flourish, Kelly sighed and rolled her chair back. That had been a good session. She felt alive, full of vitality.

As she got up to pee and get the dogs leashed up and ready, Kelly thought back over the past few weeks, since Sophia had first read her writing. Her half-sister had given her two pieces of advice, both of which Kelly had taken, in her own way.

Despite Kelly's initial misgivings, Sophia had been the perfect person to read the manuscript first. Sophia ran her own ad agency in the city now, but she'd started off as a graphic designer, and a mixed-media artist before that. As well as being a go-getter, Sophia was creative, with endless ideas and inspirations. She knew the creative process, inside and out. Her suggestions weren't at all what Kelly had expected, but they'd paid off.

Kelly leashed the dogs, who were both wiggly bundles of enthusiasm, and they headed outside. The neighborhood walking trails were mostly empty during the weekdays, and Kelly let the dogs wander.

The first suggestion had been for Kelly to find her own voice. "Your content is great," Sophia had said, "but your style is like some generic women's magazine. I mean, I was crying at the end of the Mrs. Horowitz story, but Kel, it doesn't yet sound like you. It's not you, Kelly, telling the stories. You know?"

Kelly hadn't been at all sure how to go about finding her writing voice, but she'd doubled down on reading the writing craft books and following working writers on Instagram. It had been a reel from a writing coach that'd sent her in a *fruitful direction. The woman had talked about "writing something wild every day." That and her suggestion of doing 15-minute writing sprints had opened something within Kelly that had started to let her true voice shine through.*

Soph's other suggestion was about having a theme for the book, a thread that ran through the whole manuscript. She'd said the individual stories were great, but lacked a certain continuity. This had reminded Kelly of the intentions that were set at the beginning of each of the retreats she'd attended. She'd written an intention for her book and posted it on the bulletin board above her desk. She could feel it up there sparkling at her each time she sat down to write. Weird, but it worked.

She was super happy with the way things were going. At this rate, she'd be done with the first draft in a couple of weeks. She wasn't at all sure what to do after that. Kelly shook her hair back and looked out at the river, to the right of the path. She didn't know the next steps, but somehow it felt like she was being led, as if writing this book was part of her purpose, for this next part of her life, and what one retreat leader had called "the healing journey."

CHAPTER 3:
WE BEGIN AND END WITH SPIRIT IN THE CENTER

Spirit and Creativity

The element of Spirit is the ethereal combination of all the other elements. It is the energy-matter which comprises our entire cosmos. Spirit encompasses all that we can see, and the Mysteries which are unseen to our mortal eyes. Spirit resides in the center, but also pervades the entire circle of life. It is associated with all times and seasons, and the mystical realms beyond the time-space continuum. The colors of Spirit are white, black, gold, and silver.

Each of us has a spirit, that which goes on living when our physical bodies die. Our spirit is connected to the non-physical realms and is part of a much greater whole. Spirit cannot be proven or measured. Indeed, traditional science has not yet discovered its secrets, yet somehow we know that it exists. Spirit is, in many ways, a paradox. It is exalted and Divine, and also commonplace and ubiquitous. Spirit is darkness and light, masculine and feminine, old and young, wise and naïve, active and receptive, without and within, above and below, and everything in between.

The voice of Spirit speaks to us through intuition. We sometimes "just know" things that are beyond our physical ability to perceive. The context doesn't matter, because Spirit is everywhere and always present, which can be comforting when we feel in need. The essence of Spirit is unconditional love, grace, and communion.

Some of us are in touch with non-physical beings in the realm of Spirit, such as ancestors, faeries, angels, and other spiritual guides. Spirit brings us magick and miracles beyond our conscious understanding. It is the Great Mystery.

Sacred geometry is one of the tools of Spirit. It has been taught across the ages that under the surface of all that we see, there is a web of interconnection. Each point on this web is holographic, in that it contains the essence of All-That-Is. When we recognize our own connection with everything that exists, Spirit aids us in bridging the gap between our individual selves and the unity of the eternal, infinite cosmos.

Spirit is that ineffable thing that we can theorize about all day, but can only be known by direct experience. It's that which goes beyond the physical realm. It's Nature. The Mysteries. The Divine.

Thus we begin and end with Spirit, as do all things — like our creative projects.

The word "inspire" contains the same root word as Spirit. It's often an intuitive, unexpected inspiration that moves us to write or create.

At the start of the process, this magickal inspiration carries us along on a wave of enthusiasm. We're so excited to dive in and explore this cool revolutionary idea or unique story!

As we get deeper into the process of writing a whole book, or crafting another long-form project, that enthusiasm can wane. It can become buried under the logistics of our process or lost in the overwhelming sea of words.

That's when we can tap into Spirit to bring fresh energy to our project. When I work with my clients, the topic associated with Spirit is exploring inspired persistence. This is something that we'll explore more toward the end of your first draft, but I wanted you to be thinking about how Spirit can support you in dedicating yourself to writing regularly.

By deliberately getting aligned with Spirit, you're infusing your work with a vast amount of creative energy. Spirit is pure joy and love.

When you tap into the ever-flowing wellspring of creativity, you bring back that excitement. (Yeah, I know, that's a Water metaphor — I'm a Water priestess, what can I say? Spirit can also be seen as embodied in Fire, Air, Earth, or in combinations).

When you connect with Spirit around your creativity:

- ❖ You pull in new perspectives on your project.
- ❖ You solve problems with more ease.
- ❖ You think *way* outside the box.
- ❖ You're persistent — in a way that feels natural rather than forced.
- ❖ You find that time zips by while you're in the process of creating - and you're having a whole lot of fun in the process!

With the assistance of Spirit, you can return again and again to that place of fresh inspiration and delectable ideas.

Spirit will help show you the way to becoming a Thriving Artist — and a published author! That's because, for many creatives like us, there's a strong link between our spirituality and our creative process. This has been a topic of books and essays for centuries. One of the words we use for the Divine is "the Creator." Even those who don't consider themselves creative and have shut most of the doors to their imagination know deep down that we are all innately creative.

Over the years, I've learned that creativity and spirituality are intimately connected. For a time, I thought that this might be true just for people like me, who are called back again and again to creativity. That could be true.

But in many ways, our spiritual traditions point to this connection, too. I'm not talking about heavily dogmatic religions, which don't tend to want their followers to think too deeply or question their authority. Still, many of our deities are known as creators. Human beings are curious about how we, and our amazing planet, came to be, and the meaning behind our very existence.

Religious dogma aside, if you think about spirituality, the point of it is to explore your own truths about the nature of life and the Universe. It's to discover a connection with something greater than yourself, and to ponder the Mysteries that hide behind our daily lives. Doesn't this sound quite a bit like the role of an artist?

In addition to that, many spiritual traditions posit that our Creator or Creatrix made human beings in their image. This means that we, too, are innately creative.

In one sense, it doesn't actually matter if the connection between spirituality and creativity is something that is only meaningful to artists. You're here, you were drawn to read this book about creativity, and you're open enough to spirituality to be curious about how it relates to the Five Sacred Things, the Elements. You are, deep within your soul, an artist.

Exploring your creativity will naturally pull you onto the path of spiritual growth – or, I should say, to a fuller awareness of that path, as it's one you're already walking, consciously or not. Don't be afraid. Sometimes it feels like spiritual growth will be too difficult, or boring, or unfun. Remember, tapping into your innate creativity is vastly fulfilling. The same is true of diving more deeply into your spiritual connection. Sure, there will be challenges. But there are plenty of those in daily life, whether or not you're focused on personal growth.

What is it that we artists and seekers find so compelling about the link between creativity and spirituality? This is something my clients and I discuss often. Spirituality is different for each of us. It's intimately personal. Exploring spirituality entails cultivating a connection with some power that is greater than oneself — whether you call it God, the Universe, Goddess, Nature, or something else.

When you create, you're tapping into that wider-ranging power. Many writers and artists describe being "in the zone" and feeling as if the words, sounds, or shapes are coming through you rather than from you. You are a co-creator, making something new in partnership with the Universe.

Creativity is essential for a thriving, bountiful life. The way it manifests will be different for different people — some of us love to make magick with words. Others bake, paint murals, make music, build furniture, heal others, and much more.

Creativity is a natural part of who we are as human beings. But over time, we put a lot of unnecessary baggage on top of our creative flow. It doesn't matter where we picked up that baggage — from school, peers, parents, or mainstream society.

The key to unlocking your creative flow, and making it fun and easy, is fostering your spiritual connection.

Think about how you feel when you're standing on a hillside, looking out over a gorgeous natural landscape. You connect with the wonder of creation. When you're tapped into that place of curiosity and awe, you create an opening that allows you to express *your* unique experience of life in this Universe.

You don't have to go hiking each time you want to sit down and write — although if that's your thing, go for it! By practicing your connection with All-That-Is, you strengthen your creative muscles. Your writing and other creations will be easier, and you'll enjoy the process. The baggage you'd collected around how it "should" be, or has to be, or how you need to struggle for your art, will gradually fade away.

Cultivating personal spirituality allows you to be more fully creative in your work and in your daily life. It's so rewarding. Whichever ways you enjoy creating, or even if you don't know what they are just yet, here are some ideas for using your spirituality to support your creative work:

Be playful. The concept of the Triple Self teaches us that only by appealing to Younger Self can we directly communicate with our Deep Self, allowing us to tap into the creative energies of the cosmos. The best way to get the attention of your Younger Self is to play. Yes, play. Just start doing something fun, without judgment or thought for the outcome. Experiment with playfully doing your writing for your book, blog, newsletter, or another creative project. Our culture devalues things that aren't hard or a struggle. Creativity can become easy and can flow smoothly, when you approach it playfully.

Craft your inspired intention. As I've mentioned before, having a solid intention for your writing will allow you to continue to resonate with it for the long haul. It's time to take another look at your intention – your book's Vision and Mission Statement – that you created in Chapter 2. If you haven't done it yet, now is as good a time as any! If you do have a draft intention, this is the time to edit and polish it until it feels right. When you put your intention in its final form, be sure to keep it in present tense, connect it to your life's purpose, and think about the impact you want your work to have on your readers.

Here's an example of a completed intention, so you can get a sense of what you're going for; this intention is the one I crafted while writing this very book:

"The Elements of Creativity *frees the reader's innate creativity and empowers them to play. The book embraces the reader where they are and provides an abundance of open portals through which to enter the temple and access their creative wellspring. I share the wisdom I've gained from being an author and coach in the form of a cohesive system. This allows me to reach a wider audience. I'm creating a vast network of Thriving Artists whose creativity permeates their entire world, uplifting and empowering them and their own audiences and communities."*

Make a sacred container for your time. This is the writing habit piece, which we'll explore in detail in Chapter 4. I want you to start thinking about your writing habit now, though, just playing with the notion, letting it simmer on the back burner of your mind. As with a daily spiritual practice like yoga or meditation, you'll make your creative time your own. Together we'll customize it to your needs. The way you show up for your writing will vary, and that's fine. Think of the ways that you're going to make a Writing Ritual that appeals to your Younger Self with sensual pleasures, like candles, crystals, chocolate, and sparkly pens.

Reach out to the Muses. Before you begin to write your book draft, it's helpful to purposefully craft a relationship with your Muses, whatever that means to you. It doesn't matter if you "believe in" the Muses in a literal sense. It's a useful metaphor for creating a relationship with your own unique creative expression. How do you craft this kind of imaginary relationship? Cultivate inspiration by taking yourself on Artist Dates, reading or listening to positive input, and asking for help — aloud, in writing, or in the privacy of your mind — from your Muses when you get stuck.

Try channeling. It's simpler than you might think. Do some channeled writing by asking your higher self a question and then just letting the answers flow out onto the page — maybe with your eyes closed. We'll talk in much more depth about channeling in Chapter 8, but if this immediately sounds fun and easy to you, give it a try now. As with the Muses, you don't have to believe that you're actually channeling an entity from the non-physical realm. Just pretend. If you do believe it, that's also perfectly fine. Read back what you channeled and see if any of it inspires you further or feels like it belongs in your book. If so, great! If not, check in with how you felt around the process. Play with it more or wait until I give you some further tips on it later in the book.

Capture your ideas. Creativity permeates your entire life, and ideas will come to you when they feel like it, not just when you're sitting down to work on your book. Actually, in my experience, new ideas most often come when you're doing something else entirely. Make sure that you have an easy way to capture those insights: a small notebook, a journal, and/or a notes app on your phone, voice or written. If that sounds like too much work – I can hear one of my artist friends say that as I type it – don't bother. Once you get your creativity flowing, you'll never have a dearth of ideas. They're everywhere, when you know how to look.

Be persistent and consistent. Just because we're woo-woo doesn't mean we can necessarily just wish and it will happen. That's a shallow understanding of the Law of Attraction. Wishing is the first step. Next is taking those inspired actions. Non-attachment is also useful; we'll talk about that more later on. So is not necessarily running away when it feels challenging. What do you do when you sit down to write but don't feel like it? Go back to your vibe; get in a better-feeling place before you write. Don't just give up at the first sign of trouble.

Ditch your inner editor (for now). This is something I tell clients over and over: you can't simultaneously write and edit. Don't try it. Seriously. Especially if you're a recovering perfectionist. Do something that helps you shut off that left side of the brain while you're writing. Play familiar music, shut your eyes if you can touch type, and make sure your Writing Ritual is the same or similar each day, which pleases your Younger Self.

Find community. Writers need community — yes, even those of us who are introverts. Inspiration, motivation, support, feedback, accountability — all of these things can come from community and are vital. I'm hearing that many more from my burgeoning community of writers. Find people you can talk with about your writing, whether in-person or online. Connection is key. We'll dive deeper when we get to the element of Water, in Chapter 10. For now, just have it in the back of your mind that you don't need to do this alone.

The above tips are just a little taste of the tools you'll be stacking into your toolbox as you read through this book and take your journey around the spiral of the elements. Before we move on to the next section, though, just a bit more about how the magick of spirituality intertwines with your creativity.

Books are inherently magickal. Think about it. A book, whether it's a story, a how-to, or something else, is created entirely in the author's imagination. It doesn't exist until someone dreams it up and then crafts it into the physical or digital realm.

Yes, a book is a magickal creation. And as the creator of a book — even if it's just a seed of an idea in your head right now — *you* are magickal, too. I want you to remember that as you begin this process of writing your Heartfelt Book.

Before your book exists in the 3D world, it exists in your mind. So why not love it up, right now, in that form? Don't be shy. Let's try it. Close your eyes. Take a few deep breaths and call upon your Triple Self. Get aligned with the three homes of your Triple Self: your Third Eye chakra, behind your brows; your Heart chakra area; and finally, your Solar Plexus or Sacral chakra, the ones above or below your navel – whichever one feels more like the home of your Deep Self or intuitive knowing. Now visualize your book as it will look and feel when you eventually hold it in your hands. Imagine your book in vivid detail. What does the cover look like? What font is your title and name printed in? How heavy is the book? What does it smell like? Think about how you'll feel when you've unboxed your book for the very first time.

You can also do some journaling, writing out how you'll celebrate when your readers start posting rave reviews. You could create a vision board that's all about your book and its emergence into the world. Whichever way you choose to engage the spirit of your book even before you've fully begun to write it, I want you to remember your magickal powers of creation and use them to support the crafting of your book.

It's not *just* about carving out time to write and cultivating your skills, although those things are key. Success in any endeavor includes the envisioning, the imagining, and the magick. It's the very first step. Remember that, dear one, and have fun with it!

Your Words Have Power

Think back to the intention you created for your book – especially the part about how it will change the lives of your readers, and the world as a whole. The whole notion of creating change in the world feels huge. But it's not all on your shoulders. Each of us holds a key piece of the puzzle. It will take many of us, the Thriving Artists, the conscious co-creators, to craft a new society.

When we think about power, we often think of those who are in positions of authority in government or big business. But power can be very personal, and it begins that way.

In fact, there are many different types of power. There's *power-over* others, which is what we most commonly think of in terms of society and power. That's when someone has the authority to make decisions on behalf of other beings. This is how the patriarchy has operated. It's a type of top-down power that's very authoritarian and militaristic, without much room for intuition or creativity. This kind of power thrives on making other people feel inferior, and on lots of competition to see who's going to be the "top dog" in any given situation. *Power-over* is something that most creatives and witchy types tend to shy away from. Our entire way of being is about rebelling against that sort of inflexible power model. It doesn't suit us.

There's also *power-from-within*, which is your personal sovereignty. This mode of power consists of your ability to make decisions for yourself, and to take action based on those decisions. It emerges from a connection with your inner wellspring of wisdom and creativity, or in other words, your Deep Self. This, ideally, is the power that we tap into as we write our books or take on other creative projects.

There's *power-with*, or shared power, like in groups of creative, conscious people, where each person agrees to contribute to the whole. This is what we're creating as Thriving Artists. We retain our personal sovereignty, but we also agree to contribute to the group, and support and encourage one another. This is the vision many of us have for society as we move forward.

The power of words has to do with vibration and energy. Chances are that you've witnessed the magick of the written word, by reading something that affects you strongly. Books you've read may have even helped to change your life. I know it's true for me! Are you intimately familiar with the power of your imagination to speak or write new things into being? I hope you've experienced it for yourself. As writers, this is a key part of our contribution to the whole.

The latter two types of power — *power-from-within* and *power-with* — are uplifting and positive. But we've all been conditioned by growing up in patriarchal societies and families. Our understanding of power often has a lot of old baggage around it. In my own experience and in working with authors-to-be, I find that before we can fully step into contributing to *power-with*, from a space of *power-from-within*, we have to release some of the old conditioning that might get in the way of our ability to share our powerful words.

Here are some journaling prompts that will get you thinking about your own experience of and feelings about power, particularly as they relate to creative expression:

❖ *What were you taught as a child, about the power of your words and your voice?*

❖ *Are there ways in which you've felt silenced, in your past? How does that affect you now?*

❖ *What feels unsafe or scary about sharing your deep wisdom or stories with the world at large?*

❖ *What feels most exciting about your deep wisdom?*

In the realm of Spirit, you receive the support you need to bring in the best kind of power. Not just the power you need to actually write the book, but also the power to write it from a place of deep connection with your inner wisdom. You'll learn more about how to "power up" as we go along. For now, trust that you have the capacity to bring forth the change that you're seeking. The next step is to magickally invoke that change into your life, so that it can flow through you into your book manuscript. Don't worry, I'll guide you along the way.

The Invocation of Change

To invoke means to call something forth. In spiritual and magickal settings, invocation is often associated with calling on a divine being to join us in performing a ceremony or spell. In this section, we're going to invoke or call upon our Muses. We'll request their aid in transforming some small part of the world, through the written word, in the form of a book.

First, though, let's take a look at what's behind the change you wish to create in the world with your book. One way to get a sense of this is to look at what you *don't* like or want. That's often where people stop. In fact, most of our modern political culture is built around the "don't like" part of things. There is blame, and finger-pointing, and derision, but not much actual focus on what exactly the person pontificating plans to do about it.

The next step is to use that contrast – the "don't like" situation — to propel yourself toward what you *do* like. This is the time to think about what you want to see happen in the world around you.

Here are some journaling prompts to help frame your thoughts about this part of the magickal creation of your book:

- ❖ *If your book made the difference that you'd like it to make, what exactly would change in the lives of your readers?*
- ❖ *What are the top 3 to 5 changes you'd most like to see in the world?*
- ❖ *What don't you like about the way things are now, especially in relation to the topic of your book?*
- ❖ *Who are your role models? Who do you look up to? Why?*

Words are powerful, as we've seen. They can affect change in the world, like a magickal spell. We've all read books that changed some aspect of our lives or gave us new inspiration. Imagine that you could wave a magickal wand and suddenly find that you were able to use your words to craft deep change. With that in mind, write out the answers to these questions in your journal:

- ❖ *What is your personal magick?*
- ❖ *What spells are you spinning with your words?*
- ❖ *What is the most profound difference that you want your book to make?*
- ❖ *Who will benefit most from it and why?*

Now it's time to perform the invocation. We'll begin in the realm of Earth, by crafting the sacred container of a writing habit that will carry you through the process of writing your book. Remember, it's not just about schedules and plans, although those external steps are part of the picture. It's also about calling on your Triple Self and your Muses to bring non-physical energies into the process. This will make your book writing experience easier and more fun, as well as helping you craft a book that will, indeed, create powerful change! Let's walk the winding path toward the next element: Earth. But before we get there, I'd like you to meet Delia.

THE ELEMENTS OF CREATIVITY

Delia's World

Delia lies in bed, one arm over her eyes, thinking about laundry. Well, and aliens (when will they officially introduce themselves to humankind?), *her daughter's upcoming school dance* (isn't she still too young??), *and what they did for Christmas this past year. She probably should have gotten up half an hour ago.*

She knows that most of her friends and family consider her a hot mess. Especially her in-laws, or, she supposes, her ex-in-laws. Ex-laws? Outlaws? Whatever.

The thing is, she's actually doing really well. She finally got her drinking under control - not that she was an alcoholic or anything. Or was she? She's not sure, but anyway, she stopped drinking entirely six months ago. But now the house is just totally out of control. Thus, the laundry pondering. The thought of the huge piles of it awaiting her in the laundry room, plus the clothes scattered around the girls' room, and, well - she lifts her head and takes a glance - her own bedroom... It's more than she can do in a day, which makes her not want to even bother.

The doorbell rings toward the front of the house, causing the cat to startle and unwind himself from Delia's feet. Who even rings the doorbell anymore? Must be a delivery. Did she order something? Delia can't remember. Probably.

She stretches and stirs, not to answer the doorbell - they'll leave the package on the porch - and certainly not to start the laundry, but it's well past coffee time.

Anyway, hot mess. The house is a wreck, but on the other hand, she's been seeing the same therapist for almost 3 months, and the new ADHD meds seem to be helping. Until recently, Delia had had no idea she was the owner of a, what was it, neurodivergent brain. But now that she knows, it makes sense of so much.

She pads her way to the kitchen, clicks on the radio, where the NPR host drones on about a stimulus package for something or other, and pours the coffee. The cat twines around her legs. Delia retrieves the container of salmon from the fridge, intending to drop some into the cat's bowl, then remembers the delivery.

It's super quiet today, with the girls both at their Dad's. She opens the door to find two brown boxes stacked on the porch. It's a sunny day, and actually sort of warm. She steps out onto the porch, coffee still in hand, both cat and packages forgotten for the moment.

Delia doesn't care as much anymore about how others see her, she realizes. She doesn't give any fucks about how she looks, whether her neighbors see her unmatching pajamas, or if she actually is a hot mess. She even left her phone in the bedroom. It's Saturday morning, and she's going to sit on the porch swing and daydream, for at least a cup of coffee, or maybe two.

***

Delia sat in front of her laptop and twirled one of her curls around her finger. She was about to click into a Zoom call but was feeling torn.

She hadn't been to one of these calls in weeks. Her writing coach was awesome, and encouraging, and would never berate Delia in a million years. And yet - Delia still felt super guilty about "not doing her homework," "not living up to her potential," "not following through" - all those things she'd heard over and over again all through her life.

But now she was "Give No Fucks Delia." Right? Right! And she'd paid good money to be part of this coaching program, so it made sense to attend. Plus, she was actually excited about her book idea. It was just so hard to focus on it. But that's why she'd gotten a coach. Okay.

She clicked in to join the meeting.

A screen opened and Delia noted that there were six other participants already there, but the gathering hadn't started yet. There was an Aimee Mann song playing, and Delia relaxed a bit. Her coach was cool, and so were the other women in the group.

Her office door creaked, and she heard bare feet tapping across the floor.

"Mommy?" came Zen's sleepy voice. "I had a bad dream."

Delia reached back and pulled her younger daughter onto her lap. Zen snuggled in, pushing her face against Delia's chest. Her curly hair, sticking up straight, tickled Delia's face.

Delia smoothed her daughter's hair down and hummed a comforting tune, hoping to lull Zen, who was seven, back to sleep. She'd been lucky to get both girls fed, bathed, and settled in time for the 8:00 meeting, but Zen's dreams often woke her lately, soon after she fell asleep. Even with two nightlights and a flock of stuffies, her youngest was a reluctant sleeper - much like Delia herself. She hoped Zen wasn't ADHD too, but the signs already seemed to point in that direction. It wasn't just the sleep thing; Zen was like Delia in many ways, and in retrospect Delia could see how her own ADHD had gone so long undiagnosed, yet still permeated her entire life. Or maybe, for Zen, it was just the divorce - they were nearly two years out now, but both girls still seemed rattled. She made a mental note to keep an eye on the situation.

The meeting began, and Zen was breathing steadily, so Delia left her in place on her lap and muted her video.

The book was gonna be sort of a combination of a Terry McMillan romance and an Octavia Butler vibe - more on the fantasy side than dystopian, really, though there were aliens. The aesthetic was lush, and she thought of it as a European-style faerie tale but for black women like her. More like Bridgerton but not so peppy. The plot had come to her soon after her ADHD diagnosis. Well, it was actually before that. Delia was on the receiving end of a nonstop series of creative ideas. Most of them died on the vine. Single, working mom of two with a house and a cat and an extended family and a bunch of insistent friends? Yeah, creativity. Right.

But this particular idea kept breathing down Delia's neck, until she'd impulsively joined this coach's program, after finding her on TikTok and following her silly videos.

This particular call involved checking in with each participant, and Delia steeled herself to admit that she'd done pretty much nothing. She shifted Zen on her lap - her left leg was starting to fall asleep. She listened to the other aspiring *writers checking in, and was surprised that she wasn't the only one slacking. Gina, the coach, was calm and encouraging as ever. She gave each person customized suggestions to get back on track.*

When it was Delia's turn, she unmuted herself and turned on the video. She tried to speak softly, nodding down at her sleeping kid, but Zen still stirred and opened bleary eyes. Delia was embarrassed, both at her lack of progress and the fact that Zen interrupted, asking for some water. Gina just smiled and waited patiently while Delia fumbled open her water bottle and gave it to Zen.

Gina offered her some great suggestions. Delia was glad the sessions were recorded, because she didn't have a free hand to make notes with, and all her notebooks had gone missing in stacks of paperwork anyway. Not that she'd likely go back to the recording of a meeting she'd actually attended, but it was there in case she needed help remembering some key points.

As always, Delia left the meeting feeling inspired and hopeful. Now to see if she actually put any of it into practice. Maybe she'd even get started on a new chapter tonight. It was still fairly early. Without the alcohol slowing her down, Delia found she could sometimes get stuff done in the evening, if she wasn't too exhausted. She wasn't feeling sleepy at all, right now. Writing - or dictating her words into a Google doc - could even be fun. But first, she had a kiddo to sing back to sleep.

***

Delia hadn't written a single word for at least three weeks, maybe more. Not even on the weekends when Allan had the girls. She hadn't been recording book ideas on her phone, either, like she normally did, which had to be a bad sign, right?

The thing was, life had just been so freakin' busy lately. Work at the ad agency was crazy, especially since her recent promotion. Both girls had a lot of end-of-school-year activities: a dance recital, field hockey sign ups, Girl Scout meetings with plans for summer gatherings - oh, that reminded her, she was supposed to register them both for the jamboree weekend or whatever it was called. Where was the form? Had they brought it home from the last meeting, or did the troop leader email it? When was it due? Delia had no idea.

She padded to the hallway table, piled with mail and the girls' drawings and worksheets, and started searching through the mess. Delia noticed an unopened envelope from the utility company, marked URGENT, and ripped it open. It was well past the first of the month, and obviously she'd forgotten to pay the bills. She hadn't yet spent the time to put them on autopay, either. Shit. She headed back to her office, bill in hand.

Anyway, writing. She wasn't doing it, and she felt guilty for it, but the ideas just kept coming. She'd been listening to Big Magic *by Liz Gilbert in the car, and the story about the book idea that gave up on one potential author and moved on to another had freaked her out. She didn't want her novel to leave her for another writer, one who had the ability to get organized and sit down at the laptop, maybe even at a fancy coffee shop, the one with the yummy lavender lattes.*

Okay. It was time, or past time. Allan had the girls this weekend - they'd switched so she could have them for Halloween in a couple weeks, one of her favorite holidays - and Delia was gonna double down on writing. She'd do the coffee shop thing. She'd order in (who was she kidding? She always ordered in anyway, when the girls were gone). She'd ignore the mess (except some essential laundry - it was always the damn laundry!) and focus on writing her book. Hear that, book? *she thought.* Don't give up on me yet!

CHAPTER 4:
EARTH: ESTABLISHING EMPOWERED HABITS

About Earth

The foundation of our physical existence is the Earth. This is the name of our home planet, which makes our very existence possible. Earth is also what we call the soil in which we're planted, metaphorically and, for our plant friends, literally.

The element of Earth reveals our connection with the land. Earth's direction is North, and its time is winter and midnight. The colors of Earth are dark and restful: mahogany brown, pine forest green, deep black like the night sky. Giant mountains, mighty trees, and burrowing creatures sing to us the slow, patient song of Earth.

We live in our physical bodies here on the Earth plane. We are rooted to the Earth through our cells, our ancestors, and the land we inhabit. As we observe the land where we live, watching the seasons change, we connect ourselves deeply to the energies of our sacred spaces. We notice the slow changes, the dance of time. When we are more nomadic, traveling across the surface of this vast planet, we can see the changes of the Earth's terrain as we move through space.

Earth is what we are made from, the matter of our cells and bones and muscles. Our bodies long to experience nature: to stand barefoot on the ground, to walk through the woods and feel the sun and wind, to look up in awe at the stars. We nourish our bodies with Earth's bounty: the fruits, vegetables, and grains that grow from the soil. When we lie down to rest and fall asleep, we allow our bodies to be held in Earth's embrace.

The instruments of the Earth element are drums. A slow, steady rhythm reflects the deep heartbeat of our living planet. It connects us with our own heartbeat, the personal rhythm that we dance to from the womb to the moment of our death. As we hear the beating drums, we touch the rhythms of our ancestors, those who came before us and whose bodies now sleep in the Earth. We are a part of all who have come before us. We arise from the Earth and to the Earth we will return.

The element of Earth is solid and slow-moving. In the work I do with writers, we use our time with Earth to begin establishing regular writing habits.

Now, wait a minute — don't run away! As I mentioned earlier, most creative people are resistant to the idea of a habit when it comes to their craft. The notion seems to be that habits are boring and mundane and will restrict the flow of creative ideas.

The Muses, we fear, only come calling on their own timeline.

Let's look at this a different way. If you want to build your dream house, you need to start with a foundation of some kind.

You can have the most innovative, unique, wild design, with round stained-glass windows and spiral towers, but you need to anchor it to the ground first, if it's going to last. Yes, even you treehouse enthusiasts; the tree's trunk is your foundation.

In home building, the foundation is usually made up of — you guessed it — Earth. When you take on a long-form creative project, like writing a book, your habits form the foundation. They help keep you focused throughout the process.

Writing a book without a solid habit at the core isn't viable. If you wait around for inspiration to strike, at a time when you're free to drop everything and create madly, what happens? It takes a lifetime to write just one book. If you're independently wealthy and don't have a family to take care of, it might only take a few years. Or maybe it just doesn't happen at all.

By establishing a writing habit, however, you create a sustainable container.

Writing habits, thankfully, aren't "one size fits all." They can (and should) be customized to your lifestyle, preferences, and commitments. Once you've established a habit, it can change with your needs.

For example, perhaps in the summer you love to get as much time outdoors as possible, so you plan to write in the late evening, before bed. Yet during the dark days of winter, you need more sleep, and you shift your writing time to the morning, right after breakfast.

Creating your writing habit isn't just a matter of choosing a time and a few days each week. It also includes things like where you write and with whom. All of these pieces will be unique to you and your situation.

Developing a habit around your writing or other creative projects not only creates more time for creativity, but can help you be more efficient and allow your creativity to flow more smoothly than when you're hit or miss.

Grounding yourself in a regular writing habit gives you the foundation from which to soar. Here in the realm of Earth, we'll customize and solidify your writing habit, one that works well for you in your current lifestyle. This will serve as a powerful container for your wild and free creativity, for your Muses to speak with and through you.

The Earth's Fertile Creativity

The most obvious form of creativity in the realm of Earth is the literal fertility of our planet. From the tiniest one-celled creatures, to plants, birds, and animals, to complex creatures like we human beings, Mother Earth seems to be continually growing and giving birth to new life.

But *how* does that happen? Is fertility truly continual? No, not really. It happens in cycles. The circle of life, growth, death, and rebirth goes around and around, much like the Earth herself circling the sun. The prevalence of cycles in nature can be seen in the changing of the seasons, in the moon's monthly phases, the fertility cycle of mammals, and in all kinds of other places.

What does this mean for us as writers and creatives? There's a cycle of creativity that we can tap into. One thing that we can observe about the Earth's cycles is that they are consistent. After winter, spring always comes. The sun rises each morning. The perennials that die away in the fall will start to grow again when the weather warms.

The Earth's habits can inspire us to form our own practices. These, ideally, will contain cycles of rest and nurturing, as well as productivity. When I talk with a new client about creating a writing habit, often their tendency is to go full force. "I'll get up every morning at 5am and do a couple hours of writing before the kids are awake, and then devote Sunday afternoon to a longer session." I gently but firmly rein them in.

Our mainstream culture, with electric lighting and round-the-clock schedules, trains us to put our productivity on overdrive. This isn't something we learned from Earth. When we embrace a natural rhythm, we take into account all of the creative work that is done before we actually sit down to write or create. This includes getting a good night's sleep, eating nourishing foods, moving our bodies, getting inspired by time in nature and the books, podcasts, conversations, and shows that we take in.

Adding more focused creative time to your schedule should incorporate all of these other needs, plus the things you're already committed to in your life as a whole, from relationships to work to caregiving. Earth is a good role model for this. It's the element that teaches us to have healthy habits and live a balanced life.

Earth also shows us how creativity touches every area of our lives. Once in a while I run into someone who insists that they are just not creative. What they mean is that they don't do the things that are traditionally considered creative, like writing, painting, playing music, or doing craft projects. If I talk with them for a few minutes, though, their area of creativity usually makes an appearance. It might be in the way they approach their work, or how they decorate their home, or even the unique way they've chosen to raise their children.

We're not able to forgo being creative. But some of us lock it away and resist it quite well. Earth leads us to release our grip on how we show up in the world. When we open up to our own natural cycles, a time of rest will naturally flow into a time when we're full of ideas and the energy and motivation to put them into place.

Your Life, Plus Writing

Right around the time that my partner BlackLion and I met, he quit smoking cigarettes after more than a decade. I remember him talking about how easy it was for him to quit. Most people have a really hard time with this process. But he created a way of doing it that felt easy.

The gist of his method was the decision he made. He resolved to continue to do everything he was already doing, but without smoking a cigarette. When it was break time at work, he went outside to the smoking shelter with the other smokers. He stood and talked with them – but didn't actually smoke. When he went out to meet friends at a bar, he would sit with them in the smoking section. Yes, there was a time when you could smoke indoors in public places. But he just didn't smoke the cigarette. It was a challenge at first, of course, as his system processed the release of the addictive substance that is nicotine. But his decision to only change *that one thing* helped him to stay focused.

In time, with the chemical addiction fading, he gradually put other changes into place. He eventually chose not to go out to the smoking area at work, especially when winter came and it was cold out there!

From his experience, I've taken inspiration for dealing with other changes in habits. It doesn't only work for something you're letting go, but can also help when there's a habit you want to add to your life. Most of the people I first speak with about getting support for writing their book lament that they have full, busy lives, and can't imagine how they're going to fit in time to write their book manuscript. But with BlackLion's technique in mind, think of creating your writing habit this way: this is your life, exactly as it is now, *plus* writing.

Dealing with the D Word

Before we get to the actual work of setting up your sustainable writing practice, let's talk about the "D" Word — no, not that one. I'm talking about discipline. As I've mentioned, it's a common and very old belief of creative people that discipline will kill your creativity. So how do you do this discipline thing while still honoring your wild spirit?

It's kind of a paradox. What I've discovered, through personal experimentation, is that when you build a habit around your writing or other creative projects, each session becomes more efficient. You take less time to do the same amount of writing. You're already attuned to your creative flow, so you can drop in easily. There's more fun and ease during the process of creating.

Here's what a habit of self-discipline will do for you:

❖ It helps you to cultivate an ongoing awareness of the value of your work in the world, a regular connection to your *Big Why*.

❖ It sets up an energetic container that holds space for abundant, uncensored creative flow.

❖ It allows you to do the work of writing a full-length book in small, achievable steps, without having to make it your full-time job.

❖ It helps you stay focused on what your real priorities are in life, and to devote time to them, rather than just wishing you could.

As we saw in Chapter 3, creativity and spirituality are intimately entwined. We're all innately creative. Having a regular time to get creative makes you more centered and less stressed. It's a powerful outlet. Creativity is a portal to deeper spiritual connection. I work with my book midwife clients in this way; over time, inevitably their writing practice begins to overlap and merge with a spiritual practice of some sort.

A habit is a ritual. We've already talked about the reasons that ritual appeals to your Younger Self, and why it's key to have her on your side as an interpreter for your Deep Self. As you now know, doing the sacred work of aligning your Triple Self will allow your most powerful creative work to flow forth from your creative wellspring. We're going to set up your writing habit so that it has a ritual aspect which appeals to your Younger Self. This will keep you connected to Deep Self, which dwells at the seat of that deep creative wellspring, the place where you're connected to the non-physical realms. This will involve some discipline, yes, but the kind that makes life easier, not harder.

Setting Up Your Writing Ritual

It's time to begin creating and refining your magickal Writing Ritual. We'll begin with the external steps. I'm going to walk you through the component parts of a writing habit.

When?

"Not having time" to write is one of the most common reasons people cite for not actually writing their book. Most people who haven't yet written a book imagine that it will take them hours each day – hours that they simply don't have. But writing your book manuscript doesn't have to cost you a huge amount of time from your day or week.

Before you scoff about writing a book in just minutes a day, listen. I have a client who is an entrepreneur, a busy homeschooling mom of five young kids, and an aspiring author. Out of necessity, she established a writing habit of just 20 minutes, three or four days per week. She got up before her girls woke, spending those quiet morning moments at her laptop, before even getting fully ready for her busy day. In about nine months, she finished her book manuscript, and is now a published author! So even if you only have an hour or two per week available to write, you could have your first draft done within a year. It's entirely do-able.

A word about sacrifice. We already talked about "your life, plus writing." Realistically, though, you will need to shift at least a few minutes of your time, on the days that you devote yourself to sitting down to write. This means that something else that you give your time to, even if for only those 20 minutes, will have to go. Think about that for a moment. What are you willing to give up? Here are some ideas on things you can choose to minimize or release when you plan your new writing habit: social media scrolling, Netflix or TV, video games, too much news, gossip, housework. Those are just a few suggestions. I'm sure you can think of more.

I'm not suggesting that you give up those things entirely, just that you subtract your writing time from them. For most of us, taking a little less time with our phones or other screens is a healthy choice. Housework is a tricky one, but you can choose to get help, whether from family members, by hiring a professional service, or by simply leaving it until later. When my writing space was in the corner of the great room, at the dining table, I could see all the kitchen counters from there. When I first started writing books, I felt like I had to have every dish washed and put away before I could legitimately begin writing. We all know how that goes. Dishes multiply more quickly than the tribbles in Star Trek! I soon discovered that I couldn't wait for the kitchen to be perfect before I began, not if I wanted to get anywhere with my book manuscript.

Here's another pro tip. Make sure that you tailor your creative habit to your own biorhythms. Sometimes the notion of adding a new practice brings to mind getting up at the crack of dawn, which kept me — a confirmed night owl — from doing a home practice of yoga for many years. There was no way I was going to get up any earlier in the morning than I already was! Others are deterred by adding a creative practice at the end of the day when they're feeling sluggish and ready to sleep. Explore your own rhythms and when in your day you feel most creative and design your plan accordingly.

It takes about 30 days, give or take, depending on which scientific study you believe, to establish a brand-new habit. I suggest setting a slightly longer goal for yourself at the start. Pick a length of time that makes sense. My clients find that they have success with committing to three months of doing this new writing practice. This gives you plenty of room to fall off the wagon, which you most likely will, and then get back on again.

It's time to break out your journal or notebook once again. We're going to brainstorm about times and days that will work best for you to do your writing. If you have a super-full life — don't we all? — it can be tough to keep up with a regular creative practice. Answer the following questions:

❖ *When will I do my writing for my book project?*
❖ *How am I going to make writing a priority?*
❖ *How will I get back on track when I go astray?*

Once you've pinpointed when you'll write, add the days and times to your calendar or planner. These scheduled dates are your appointments with your Muses, with your book, with your author self. Take them as seriously as you would a client call or a visit to your doctor or therapist.

Where?

The next thing to figure out is exactly where you will physically be as you write your book. Here are some ideas: in a quiet space in your home, in a coffee shop with headphones on, at the library, on a train, by the pool or lake, in bed, at a rented desk in a co-working space, at a local cafe, or at your work desk during your lunch break.

It helps to think about the types of environments that inspire you. Some people love to write at a busy restaurant or bar, but for me that would be way too distracting. That said, I do enjoy writing in coffee shops from time to time. I don't even drink coffee – chai tea latte with oat milk is my go-to coffee shop order — but I like the busy yet focused energy, sometimes.

Writing in nature appeals to me, too, but it might not be your cup of tea. Where do you feel most creative?

Having "a room of one's own" for writing can be helpful — but if that's not possible for you, don't let it be an excuse not to do the work. Most of the writers I know don't have a dedicated office, but that doesn't keep them from writing productively.

Writing is a very portable activity that you can do just about anywhere — just not while you're driving, please.

Get out your journal again. *Pick three places where you'll do your writing and note them in your notebook.* One will be your "usual" spot, like my little corner of the dining room used to be for me (now I have my own office!), while the other two should be attractive alternatives. For example, my three places are my office (my new default), the hammock in my backyard (when the weather permits), and my favorite local coffee shop. If you don't yet know where you like to write, jot down some ideas to try in the weeks and months to come.

With Whom?

Writing can feel like a completely solitary activity. The popular culture's image of writers certainly reflects this, and I think that's where our minds tend to go when we think about writing a book. But even though many writers are introverts, and there are certainly plenty of times when you'll be writing alone, that's not the entire picture. Over the course of my career as an author so far, I've discovered that it helps to have some kind of human connection around my creative work. The process goes more smoothly when you have some form of support.

Who's going to be there at your side, figuratively and/or literally, as you do the work of nourishing and then bringing your book to life? Perhaps you have online friends or acquaintances who write or create. If you don't yet have those connections, there are many groups to check out and join. Maybe it's a partner, a family member, or a close friend. Getting someone in your life, someone you see in person on a regular basis, on board also makes what you're doing more real. It makes it a solid part of your life.

Here's a piece of advice I've discovered from personal experience: don't even involve the doubters. As you get started, you're still tentatively building your confidence in your work. If you have someone in your life who tends to be skeptical, don't pick them to confide in. They might mean well, but you don't need that type of energy around your creative work, especially just starting out.

For me, it's my Dad who was the main voice of doubt in my life. He meant well. He wanted to protect me from failure or disappointment. But that's not the energy I need when I'm taking on a Big Project. I didn't even talk with him much about my writing until after my first book was published, because I knew he'd deliver a hefty dose of skepticism. Later on, he was proud of me and knew I could successfully write books — because I'd done it before. As you get started, it's best to choose supporters who are, you know... supportive.

Another word to the wise: remember to call upon your non-physical helpers. This could mean your ancestors, spirit guides, power animals, your higher self, or your guardian angel. The things I've experienced lead me to believe firmly that each of us has a whole team of non-physical guides who are there to support us. They're cheering us on from behind the scenes. If this resonates with you, make sure you tell them you're taking on this project and would like their support. If it's not your cup of tea, you can skip this step – or suspend your disbelief and try it anyway. Remember, we're bringing in playful experimentation. Trying new things is part of that process.

When we get to the chapter on Water, we'll be focusing more deeply on creating a support network for you and your book. In the meantime, start small. Choose one person in your life and share your book idea with them. It can be someone you've talked about it with before, and this can be a chance to let them know that you're committing to your book. It might be someone you've never said it to before, but you sense that they'll be supportive and encouraging. Write their name down in your journal or notebook and make a note to reach out to them this week.

If you're going to choose a non-physical helper or two to connect with, make a note of that as well. Reaching out to them is as simple as talking to them in the privacy of your mind or saying a little prayer or invocation. If you have an altar, you might make an offering. Incense and chocolate are usually welcome.

What Ritual Tools?

Remember, we're going to involve ritual as part of your new writing habit. Doing this makes the process of sitting down to write playful and fun. This will appeal to Younger Self, which entices her to show up. She'll bring Deep Self along, which makes your writing easier. Creating a fun ritual to signal yourself that it's time to be creative will also bring you back to your desk again and again, rather than putting off your writing for another time.

Rituals appeal to the five senses. Here are some ideas of things to include that touch on the senses: candles, crystals, shells, incense, herbs, flowers, a tasty beverage, some chocolate or fruit to nibble on, a cozy spot in which to create, a creative music playlist, sparkly pens and a pretty notebook, or a particular scent that you use just for this book project.

Get out your journal and write down some ideas that really appeal to you for your Writing Ritual.
- ❖ *What tools will you use?*
- ❖ *What do you have on hand already?*
- ❖ *What do you want to acquire?*

Next, it's time to create and refine your plan for integrating your Writing Ritual into your life. Look over the notes you've made so far and add to them. Consult your calendar and see when would be best to write as you get started. Write down the when, where, and with whom parts that we've just talked about, as well as the tools you'd like to include.

If you're especially ambitious, or perhaps a recovering perfectionist like myself, I want to caution you to rein yourself in. It's common to decide that you're going to write every day for an hour or two, especially when you're excited to begin. Don't do that. It's too much. You'll most likely get overwhelmed and then not meet your goal, which can make you disappointed in yourself, and then you avoid writing. Let's not go down that particular spiral of shame. Restrain yourself to two or three writing sessions per week as you first begin. Seriously!

Okay, now that you have a rough plan, it's time to take action. First, put all of your writing times into your calendar. If you don't keep a calendar, set alarms on your phone that will remind you to write at the appointed time — give yourself 10 minutes or so to get ready. I keep a Google calendar which includes chunks of time to write, and I also have a bullet journal where I list out daily tasks. My writing times get put into both. It's good to have a backup, just in case.

Decide how long you're going to commit to your plan, initially. I suggest three months. At the end of each month, look back and see what has worked for you and what hasn't. Your habits will change as your life does. You might have a different schedule at different times of year, and you'll need to tweak your plan to accommodate your needs. This is a good thing. We don't want a rigid form of self-discipline here. Your writing habit is a sacred container, remember. It is meant to serve you and your writing project.

The Elephant in the Room: Procrastination as Resistance

You've gotten your writing times planned out and scheduled them in your calendar.

But are you actually sitting down to write at the appointed time? Or are you procrastinating?

Procrastinating can look like: doing housework or business tasks instead of writing, forgetting entirely that you'd planned to write, deciding you just have to run that errand or return that call *right now*, getting sucked into a new Netflix series, or any number of things. There's no shame in it.

Making a change, such as starting a writing practice or beginning to write a book, is a Big Deal. There will be some internal resistance, especially as you get started. It takes a while to create a new habit.

How can you ensure that you'll actually *do* your writing rather than blowing it off? Here are a few tips.

First, set a phone alarm to alert you ten minutes before your scheduled time. Do this in advance for each session. Use a special sound or song just for your writing dates.

Next, make your writing session fun — the ritual part, remember? Purchase a sparkly new gel pen or break out a new lined journal. Find some writing prompts that get your creative juices flowing. Plan for a little reward for yourself after you've finished. You can also convert a writing date into a blue-sky brainstorming session. Make a list of all the things you want to write about. Add them to your Flexible Outline. That way you'll know what to look forward to in the next session. I find it helpful to plan the topic ahead of time, so my ideas can simmer away in the back of my mind before I sit down to write them.

Another useful technique is to stop in the middle of a scene or section. That way you're not out of fresh ideas, and when you return to the page, you can pick up where you left off.

Finally, tell someone you trust that you're going to write today. Remember to pick someone who's naturally encouraging and optimistic. Ask them to check in with you later in the day. Having to be accountable will make you more likely to follow through.

Feeling like these little hints won't even begin to break through your procrastination? Don't worry. I've got your back. Read on.

You already have plenty of habits in your life that you do successfully, from brushing your teeth to taking care of your pets. You may have thought, "There's no reason I shouldn't be able to do that with my writing habit."

And yet... Resistance does come up, and it's often around inner work rather than just the external pieces or distractions. Or maybe the external things that seem to get in the way —

like housework — are actually reflections of some inner limiting beliefs or doubts.

When you're working with the element of Earth and setting up these solid writing habits that will carry you through, resistance often arises in the form of procrastination. You intend to sit down to write, but somehow it doesn't happen. You put the writing times in your calendar and set your phone alarms, but something else always comes up and gets in your way.

Despite your best efforts, you're not writing.

On the surface, it looks like the external pieces of life get in the way. The dishes, the laundry, the day job, your family – there's always something that needs to be tended to, and your writing falls further and further down the list. But there's usually more to the story.

All writers have resistance, which can often show up as procrastination. The parts of writing that you tend to procrastinate on will tend to be unique to you. For me it's editing, and also fiction-writing projects, since that type of writing is newer for me than nonfiction.

Resistance is the elephant in the room. It's not something that most people tend to talk about much, but we all have resistance to our biggest dreams and goals. Yes, you too. Otherwise you'd already be celebrating your success! You have your own particular forms of resistance that you're dealing with at this point in time. There are also those "life happens" moments, like illness, family members who need you, changes in your job or home life, etc. Sometimes it's the bigger-picture things that serve as distractions. As I began writing this book, we were collectively dealing with the big Coronavirus/Covid-19 health pandemic and its profound effect on our lives.

The resistance that keeps you from writing regularly comes from, at its root, a belief that you've internalized. Why is it, exactly, that your desire to create comes last? How, through your own actions, have you trained the people in your life to rely upon you? What still feels scary about devoting time to your writing project?

When resistance shows up, it's time to do some Shadow Work. Are you familiar with the concept? I'll share with you how I understand it and work with it. When there's something in your life that you want, but don't have, there's a hidden part of you that actually *doesn't* want it. You have a divided will. You want to write your book, working on it three times per week – but you're not doing it.

When you take the time to explore that part of you, the one that's hidden in the shadows, you can start to get clues about why she — yes, we're going to personify your shadow self, for effect — isn't playing along. Your shadow self is often a part of you that's trying to protect you, in her own warped way. She represents a belief that you internalized, often in childhood or as a young adult.

You can start by engaging in a dialogue with her, either in your mind or in your journal. Ask her why she doesn't want you to write your book. Why does it feel unsafe? What is it about devoting time to your own creative project that sounds scary?

You might uncover some answers that seem unrelated, or even strange. It could be that as a kid, a parent yelled at you for taking the last three cookies, and not sharing with your siblings. They shamed you for not thinking of others and for being selfish, and in the fight-or-flight part of your brain, this is still the standard. If you take time to write when the house is a mess or your friend wants you to get coffee, you're being selfish. Bad. Wrong. And of course, everyone will hate you and you'll get expelled from the community and die alone and hungry.

What?! That's precisely how our shadow selves tend to catastrophize. They think of the very worst outcome, so they can protect you from it. I told you it was warped.

So yes, you might unveil some wacky beliefs when you engage in Shadow Work. The good news is that once you shine the light of your awareness on them, these beliefs will start to shift. When you become aware of them and they're no longer hidden, the grip they have on you begins to release. As my biz coach, Britt Bolnick, says, "The shadows can still make their opinion known, but they don't get to drive anymore. They can sit in the back seat, and they don't get to choose the radio station."

Next time you have an appointment with yourself to write and you start to get that panicky feeling that makes you want to go walk the dog or empty the dishwasher, you'll be aware that this isn't coming from all parts of you. You'll pause. You'll remember the intention you set for writing your book, and why you're doing this. You'll pat your little shadow self on the head and tell her to buckle up, because you're going for a ride – and you're the driver. Maybe it'll be just that tiny bit easier to sit down and put your fingers on the keyboard.

Once you've had that writing session — the one where it wasn't actually so bad, and you know, it was kind of fun, and your partner or kid walked the dog while you were writing, and the dishes were still there after dinner and only took a few minutes — it'll be even easier next time. You're asserting your will – your true, deep, united will. With practice, your shadow self will learn that writing your book isn't life-threatening and won't throw a fit every time you do it. The various parts of you will come together in unity – or at least neutrality! Then your customized writing habit becomes just something you do. That's what you want. Creativity will no longer be a scary prospect or something that other people do and you just wish you could. It will become a natural, even joyful, part of your everyday life.

It's time to dive into exploring *your* particular form of resistance to your regular writing sessions.

First, close your eyes and take a few deep, intentional breaths. Let your attention drop down from the head, where Talking Self endlessly chatters, into the heart center, where you can call on your Younger Self, the universal translator. After a few breaths here, drop your awareness further, down into your abdomen. Focus on aligning your Triple Self. This will allow room for the wisdom of Deep Self, your intuition, to bring insights to your conscious awareness.

Next, take a look at what you wrote as your intention, your book's Vision and Mission Statement. Read it to yourself. Now take out your writing journal or notebook and answer these questions.

❖ *Does your written intention still feel relevant now? Why or why not?*

❖ *Do you have any questions or concerns around your intention?*

❖ *Are there any tweaks or changes you'd like to make to it? Make note of these.*

We're going to take a closer look at your particular resistance to writing your book project at this current time. Remember, this could consist of both external things like your day job or your family's needs, and internal fears or stress that are getting in your way. It's most often a combination of factors. In your journal, write your answers to the following prompts.

❖ *Write down the top three things that you feel are holding you back right now.*

❖ *Take a look at any beliefs that might be hidden behind them.*

  ○ *What limiting beliefs are influencing you right now?*

  ○ *How might you shift them to make room for your writing habit?*

For example, say that you wrote that you don't have time to do your writing because your kids need you to drive them around, and one of them has some extra appointments due to a medical issue. You might ask yourself why you're the only one who can drive them, or why those appointments aren't scheduled at another time of day. Looking more closely, maybe there's a belief that no one else will be as supportive or caring as you, that your first priority is your kids (not a bad thing!), and that you believe you can't spend time doing what you love or pursuing a big dream when loved ones are suffering. Ooh, that's a juicy one! You could then follow up by asking yourself how the loving nurturing of your children and your writing project could co-exist in your life.

❖ *Tap back into your Triple Self and make sure you're aligned. Listen for wisdom that's coming from your Deep Self, your intuition, your gut wisdom.*

  ○ *Write down what you discover there.*

  ○ *What are three small inspired actions you could take this week that you feel will help you move through this resistance?*

Here are some suggestions to get your flow of ideas started about which actions to take:

Reach out to someone for a bit of accountability. Who is your chosen writing supporter? Can you ask them for assistance? Be clear and specific about what you need. "Please text me on Wednesday and Thursday afternoons and ask if I've done my writing session for the day" works much better than "make sure I'm writing."

Find some support with real-world situations that are distracting you. In the example given above, you might ask your partner, co-parent, or caring family member to help you drive your kids to their appointments. Or if it's important for you to be the one who takes them, you could ask someone else in your family, or a good friend, to make a meal or two for your family so you can take an extra task off your own plate.

Sign up for a co-writing session or two. What do I mean by that? I'll use the example of the session I run, but I'm far from the only one offering this. It's become quite popular as a productivity technique as more and more people are running their own businesses and working from home. My version is called the Parallel PlayDate. Each week, a group of us gather on Zoom for two hours. At the start, we introduce ourselves and tell the group what we've brought to play with that day. As you might expect, many attendees are writing a book. But we also have people who are designing courses, making an art journal spread, or knitting. Then I lead everyone on a brief guided meditation journey to get grounded in creative mode. I offer a writing prompt that follows up on the meditation. We spend about five minutes writing, then I offer the chance to share what you've discovered. This is many attendees' favorite part, as the shares often inspire or uplift everyone. Then we mute ourselves, turn off the cameras, and get creative. Just before the end of the two hours, we come back on camera and share how it went. These sessions are great for accountability, and there's also a group energy that carries you along into the creative zone.

Devote yourself to some Shadow Work if you have a lot of internal resistance. Decide to do "morning pages" in your journal, writing three pages of whatever's on your mind and heart as you start your day. I know, doing more writing seems counterintuitive when you're trying to get to the sessions you've already committed yourself to – but this is different. Getting some of the emotional toxins out of your system and onto the page frees up more space for awareness.

If there is a lot of stuff there, be patient. In Chapter 5, we'll take a deeper look into hidden beliefs and how to transform them. For now, know this: it's completely normal to have a big shadow around your creative goals. The voice of the inner skeptic is loud and insistent. It comes to the forefront even more when you try something new.

You can bet that when you've decided to write your book and you start to take action toward that goal, your shadow self is gonna be screaming, cajoling, whining, objecting, and otherwise trying to hold you back. It's not a design flaw. It's just your ego trying to do its job, which is to keep you safe.

What's the best way to deal with this inner skeptic? In my experience, it's best to start by listening to it and letting it know you've heard what it has to say. There's this thing that I love from Star Trek (yep, I'm a huge Trekkie). When a commanding officer gives an order, the recipient of the message might be busy doing some other vital task. They often respond by simply saying "Acknowledged."

This shows that they heard the order — but doesn't imply that they're going to drop everything to follow it, or even that they agree with it. It's like a polite, "I hear you." Try that with your inner skeptic.

When it starts ranting about how you don't know what you're doing, you don't have time to start writing a whole book, and you really need to go deal with that sink full of dirty dishes instead, just reply "Acknowledged." Then continue on with what you were doing. Sounds too simple? Try it. It works.

Other effective ways to soothe the inner skeptic include:

Starting with brief writing sessions as you develop the habit. Keeping it short at first, and easy to fit in your schedule, helps keep the inner skeptic from freaking out.

Have a Writing Ritual that appeals to your Younger Self. You can totally keep it simple, like burning a candle or some incense and putting on your favorite music playlist.

Set a mini-intention for your writing session. This could consist of a word or page count goal — we'll talk more about those in the chapter on Air — or deciding to finish a particular section or scene. Look back at your intention for writing your book and connect what you're doing with your Deep Why and your calling in the world, like: "Writing this section about my unique take on customizing the Reiki symbols will help other healers and those in need of healing, when they read my book."

Reward yourself. For each writing session, you get a healthy, self-nurturing treat. It might be a luxurious bath, a walk in the woods, reading a chapter in a novel, or watching an episode of your current Netflix show, perhaps with some dark chocolate or a handful of blueberries. Figure out what type of healthy rewards work best for you and use them to motivate yourself as needed.

The key to overcoming the worries of your inner skeptic lies in becoming aware of them. When you can see your fears clearly, they start to lose their power. Your resistance becomes a tiny blip on the screen of your creative life. In writing your book, you know that you're doing something that's of deep value to you. That's the key. Learning to soothe that inner skeptic allows you a more abundant experience of your innate creativity. You've got this.

Spirit in Earth

In Pagan traditions, many indigenous cultures, and other forms of Earth-based spirituality, the Divine is described as being immanent. Rather than some anthropomorphic figure who lives on a big throne somewhere else, these traditions believe that pieces of the Divine, parts of a greater whole, inhabit everything we can see and touch. Everything has a spirit, a form of consciousness that may be hidden from us but is nonetheless alive.

This means that the beings of the Earth element, like the Earth our planet, are composed of and connected to Spirit. We can establish relationships with trees, birds, boulders, rivers, mountains – and even buildings and cars. Another word for this is animism.

Most children are naturally drawn to animism. It's not just the invisible friends and beloved stuffed animals who are real to them. Kids connect with everything in their surroundings – sometimes in a fearful way, but most often experimentally.

Your Younger Self, or inner child, might still look at the world that way. Those of us who have an open channel to an active imagination often talk to our plants, our car, the dishwasher, and of course, our pets — even when they don't seem to speak our human language. Do you see little faces in patterns, like wood grain or clouds? There's actually a name for that: facial pareidolia. Our brains are predisposed to attribute personality to random patterns that we encounter. We know that the whole cosmos is made up of energy, and not just chaotic energy, but patterns of consciousness.

There's more to this notion than I can cover in the scope of this book, but to return to the subject at hand: the element of Earth is connected to Spirit because all of the manifestations of Earth contain some form of consciousness.

In terms of how we can use this connection to expand our creativity, think about the rituals I've encouraged you to create around your writing habits. They are designed to appeal to Younger Self, and thus are related to touching the senses. But these little rituals also infuse your practice with magick, or in other words, Spirit. They connect your habit with the energy behind wanting to become an active creator.

Consciously infusing your grounded habit, a creature of Earth, with magick and mystery, the children of Spirit, makes it more fun. That in turn makes you more likely to want to engage in the practice. Younger Self's motto might be, "only do it if it's fun!" As you know, Younger Self is close to Deep Self, the part of you that is plugged directly into the electric current of All-That-Is. When they have a tea party, your creativity will flourish, and that powerful energy will ripple out into all areas of your life.

CHAPTER 5:
THE BORDERLANDS: THE SEEDLING EMERGES
(EARTH TO AIR)

About This Transition

At the beginning of the book, I shared an overview of the main five elements of Earth, Air, Fire, Water, and Spirit. You've gotten a glimpse of how they feed us in various ways as we move through life and creativity. My initial study of the elements led me to thinking about the transitions between the elements and how they interact with one another. These transition points, also known as The Borderlands, are full of possibilities. We can use their unique energy to support us as we work our magick and walk a spiritual path.

Moving deosil, clockwise, around the circle starting in the north, the first transition we encounter is the move from Earth to Air. On the surface, it would seem that we more often change between these two elements in the other direction – first we come up with new ideas (Air), then we bring them to fruition in physical reality (Earth). Yet the wheel is actually a spiral path that we traverse more than once. The transition from actualization to thought is an important part of the cycle of creation. Once we've manifested one of our goals, we can evaluate it using our intellect. Can it be further improved or refined? How well does it fit with our life as a whole? What comes next? What new ideas are inspired by the completion of this project?

The intersection of Earth and Air lies in the northeast. A long, cold winter season gives way to the fertile promise of a warm spring. I imagine the landscape as much like that of New England – rugged, rocky terrain that nevertheless supports trees and plants which flourish, even in a fairly short growing season. Traversing this transition is like going on a hike; we climb the mountain, up through the forest, emerging at last on a stony peak where we can feel the refreshing wind in our faces and watch the clouds sail across the sky. It is the energy of Imbolc, a Pagan holiday of Celtic origin that takes place in early February, when the days have lengthened and our thoughts turn to planting the seeds of spring, yet the land is still caught in the throes of winter.

Where does this transition point emerge in time? The part of the day represented is the time between midnight and dawn. "It's always darkest before the dawn," as the saying goes, and this time is that of a deep quiet, of taking our solitary inner contemplation and turning it slowly outward into the dawning of a new beginning. The moon cycle as we turn from Earth to Air is Diana's Bow – a brand-new waxing crescent. Our new dream has been born, and is still a slender crescent, slowly gaining in power and energy, fed by our inspired thoughts.

The stage of life represented by the intersection of Earth and Air is rebirth. As a soul moves from death to being reborn, there is a time of limbo. We rest within the womb, helping to create our new body, or perhaps we hover nearby, exploring the energy of our new family. A plant, once it has burst forth from the seed, grows those long slow inches, readying its energy to send shoots up through the ground and emerge into the sunshine and rain. This "pregnant pause" is an important part of the ever-circling cycle of life, death, and rebirth. It allows us to gather energy for the next phase of our growth.

There are resources available to help us in exploring the Earth to Air transition, such as spiritual practices, tools, and symbols. Here are a few ideas:

❖ Yoga is a helpful practice for working with these energies. The combination of physical stretching (Earth) and breathing exercises (Air) bring us a more tangible awareness of how our body and mind are connected.

❖ In the Tarot, the card that represents "Earth of Air" is the Page of Swords. The card speaks to the grounded, or Earthy, aspect of the Air element. The Page of Swords cuts through depression and stormy thoughts. It heralds a time of activity and starting new projects – like writing a book!

❖ The mythical creature related to this transition is Pegasus – a horse, very much a creature of Earth, who has wings to fly through the Air. Pegasus embodies qualities of both of these elements and can fly over the Earth, bringing a new perspective to physical reality.

❖ A sample of an affirmation to use when working with this transition might be "The things I have manifested now inspire fresh new ideas."

How do Earth and Air interact in *your* life? Most of the people who come to me for help writing their book usually fit into one of two categories. They're either people who don't consider themselves "real writers," yet nevertheless have conceived of a kickass book idea. Or they're aspiring authors who have reached some kind of stuck place, like a barren wintry landscape where the words just aren't coming.

The Earth to Air borderland is, for those in that second category, like walking through that wintry landscape and beginning to see the first signs of spring thaw. There's still snow and ice on the ground, but the air and the quality of the sun's rays both feel different. By giving up your resistance to the stuck place and staying on the trail, you see more and more signs of re-emerging life. Your creativity begins to stir and awaken, like a seed buried deep in the soil that somehow knows that conditions in the world above have shifted.

These borderlands can also be a welcoming place for those who think they're "not writers." Those in that first category are moving from a frozen field of possibility to an amazingly fertile garden of the mind. You'd be surprised by how powerful this first turn of the wheel can be. Deciding to write your book opens up your creativity in many areas of your life, and that awakening can be as delightful as the return of spring after a freezing winter.

No matter which category you fit into, here we are. We walk the creative path, moving through this borderland between Earth and Air, the place where these two elements interact. You've begun to establish new habits that encourage you to write and create. You've now planted the seed of your book in the nourishing soil of a writing practice that is personalized to your needs.

When we reach the realm of Air, you'll be learning to tend this seedling as it becomes a first draft. But as of yet, the seedling hasn't quite pushed its way up through the Earth to emerge into the Air. This is a time when trust is essential, yet it doesn't come naturally just yet.

When we loop back around to Spirit near the end of the book, I'll share my thoughts on trusting your creative process. But at this point, at the very beginning, I know it's challenging to trust that your seed will sprout. Your book in its final form is still hidden from you, there below the surface. Your efforts may feel tentative and unsteady. How can you trust that you can do something so huge as write a book?

Pause for a moment and think about some of the other big creative endeavors you've accomplished. Maybe you've had a child, so you're intimately familiar with how tenuous it feels when you first discover that you're pregnant. You might have launched a business or led a project in your workplace that took a lot of energy and focus. Perhaps you're an artist in some other medium, and you've produced a play, painted a complicated landscape, or sewed an elaborate costume. Maybe you've built a garage or shed, planned and managed an entire food garden, or designed a website.

Let your previous accomplishments reassure you that you *can* do this – and also that, during the process, success might sometimes seem impossible or unlikely. Think about the resources you have that can support you.

In the realm of Earth, you've established a basic writing habit – or learned how to do so. This is the foundation that will carry you through the writing of your entire manuscript. Looking ahead, in Air you will practice your craft through repetition, and acquire new tools to track your progress.

Here at the borderland, let yourself rest after the first steps of your journey. Think about what you might need as you continue forward. Maybe you set up a time to write on Wednesday evenings, but forgot you'd be starting a class that will soon occupy that slot, so you need to adjust your schedule. Do you want to find an accountability partner, someone to check in with you each week to see if you've done your writing as planned? Maybe you need to block off some time on the weekends to make meals for the coming week, so that you can free up that time in the late afternoon for writing and other creative practices.

Reflect on your journey thus far and allow yourself to envision how your creative path through the process of writing a book will unfold. Visualization has been shown to positively affect success in endeavors ranging from high-performance sports to leading a huge corporation. Your mind and body don't know the difference between what happens to you in waking life and the things you imagine. Rather than worrying, which is visualizing things you don't actually want, take some time to picture yourself at the point of your book's completion. Imagine your smile, your feeling of triumph, the readers who love what you've written, the impact your book is having. If the intention you created came true, how would it feel? How would your life change? What would you have that you are wishing for now? What will it be like to hold a hard copy of your book in your hands?

If that all sounds far too good to be true, relax. In the next section, we'll dive into releasing some of the old beliefs that might be holding you back from even imagining that you'll succeed in becoming an author. Join me in the shadows, for our next round of uncovering — and shifting — the inner resistance that's holding you back from working on your book.

Rewriting Old Core Beliefs

In 2010, my partner BlackLion and I launched a new creation into the world: *The 30-Day Core Belief Kit*. It came from an idea we'd brewed up in 2007, after reading *The 4-Hour Workweek* by Timothy Ferriss. The author's challenge was to create a product that you could sell electronically to generate passive income. Our kit had 30 recorded audio guided meditations and an e-book with a page of instructions and exercises for each day. Little did we know when we came up with the idea how much the process of creating the kit would change our own lives – and how far we still had to go when we launched it! The kit was the very beginning of our journey as entrepreneurs, and I'm so thankful that it led to where I am now, doing what I love as my second career.

What are core beliefs, and why would you want to examine them? I don't remember where I first heard the term "core beliefs." The idea, though, is that your brain's operating system runs on a set of conditions, underlying beliefs about yourself and the world you inhabit, and this process is mostly unconscious. In fact, the beliefs that you would list if someone asked you exactly what you believe in are only a small part of the picture.

Many of our most foundational beliefs about reality originate from our earliest years on the planet. From birth to age seven or so, we are busy absorbing all the knowledge we can. Babies and young children, which you know if you've spent any time around them, are basically learning machines! They observe what's going on around them and soak it up like a sponge.

The trouble with this is that, at a young age, we don't yet have any filters in place to judge the input we're picking up. We haven't begun individuating from our parents or other caregivers. Logic doesn't kick in fully, either, until later. You've absorbed beliefs, unknowingly, from your family, your culture, your peers, and the media – ones that you might find absolutely ridiculous if you heard them from someone else. Some of them, of course, are valuable beliefs that serve you even today. Some are neutral and don't hold much of a charge one way or another.

We're each a wild jumble of beliefs, some of which even contradict one another! You can see how that could hold you back, right?

At this point in your creative journey, you've set up a custom writing habit, and started to examine some of the resistance that's been keeping you from writing your book up until now. When we move into the realms of Air, we'll be practicing some of the basic skills you'll need to write your manuscript. Here in the borderlands between Earth and Air, it's time to recognize that this journey of writing a book will involve overcoming some of your old programming.

Examining and changing your core beliefs is part of the Shadow Work we talked about earlier. Don't worry – it doesn't have to be scary. I admit to having a weird aversion to seeing the insides of things and how they work. I don't want to see the engine of my car or look at what's inside the walls of houses when they're being remodeled. It gives me the creeps. Even so, I've found examining my foundational beliefs to be rewarding and transformative.

It's not something that's going to be done in a day or a weekend – or even 30 days — I told you we had a lot to learn, even after launching our kit! But by incorporating core belief work into your personal growth, you'll find that achieving your goals and dreams becomes easier and more enjoyable.

How do you go about examining and changing your core beliefs? When BlackLion and I created the Core Belief Kit, we came up with a technique called the Drill-Down. Recognizing your core beliefs requires letting go of your conscious surface views and drilling down to their deeper source. Once you are able to recognize and acknowledge the core beliefs that guide your routine thoughts and feelings, you can understand their influence on your daily life. Then you can decide, for each core belief, whether you want to release it, affirm it, or transform it.

The Drill-Down technique involves focusing on your current thoughts on a specific topic, noticing what you think and feel about it. Next, you'll come up with – and then answer

— a question about that topic. Look at your initial answer and focus on it, observing the next thought or feeling that arises in response and noting it down. Ask yourself "why?" Repeat this process several times, writing each subsequent thought or feeling until you come to a phrase or sentence that best describes the essence of your views on the topic. You have now found your core belief.

You may initially have multiple surface thoughts on each topic, but when you examine these thoughts more thoroughly and deeply, you'll notice a belief that is the basis for each of them. This is a core belief and will be the gem you find at your center.

Once you've discovered a core belief, you can examine it and acknowledge your deepest feelings about it. You've been taught many different things in your life, some of them conflicting. Your core beliefs may involve ideas you would not consciously associate with the subject at hand. You will find, with varying levels of intensity, that you have fears, expectations, or assumptions about each of these topics.

You may also find core beliefs which are beneficial or comfortable. Ultimately, the goal of working with your core beliefs is to replace any negative or detrimental core beliefs with ones that are positive and rewarding. The purpose of the Drill-Down technique is to uncover your core beliefs so you can work with them consciously.

Since this is a book on creativity, I'll give you an example related to that topic to get you started. Don't let yourself be limited to this topic, though. You can use the Drill-Down exercise to figure out your core beliefs about any area of life. I've found it highly useful in examining my beliefs about money, work, and prosperity.

Are you ready to try it? I'll give you the question this first time, and then you can take it further by making up your own questions on various areas of life where you feel stuck.

Write this question at the top of a piece of paper or a blank document:

What's keeping me from actually doing the work on my creative project?

Now, using free-form, stream of consciousness writing, answer the question. Then take a look at your answer and question it. I find that using the further question "why?" is very helpful to keep the flow going. Something else that helps is to time your Drill-Down. Set a timer for five minutes and keep writing, answering and questioning until the alarm goes off. Keeping your pen moving will help you to avoid overthinking. The answers are present already, below the surface, where your core beliefs reside. The Drill-Down just helps you consciously gain access to them.

When you've come up with the essence of your belief on the particular topic you've chosen – which in this case is what's holding you back from a free flow of creativity – examine it. Is this something that is serving you in some way? Is it outdated or ridiculous? Is there a partial truth hidden there? Do you want to get rid of it? Or adjust it so that it makes more sense in your current situation?

Often you'll be able to see how this hidden core belief once served you. Even so, chances are that it doesn't serve you now, as you actually commit yourself to writing an entire book. Now that you've unearthed the belief, you can work with it in ways that make sense to you.

If you want to release the belief, you can choose to do some ritual around it. Maybe you write the old belief on a piece of paper and burn it (safely, please!) or bury it in the ground. Perhaps you re-write the belief, converting it into one that will support and encourage you in your writing practice. You might want to create a brand-new belief around this topic, writing it and posting it at your workspace, or making an affirmation from it that you repeat to yourself each morning. There are many ways to ritually work with your core beliefs. The key is to bring them into the light so you have the opportunity to consciously engage with them.

This aspect of Shadow Work can be a total game-changer. Combine it with the work of uniting your divided will, which we'll talk more about when we reach the next borderland, and you'll be well on your way to achieving your dreams. Yes, I mean writing your book, but it doesn't stop there. Examining and shifting your core beliefs means that you won't sabotage your success. Well, you'll probably still *start* to do so, but now you'll have developed the priceless gift of awareness. You'll be able to tell when an old belief is running the show and take the steps necessary to shift the power dynamic.

If you feel like you have a lot of core belief work to do and would like some guidance, I've included our kit, which has been renamed the Alchemy of Core Beliefs and is offered as a self-guided e-course, in the Resources section at the back of the book. Most good life coaches and therapists will also be able to help you dig into your underlying beliefs. If you're being called to dive full-on into this process, I recommend getting some support with it.

As for BlackLion and I, ten years later, we're both fully in our creative flow and enjoying success as writers and entrepreneurs – although it doesn't look exactly like we thought it would! Uncovering and examining your core beliefs will free up the energy to follow your callings. This is an essential part of being a Thriving Artist. You need to be ready to follow your Muses wherever they lead. When your core beliefs encourage you to create, thrive, and be led by your intuition, you'll live a purposeful life and accomplish the things you set out to do – like writing your book!

Thinking Outside the Box

What happens when you really, truly want to write your Heartfelt Book, but just contemplating the actual process of writing makes you break out into hives?

Maybe you want to write in a language that isn't your first, and you're nervous about "getting it right." Perhaps you have dyslexia or other challenges that mean the writing process is extra difficult for you. You might, like Delia, be neurodivergent. Maybe a chronic illness means you have limited energy. It could be that you had awful experiences in school that convinced you that your writing is terrible (that's me when it comes to math, so I feel you!). Or you might just type super slowly and fear it would take forever to capture your ideas.

I'm here to assure you that there are many alternate ways to "write" a book. You get to do this in a way that works for you. Here are a few alternative methods that my clients and friends have used successfully.

Speak your book out loud. Technology is your friend. You can use software like Dragon or an app like Otter. Google docs even has a tool for this; look for Voice Typing in the Tools menu or the little microphone icon. Speaking aloud is much easier for some people than trying to type it out. It also makes it easier to work on your book when you're on the go. It's easiest when the option you choose will also transcribe the audio into written words for you. But if all you have right now is the little voice recorder that comes with your phone, use that.

Record your offerings. One client had fantastic ideas and years of experience about the topic of her book. She's also dyslexic, and writing was a challenge for her. She knew she was at her best when talking to actual students and responding to their questions and feedback – so she came up with a series of online classes, recorded them, and had them transcribed. This comprised the bulk of her book's first draft.

Collaborate with someone. If you struggle with writing but have amazing ideas to share, find a colleague, friend, or acquaintance who's willing to collaborate with you on a book. Take your time and find someone whose values, process, and attention align with yours. There's no rush. When you find someone who wants to collaborate, talk with them in detail about how you'd like to work together. Brainstorm with one another. Agree now how you'll each be credited in the book and how you plan to split the eventual royalties. Put your agreement in writing.

Break your writing down into smaller chunks. Maybe it's the idea of writing a whole book that feels intimidating. But you still have something to say, so start a blog or write a series of short emails that you'll later compile into a book manuscript. It's better to take three years (or more) to write your book in little chunks than to keep putting it off forever!

Practice, practice, practice. This is especially helpful for those who were told they were bad at writing, or who are exploring a new language. Reclaim your words! Start by writing just for fun, perhaps in a journal. Let yourself be as creative and wild as you dare — you don't have to show anyone. Keep practicing until writing feels a little less scary. Eventually you'll feel comfortable enough with your writing to move forward with your book project.

Get tailored support. In our fictional example, as you'll soon see, Delia has a therapist who translates mainstream tools from her writing coach into ADHD-friendly techniques. I got this idea from a friend and client who hired an ADHD coach. This professional has helped her in the process of writing her first novel (among other things). Find someone who is experienced in helping those who have the same challenges you do, and get their assistance.

There are many other alternate ways to accomplish your goal of writing your book, even when writing itself feels out of reach. Tap into the energy of this borderland, welcoming the inspiration of Air as you ground yourself in the practicality of Earth.

So many people have a powerful book idea but think that it's impossible for them to actually write it. If this is you, it's time to think outside the box. As you've seen here, there are many ways to craft your book that don't involve you staring at a blank page and a blinking cursor.

Remember that you're a Thriving Artist, and that we're approaching this whole process with an attitude of playful experimentation. Try some of the ideas above or make up your own. Give it a little time and see how it impacts your progress. Adjust as needed.

What if the physical act of writing isn't an issue for you, or you've now adopted a useful alternative, but resistance is still blocking your way? Read on...

Who Am I to Write This Book? The Resistance

In this first borderland, you're setting out on a new kind of journey. Chances are that you've never written a whole book before. But even if you have, each new manuscript will present unique challenges, because you're at a different point in your life, writing about new topics or telling a fresh story.

It's normal to feel tentative when you're entering new territory. In the realm of Earth, you created a writing habit, with associated rituals that appeal to your Younger Self. But chances are these habits are still too freshly born to fully lean on. When we move into Air, you'll be learning (or re-learning) some solid skills that will help you with your writing project.

In the meantime, you might not trust your expertise just yet. Maybe you set out to share your wisdom about something cool you know how to do, a healing technique you invented or refined, or ideas that challenge the status quo in your field. When you first begin to write, perhaps you suddenly doubt that you have anything original to say. How did all your confidence suddenly evaporate?

If you're writing fiction, it could be your writing techniques themselves that are in question. "Do I even know how to write dialogue? I thought it was just a matter of writing the way I talk, but now it feels all stilted." "This chapter is all over the place! How will the characters meet up at the soup kitchen like they're supposed to for the next scene?"

Questioning your ability to write the book you'd imagined is completely natural. If you were going to climb Mount Everest – or even Mount Katahdin here in Maine – chances are that no matter how much research you'd done, how much highly-recommended hiking gear you'd ordered, how well-packed your backpack, you'd still be nervous. This is a good thing.

Writing a whole book is a Big Deal. It truly is. But you're not doing this alone. I'm walking the path with you, and between my own experience and that of my clients, I've got you covered. You don't actually have to know how to do it, not yet. You'll be guided along the way. For now, rest assured that you've packed everything on the equipment list, you've customized your gear, and your experienced guide stands ready to help.

Your responsibility at this point in the journey is simply to keep showing up.

Spirit Walks from Earth to Air

As you walk from Earth to Air, embracing the warming air and watering the seedling of your book, the energy of Spirit is there to bless your journey. No matter how much we human beings have learned about the process of creating new life, there's still a bit of magick and mystery that is an essential ingredient. We can't truly predict which seeds will flourish, or why.

It's the same with the creative process of writing a book, or any other form of art. You can have the best technical skills, the most powerful Writing Rituals and unique ideas, and yet your creation might not have that spark of life that makes it alive. Don't worry, though. What you *can* do is nurture the conditions that allow your project to thrive.

The presence of Spirit is there for you as you make the transition from the foundational pieces of Earth to the solid skills of Air. You might not be consciously aware of the influence of Spirit, but it's there. Spirit directs the energies that you need in order to manifest your book project into the world. It also helps to inspire you, constantly suggesting inspired actions you can take in your creative work. It might take some practice to listen closely enough to hear the suggestions coming to you from Spirit, and we'll work on that as we walk this sacred path. For now, just know that Spirit in the Center is holding space for you to grow and expand as a writer and as a person.

In the Earth to Air borderland, you've taken the first steps toward truly trusting your own process. You've uncovered and transformed old beliefs that affect your writing and the choices you make regarding your book project. You've learned the value of thinking outside the box and letting yourself explore the boundaries of your creativity.

Now, entering the realm of Air, you'll be practicing some of the tools of the writing trade. Through regular practice, you'll hone your writing craft. Your confidence will increase and you'll find the words flowing more smoothly onto the page.

The most important things for you to do now are to continue to cultivate trust in the process, and to dedicate your time and energy to your book project. Stay the course. You're becoming an author, slowly but surely.

Delia's World

Delia danced around the kitchen, whooping and shouting, waving her phone. The girls were looking at her like she was insane, which she supposed made sense as there was actually no music playing.

"Mommy got in! Her story's gonna be heard by some bigwig agents!" she sang to the girls, who grinned. Zen started dancing, doing ballerina twirls. Shauna, who was 10, found one of the bluetooth speakers behind some throw pillows on the couch and put on a music playlist.

Once Delia had finally gotten into her writing groove, her coach, Gina, had encouraged her to share pieces of it with the group. That had led to one of the other writers reaching out to share an invitation to a contest she'd found on Instagram. Delia, in a burst of inspiration, had applied, and now she'd won one of the spots at an upcoming virtual "meet the agents" event!

This was so exciting - and kind of nerve-wracking, too. Delia's brain started running through the details, even as she celebrated. She wondered if Allan would take the girls that night, so she could have a quiet space for the event. She'd have to clean up her office, or better yet, find a good Zoom background - maybe one of those ones that looked like a library in a school for wizards. Or maybe a spare, elegant look would impress them more. What would she wear?

Delia ordered takeout for dinner, to continue the celebration. Her writing coach had drilled into them the importance of honoring the little wins. Delia found it hard to celebrate finishing a chapter, but this was different. She hadn't finished the first draft - not even close - but meeting agents was huge.

Maybe she'd have to do the November writing challenge thing after all. Her coach had suggested that Delia take part in something called National Novel Writing Month, where the goal was to write 50,000 words in 30 days. Delia had declined - it sounded too intense, in a month with Thanksgiving, the start of her Christmas shopping, and the end-of-year wrap-up process in full force at work. But now she felt like maybe it was a good idea. If she was gonna be talking with agents, it was probably best to finish the book sooner than later. That many words would get her close to the end of her novel, if not allowing her to wrap it up. She'd talk to Gina about it again and see what her coach could recommend in terms of making sure there was time to write every day, while still keeping all the other balls in the air. Well, as much as she ever did, anyway.

***

Sighing, Delia clicked the button to join another writing sprint. She checked the clock on her laptop - 11:16pm. She really needed some sleep, but one more round would most likely get her back on par with her word count goal. Listen to me with all the author lingo, she thought, smiling blearily.

The sprint wouldn't start for another couple of minutes, but Delia didn't get up, because if she did, she knew her body would take her straight to her bed, and that would be that. She closed her eyes, resting her head on her hands, waiting for the loud "ding!" that would signal the start of the sprint.

Back when she'd started writing the book, Delia had listened to the other writers in her coach's program and felt like she didn't belong. They talked about their book's voice, how the characters took on a life of their own, and mentioned sprints and late nights. But now, here she was.

It was November 16th, and Delia now had a total of - she looked at the corner of her document - 77,000 words written, 27,000 of them just this month! Gina was right about NaNoWriMo. It was hard, but committing to this challenge had made Delia write more feverishly than ever before. Not only that, but now her own characters had taken charge of their stories.

Writing this novel was more satisfying than Delia had ever thought anything could be. She'd never really done a huge project like this - well, unless you considered graduating from college a project. That she'd done by the skin of her teeth. This project was actually fun. She grinned, imagining what the "Delia's a hot mess" crew would say when her book was published.

She hadn't heard back from any of the literary agents at the pitch event, but her new writer friend, Holly, had assured her she'd done well when it was her turn to present her work and answer questions about it. Plus Gina said that it was essential to keep putting herself out there. Each event she did was good practice. So Delia had looked up some other events and signed up. Allan was even being supportive, changing the schedule so he'd have the girls on those nights. She wasn't sure why he was being so cooperative, but she'd take it. He was one of the few people she'd told about the book. Delia was just glad he hadn't rolled his eyes or made fun of her for it.

The starting bell chimed, startling Delia from her thoughts. She focused on her screen, biting her lip as she imagined her way back into the scene she was writing, forgetting the rest of the world as she immersed herself in the story.

CHAPTER 6:
AIR: PRACTICING SOLID SKILLS

About Air

Now we once again traverse the compass in a deosil or clockwise direction, arriving in the East, the home of Air.

The element of Air swirls around us, unseen but essential to life. Air's direction is East and its time is spring and dawn. Air's colors are light and peaceful: sky blue, pale yellow, and pure white. Air's essence is expressed by capricious winds, the flight of birds, and music of all types.

We need Air to exist. We can live for a time without sunlight or food or even water, but when we cease breathing for mere moments, that is the end of this lifetime. The physical process of breathing is complex, yet we do it all the time, unconsciously. Deliberate focus on the breath is an ideal way to calm our thoughts and emotions when we are in turmoil. Air brings us back to center.

The Air element has long been associated with communication. Our spoken words literally travel on currents of air, from our lips to the ears of our listeners. Communication is an integral part of our relationship with Air. We can only see Air as it interacts with the other elements: we observe the smoke rising from a campfire, the clouds as they travel through the sky, the rippling leaves on the trees as wind moves past. Air can be tricky – when we express our thoughts and ideas, that which seems perfectly clear to us can be confusing or even hurtful to those receiving our message. We can use the power of Air to see through the illusions created by the mind.

Air brings new beginnings. Change is a constant part of our lives. We long for growth and progress, yet at times we resist it. Air brings us a reminder of how fresh and exciting a new phase of life can be. When we allow new ideas to breeze through our minds, we are cleansed and refreshed.

The tool of Air is the athame. This sacred knife slices through old energies, cuts away that which is no longer needed, and defines our boundaries. We hone our thoughts to a pointed focus, take a deep breath, and move into action. Air is our constant companion, from the first inspiration at birth until we expire and meet our death.

In some ways, the element of Air is like the patron saint of creative endeavors, particularly those that make use of the written and spoken word. Writing and other forms of creativity are shared in various ways, but they originate from the artist's thoughts.

Over time, the artistic expressions of our planet's various cultures have evolved to the forms we're familiar with today. Even so, new ways of expressing ourselves are continually being invented.

I'm a fan of inventing new ways to be creative. Yet most art forms have some basics that, once learned and assimilated, will aid you in crafting unique expressions. This is true in writing, and as we explore Air, I share with my writing clients the solid skills that will help them as they write.

Using our "building your dream home" metaphor from earlier, you may wish to build a structure never before seen in your neighborhood, or anywhere! Before you design and execute your vision, knowing how to draw up the blueprints, choose your materials, and create a framework that won't fall down — and those are some essential skills to have.

Just as you need the foundation of Earth, the external skills of Air will come in handy as you build.

For writers, these skills will include things like doing research, varying the lengths of sentences, and the creative use of language. A basic understanding of grammar, particularly how to be consistent with tense and dialogue, are also necessary. Spelling? Well, it's not as crucial these days, thanks to spell check. But you get the general idea.

The good news is that you don't need to have a MFA to master the craft of writing. Practice is the best way to get better at the basics. The same is true for most other creative passions. Life-long learning is a Thriving Artist's best friend, but it's ideal to follow your own learning styles. Some of us thrive in a classroom setting, but that's only one of many ways to get the solid skills you'll need in order to do your best work.

The element of Air gives support as you master the basics of your chosen craft. Like the "wind beneath your wings."

Are You *Sure* I Don't Need a Degree?

Air is the realm of the mind and the intangible power of our thoughts. The word "inspiration" comes from Air, and the actual process of breathing it into our lungs. As a creative person, chances are that you have a lot of ideas. If you don't, that's okay, they've just been hidden by old beliefs – you'll reclaim your creative flow as you move through this book. This is your imagination in action.

Our Talking Self is active all the time. We have thousands of thoughts coursing through our minds on any given day. Those thoughts are like wind currents moving through the atmosphere. They loop and swirl, and sometimes circle in on themselves, while other times the thoughts and ideas move so swiftly that we can barely keep up.

Not all of these thoughts are useful. Not all of them serve us. However, just wait a moment or two and they'll pass by, with others coming along to replace them. This is never more evident than when you sit down to meditate. Many people mistakenly think that the idea of meditation is to somehow stop the thoughts. Truly, meditation is a practice of observing those thoughts, and detaching from them so that they flow across the sky of your mind like clouds or air currents.

In this chapter we'll be diving into the topic of the solid writing skills you'll need in order to write a book that people want to read. These are the tools of the writer's craft, from grammar and spelling to word choice and the arc of a story. Don't panic if these concepts seem foreign to you, or boring, or even intimidating. We human beings have cultivated the powers of our Talking Self, to the point that many of us live much of our day in our heads, often forgetting we have a physical body until it gets thirsty, hungry, or tired of sitting in the same position. Like it or not, you already have many of the mental skills you'll need in order to succeed as a writer. The chief among these is that you know how to learn.

While it's not the purpose of this book to teach you to write a grammatically correct sentence or even to plot out your novel, we'll touch on these things while we reside in the realm of Air, and I've included resources for further study and exploration at the back of the book.

Some books on writing would take this opportunity to delve into things like grammar, the parts of speech, and so forth. But that's what *Elements of Style* is for. I must confess, I'm not convinced those things are necessary for writers to study, unless you're drawn to them.

As I shared in the introduction, I have a B.A. in Broadcasting and a minor in English from the University of Maine. I've long been passionate about words and stories — but even so, diagramming the parts of a sentence puts me to sleep. Here's my unconventional take on the subject: I don't think you have to have *any* sort of formal education to be a successful writer. I believe that it's much more important to master the art of writing through experience, feeling, imagination, feedback, play, and practice.

I find it interesting that this is the area where most aspiring authors have grave doubts about their writing abilities. They think that they need to go back to school and get that Masters in Fine Arts, specializing in creative writing, before their book is any good. That's because industrialized schooling has a really good propaganda machine; of course colleges want you to think that you need their expertise in order to succeed. Who would pay them otherwise?

Don't get me wrong – I'm not against colleges, though I have my doubts about the public school system for younger kids and chose to homeschool my own children. I just don't want you to believe that your life experience is innately inferior to having a fancy degree. While schools can certainly help you improve your technical skills, often they squash your imagination in ways that take time to reclaim.

Perhaps the best analogy to use here is music. You can learn to play an instrument in the most precise way possible, practicing for hours, reading sheet music, studying music theory. You can attend Julliard and become one of the best acoustic guitar players in the entire college. Then you meet someone at a party who also plays. They even have the same kind of guitar as you. You go off to the corner and start playing together, sharing songs. This person keeps up with you easily, and even has their own unique style, a sound you haven't heard before, or not exactly. You ask them where they went to school, who they studied under, and they give you a puzzled look. You're amazed to discover that this person is entirely self-taught. They started as a street musician busking for change, and in fact can't even read music. Yet before you knew that, you would swear that they are easily your equal.

What's the common denominator, the thing that you each have in common? The hours of practice that you both put into learning and mastering your instrument.

The same is true for the writing craft. The best way to become a writer is simply to write – and, I would add, to read. Both of the excellent musicians above have likely spent countless hours listening to music, as well as creating it. By immersing yourself in the realm you're working to master, you're learning. You're moving ever closer to mastery.

A degree is not required. Your brain is just that clever.

In the realm of Air, we'll explore and practice the skills you'll need to write a powerful, inspiring, life-changing book. You'll make these skills your own. You might still decide that a graduate school is the way to go, for you. Or you might embark on your own self-designed course of study. The choice will be entirely your own.

Tools of the Trade

Rather than talking about grammar and theory, I'm going to share with you some ways to develop your writing skills joyfully. These are the tools of the trade, as it were, that you'll use to write your book manuscript. We'll begin by talking about three key areas to focus on as you begin to enhance your writing skills: write for just one person, write uncensored, and read (or otherwise consume stories) with a curious mind. Then we'll add some more specific tools to use as you write your book.

1. Write for just one person.

Writing for just one person keeps your writing both focused and personal. Creating an "ideal client avatar" is a common starting point in the entrepreneurial world. This is very similar. We already worked a bit on figuring out who your ideal reader is when you crafted your intention for your book project. Get out your writing journal or notebook and take a look at your notes from that process. Does what you wrote about your ideal reader still resonate with you now? Why or why not? Through the process of beginning to write your book draft, have you discovered more about your book's ideal reader? Make some notes now on what comes to mind.

There's a tendency to think that getting really specific about your ideal reader will limit your eventual readership. That's not something you need to worry about. Homing in on one particular ideal reader will serve the purpose of helping you improve the focus of your book. Your book will naturally appeal to readers who share some of those qualities, *and* to those who possess other traits you hadn't thought of yet.

Here are some more questions to answer in your journal or notebook as you imagine the ideal reader you'll be addressing as you write.

❖ *What does your ideal reader look like? What is their gender? How do they dress?*

❖ *What does your ideal reader do? What is their work? What do they like to do for fun? Who lives with them? Do they have pets?*

❖ *What does your ideal reader dream of accomplishing in their lifetime? What do they worry about? What are their fears? Their hopes? What do they long for most?*

❖ *What emotions does your ideal reader feel on a day-to-day basis? Are they optimistic or pessimistic, or somewhere in between? What do they feel about the world around them?*

❖ *Who does your ideal reader hang out with most often? Do they get along with their family of origin? Have they started a family of their own? What are their friends like?*

❖ *Where does your ideal reader live? What type of home do they have? What's their favorite vacation spot?*

You can even get super specific, if that helps you to focus more clearly on who they are. *What is your ideal reader's favorite food? What is their favorite book? Movies or shows? Music? Color?* Include any other details that will help you to see them very clearly in your mind's eye.

Good work! When you next sit down for a writing session, start by reviewing your responses to the above questions. Using your imagination, picture your ideal reader. Imagine them reading the part of the book that you're about to write. Get into the mindset of them receiving your words. Now write those words that they will eventually read. Don't get too serious about this. It's a game that can get you started, or one you can play for the entire writing session. Let your Younger Self take the lead, and playfully create alongside her and Deep Self.

2. Write uncensored.

As part of working with my biz coach, I get to attend her three-day retreats, three times a year. The thing I love most about my coach is that she offers guidance through the inner work — the magickal, witchy woo-woo stuff that you know I adore — as well as the external steps for creating a successful business.

At one retreat a few years ago, we sat in a circle on the hardwood floor of a sunny room. In the center was an altar, and we'd already been consulting Tarot and oracle cards for feedback on what inner shadows were holding us back. Now it was time for a guided meditation. I often lead them for my clients and friends, so it's extra special when I get to be guided into my own inner realms.

In this meditation we were to meet a future version of ourselves and see what advice she had for us. Since I'd been focused on building my business and expanding its reach, I expected that my future self would focus on those topics when sharing her wisdom. I should have known better. It makes sense that the gem she offered would center on my original calling, writing.

My future self's best advice for me: *Write something wild every day.*

I was a bit stunned, but also intrigued. What did that mean? What is "something wild?" How would writing wild stuff help me to grow as a writer and entrepreneur? How would it serve me?

I still don't fully have the answers to those questions, but I've kept this advice in mind, and followed it sporadically. When I started taking Carolyn Elliott (Lovewell)'s alchemy course and adopted her suggested method for keeping a magickal journal, one of the topics to address each evening is: *What is the most profound thought or experience you had today?*

That question offers the chance to explore some wild writing. Other types of writing that seem to naturally fit this theme are poetry and channeled writing. Beyond that, just the experience of writing in a stream of consciousness manner invites the wildness at the core of creativity to join me at the table.

Ernest Hemingway's famous saying was, "write drunk, edit sober." Since I don't drink much alcohol – because it gives me an upset stomach and headache – I take the notion of "drunk" metaphorically. It's a shift in consciousness. When you write "drunk" or "wild," you take away the constrictive filters that normally take up space between your imagination and the words you allow onto the page. I think my future self was advising me wisely. By playing around on the edges of waking consciousness, it's easier to encounter ideas that are unique and ways of describing things or events that are unusual. This makes your writing both more your own, and also more universal. When you tap into the Mysteries, you're entering the realm of myth and dream. In the collective unconscious lies much wisdom, and stories which will resonate with others besides yourself. Taking off the masks of daily life and letting your creativity be wild and free is a good way to get to the essence of what you want to share in your writings.

After playing with this wild writing concept, I came up with another way to describe it, which forms the title of this section: write uncensored.

Let yourself flow as you practice this method. Remember that you're keeping your editor's hat on the shelf. Don't let any thought of the final product into the mix as you're drafting. This is perhaps the best thing you can do to make your writing uniquely yours. At first, it will feel hard to write without censoring yourself in any way. Make sure you get aligned before you do your writing. Do a bit of meditation. This technique is good to combine with channeled writing, which we'll come to when we enter the realm of Fire. It also works very well as a timed writing exercise.

3. Read with a curious mind.

My fellow bookwyrms who also wish to write are going to love this tip... One of the best actions you can take, if you want to write a book, is to *read*.

Reading — or listening to audiobooks, or watching movies or shows — with a curious mind is a terrific way to begin enhancing your own writing skills. It translates well between genres, though it might spoil some of your enjoyment of movies.

To get a little more specific, I advise my clients to read books in the genre they wish to write. Readers of differing genres, and I'm particularly talking about fiction, although this applies to some nonfiction genres as well, have certain expectations. It's okay to push the borders of a genre, not conforming precisely to the usual format. But before you go there, you need to get familiar with the genre you're writing in – it's best to break the rules once you know them inside out. I say that as a confirmed rebellious soul. Besides, if you don't enjoy reading or listening to the genre you're writing in, I would suggest you journal about why that is.

Don't worry, bookwyrms. All forms of reading count towards your writer's education. You've probably got stacks of books in your "to be read" pile that will all help you, in one way or another, improve your writing skills.

Not a bookwyrm? Used to be until life got busy? Here are some more ideas for you: Read novels, just for fun. Read poetry, to absorb the lyrical use of language. Read something you wouldn't normally choose and notice how it's different from your usual fare. Re-read your old favorites.

Don't enjoy the actual process of reading? We talked about this before in terms of alternative ways to write, and the same holds true for books and stories. You can also practice these techniques with audio books, movies, documentaries, podcasts, and TV series.

What do I mean by reading with a curious mind? Instead of getting absorbed into the story or text, keep an extra layer of awareness about the writing itself. Notice what's going on as you're drawn into the world the writer creates. The key is to get curious about *how* the author created this experience for the reader. Be an active reader. Read (or listen or watch) with an eye toward the architecture that underlies the story.

At first, just let your awareness be pulled along and use your observer self to get the bigger picture. It's like in one of those fantasy movies where you see the hand-drawn map of the land, and then it seems like you're flying over the terrain as it becomes real.

As you practice this type of reading, your awareness of the writing craft will get more pointed. You'll notice how the author uses words. Admire the sentence structure. Follow the thread of the narrative. See sub-plots or side tangents.

As you read, ask yourself questions about the way the author has written the book: *How could she have written this part differently? What if he had included more description, or more dialogue? What works so well about a chapter or section that you admire? What's not working here, and why? How have they succeeded? How have they failed?*

Explore the images that the work creates in your mind's eye. Evaluate the feelings that arise from deep within. *What inspiration, emotions, or thoughts does this piece of writing evoke? How did the author take you there?* Tune your creative powers to the craft behind the book. You might also want to read books about writing; I share some recommendations in the Resources section at the back of the book.

Does this suggestion sound almost too good to be true? Sure, reading alone won't make you a writer. I wanted to be an author from a very young age, and it took me several decades to get there. But I was a voracious reader that entire time, and the writing craft I absorbed from reading so much serves me now, as I write my own.

When you immerse yourself in the books you love, with an eye to "how they did it," you'll be nurturing your own writing process. Want to get especially meta? Examine how I crafted *this* book. Evaluate it as you read. *What could I have done better? What do you like about the structure? What is confusing or too repetitive?*

Get started on reading other books with a curious eye, too. Start by picking one book to read this month. You might choose another writing craft book, something in the genre you're writing, or something else to read critically.

Whenever you finish reading a book with a curious eye, make some notes about your findings in your writing journal. Include suggestions for yourself about things you want to include in your own book. As you do this, you're already beginning to cultivate your writer's voice, which we'll delve into more deeply in the chapter on Fire.

More Tools for the Writer's Toolbox

Once you've had a chance to implement a practice of the three main tools from the previous section, experiment with some of these other tools. Not everything on this list will help you as you write your book draft. Some will be more useful when you're in the editing phase. Others just won't resonate with you. Get playful as you try out various things. Keep what works for you and leave the others in the bottom of the toolbox. Remember, we're customizing this journey for *you* every step of the way.

Keep your Flexible Outline updated. The Flexible Outline is not only one of the containers in which to write your first draft, it's also a useful tool along the way. Taking some time – outside your usual writing time – to keep your outline organized will help your creative process. It frees up your mind with space for inspired new ideas. It allows you to capture those ideas when they appear outside your regular writing times.

I suggest that you keep three working documents as you write a book. One is your Flexible Outline itself, which should be its own document. The second is the document where you do your actual writing. Remember, the writing you do doesn't have to be in the order that the reader will experience. It's fine to jump around and write the sections and/or chapters out of order. I do it all the time, more often with nonfiction, but sometimes even when I'm working on one of my fantasy novels. Think of this second document as the developmental lab where you're bringing together the very first stages of your book's existence. You can do stream of consciousness writing, channeling, and writing sprints here. If the document is riddled with spelling errors and questionable grammar, excellent! This is the messy first draft. It's a playground. Revel in its chaotic nature. You're writing something wild!

The third document is where you'll put your writings in the order reflected in the outline. You may choose to do some editing before the draft is complete, which can be done in that third document. Even if you decide not to edit at all until your first draft is written, having that third document with things in order will help you get ready for those eventual editing sessions. It's also a good idea to back up your work, and this method helps with that process (my Tech Guru, BlackLion, wants me to tell you to have other ways to back up your work, like attaching files to an email to yourself, having an external drive, using the cloud, etc.).

When one of my clients was writing her first book, she had times when she wasn't sure what to write next, or she felt uninspired. She tried various techniques, and then stumbled on one that worked well for her. She'd schedule a book organization session for that week. In the session, she'd get into sacred space and then take a look at what she'd written so far. This was the time when she updated her Flexible Outline and made notes on what was done and what still needed to be written. When she reported back on this process, she was surprised by how much fun she had in these creative planning sessions. They inevitably got her back on track, feeling inspired to write the next part of her book. Try it for yourself and see how it feels.

What if you sit down to write and all the items on your outline sound boring or hard to write? Return to Chapter 2, Making the Map, to brainstorm some new ideas. Create a mind map. Visualize your book in blueprint form. What's missing from your outline? Add to it. If you find that you've already written all the ideas you've listed in your outline, and yet the book doesn't feel complete, use the following tools to flesh out your outline.

Imagine that your writing is music. One of the tools that has helped me develop my skills is finding the rhythm of written text. You'll probably see this suggestion in many different writing craft books: vary the lengths of your sentences for better readability. I've jazzed that advice up by thinking of the writing as music.

You can also think of your writing as poetry. The key is to notice a rhythm here. If you're not sure what I mean, try reading a paragraph or two of your writing out loud. If all of your sentences are about the same length, it will sound monotonous. Don't worry about correcting anything you've already written. You'll do that in the editing phase. Right now, you just want to practice doing this as you write.

If you play (or have played) a musical instrument, this will be easier to implement. I play hand drums, like djembe and doumbek, and I can touch type. Sometimes my writing feels like drumming. When I get into the groove, I can tell by the way my fingers dance around the keys. Adapt this writing-as-music suggestion to your own experiences. If you can find a way to be playful with sentence length, try it.

Be aware of throwaways. As you begin to build a body of writing, you can start to become aware of your own particular shortcuts and throwaway words. Read through some of what you've been writing for your book. Schedule a separate session for this, rather than taking up one of your regular writing blocks. As you read, look for repetitive and throwaway words. What do you tend to write while you're waiting for your brain to come up with the words for the next sentence? Look for words or phrases that you use a lot in your text. These might relate to the topic you're writing about, or they might just be your favorite adjectives.

Don't come down too hard on yourself for doing this. It's extremely common. In fact, some of your throwaway words might be found in this list: very, really, so, well, and, actually, best, as, also, again.

You're not alone in this. It'll get fixed in the editing process. The point of becoming aware of it now is so that you can learn to skip some of these fillers before they even reach the page. I know that I'm also advising you to write uncensored. If you're still at the place where you need to *not* think about any of this stuff while you're writing, that's perfectly fine. As you practice your writing more and more, these types of suggestions will make more sense. They're also part of the process of developing your voice, which I'll go into more in the Fire chapter.

Blend creativity and convention. This idea could also be paired with the process of finding your voice. But I've put it here on purpose, so you can begin to weave it into your process, or at least know it's an option. Each of us has particular turns of phrase that we bring to the page. Many of these come to us through pop culture, literature, and conversation. You'll also come up with metaphors and phrases – and perhaps even words – of your own original creation. In my opinion, good writing is a combination of these.

If you rely too much on cliché, your book will sound generic. Readers don't want to read a whole book of familiar-sounding pontification. They want something new. At the other end of the spectrum, if your book is completely unique to you, it could be too confusing. Your reader will be slowed down by the process of figuring out what in the world you're talking about. They won't be able to immerse themselves in the story or narrative.

By combining familiar metaphors and your own poetic language, you're creating a book that's both relatable and innovative. How do you do this? Through practice. I suggest experimenting with poetry if you want to get good at this technique. Reading books by writers who have an especially lyrical way of writing can also help you gain a more complete idea of what I mean. I suggest starting with the works of authors like Neil Gaiman, Patricia McKillip, Erin Morgenstern, Isabel Allende (yes, her voice shines through even in translation from Spanish to English), and Alice Hoffman.

Here's a little game to get you started. Get into alignment, so that your Younger Self is excited about some wordplay. Go outside if the weather permits, or find an interesting indoor spot. Now describe familiar objects and scenes in ways that are unusual or new. A vivid sunset might become a drop of ruby in the glowing embers. An early breakfast is bliss cakes at sunrise. A hole at the bottom of a tree looks like the grand entrance to the faeries' ballroom. You get the idea. Play the game for a specific amount of time, coming up with as many new phrases as you can. This will limber up your imagination. As you practice this game, you'll begin to incorporate some of this process into your writing.

If you're writing fiction, especially genres like fantasy or the paranormal, where there's a lot of world-building, you'll get a bigger chance to play with inventing new metaphors. Some authors, like Brandon Sanderson, are masters at this. How did they get to be masters? Lots and lots of practice. Be patient with yourself as you learn to bring your unique ideas to fruition. A caution: don't try to pack your book with *too* many made-up words, including names of people and places. You want to be unique, but at the same time to keep the reading process smooth, so that your reader can immerse themselves into your book's world. Having too many unfamiliar words and concepts will jar them out of the flow, and perhaps even cause them to set the book aside. Be conscious of the need for balance.

Again, much of this work can be done in the editing phase. Don't go back and work on the parts of your book draft that you've already written. Not yet. I offer these suggestions here to give your imagination something to play with as you begin to grow more comfortable with writing. Not there yet? Don't worry. Take the journey one step at a time, and only implement a new tool if it feels like something fun to try.

Let research serve you and your book. Some book manuscripts will require a bit of research on your part. Research, like editing, should be done separately from your scheduled writing times. Otherwise it will become an excuse to procrastinate, or a distraction that eats up your time. The idea is to have the research serve *you*. Don't let it lead. This is *your* book. You choose which facts, anecdotes, case studies, historical trivia, etc. will enliven your manuscript. Don't let it overshadow your unique ideas.

The types of research you might do for your book vary. This could include looking up the results of a scientific survey you want to quote, reading various definitions of a particular term, or re-reading your old journals. In the process of writing the introduction for this book, I read back through several of my personal journals. This sparked my memory and inspired some new content, as well as answering the questions I'd posed myself, about how I freed up my creativity and began to write full-length books. It was a worthwhile endeavor. I made sure to keep my research sessions separate from the time I'd set aside to actually write the intro. Try to do the same for your own research.

When you're in the middle of writing your book and you come up with a fact you'd like to include or a study you want to quote, if you don't already have it at hand, just make a note. I use [brackets] within the text to note places where I need to come back and include some additional information. Whatever you do, resist the temptation to "just google it really quickly." That never works. You'll find yourself headfirst down the rabbit hole. Save the research for after the writing session.

Tracking Your Progress: Using Word Count and Other Techniques

As you move through the journey of creating your book draft, your writing is improving. No, don't give me that look. It truly is. How do I know? Because the more you write, the more practice you get, and practice is the best way to improve any skill. So there.

At this point, you've probably racked up a significant chunk of your book's first draft. If that's not so, please don't scold yourself. The most important thing you can do for your book is to show up. If reading this book is helping prepare you to do that, but you're not yet fully ready, that's perfect.

Writers who are new to the process of creating an entire book often refer to how many pages they've written so far. This isn't actually the best measurement to use, though. Pages is a highly relative measure. You're probably writing in a Word document or Google doc or other word-processor style software. The size of those pages, if you actually printed them out, is bigger than most printed books. To complicate matters further, what size font are you using? That will impact how much writing is actually found on a given page.

Word count is a much better way to gauge your progress. This is what publishers and professional writers use. It's a helpful way to track how much you've written.

Books of many genres have an expected word count range. This is a thing. Look it up. If you're writing a science fiction novel, for example, google "word count sci fi genre," take a look at several of the top results, and you'll learn that this genre generally has a word count range of 90,000 to 125,000 words. If you're writing nonfiction, there's generally a wider variety of lengths. Still, unless your book is meant to be a shorter-form ebook or a novella, you'll likely want to have at least 50,000 words. That's just a guideline, not a solid rule. But it does give you a place to start as you determine when you'll consider your book draft "finished."

Once you've determined a tentative word count goal, it'll be easier for you to break your writing down into smaller chunks. Most word processors or similar software have a word count feature. Begin to play with this. At the end of each writing session, take a look at how many words you wrote. Also note how long you were on task, writing. Make notes of these things in your writing journal. When you do this over the course of a few weeks, you'll get a sense of how many words you usually write in a given hour — or half-hour, or whatever length session you're working with.

That makes it easier to figure out how long it's going to take you to finish certain chapters, or even your entire manuscript. I advise writers to always give themselves plenty of leeway when setting time-based goals, though. Remember, there's an ebb and flow to creativity, and there's no point in forcing yourself to create when you find that you're in an ebb tide – or perhaps, since we're in the realms of Air, the image of a sailing ship in becalmed waters would be more appropriate.

In order to get comfortable with word count goals and pushing yourself just a bit, you might want to try doing some writing sprints. I discovered writing sprints a few years ago when hanging out in a virtual community with other NaNoWriMo participants, and wish I'd known about them sooner. A writing sprint can be as simple as setting a timer for, say, fifteen minutes, and resolving to write nonstop until the bell goes off. As one friend with ADHD says, "I like them because you only have to be uncomfortable for 15 minutes, and I'm willing to do that." It gets those creative juices flowing and keeps you from trying to edit as you go. The goal is to write as many words as you can during that time. I like the way the

NaNoWriMo crowd runs sprints while in community. There's generally a place to chat: some people do sprints on Twitter, and I've often participated in sprints on the Discord app. When the sprint begins, everyone writes furiously. Then there is a five-ish minute break, when you can report how many words you wrote, chat with other writers, and take a bio break as needed. Then it's time for another sprint! The pace is fast and the attitude is generally playful. I've found sprints to be an excellent way to write a lot of words in a relatively short time. I can usually manage 2,000 words in about an hour and a half, writing for 15 minutes, then breaking for five, and repeating the process four times.

Doing sprints in community provides an extra layer of momentum and accountability. If you've shown up for a session of sprints and chatted with the other writers, they'll be looking for your results. In the sprints I've done, when someone laments that their words aren't flowing, there's a lot of encouragement. Writers aren't competing with one another; they're usually there for the supportive vibes. It's fun to talk about the writing craft with others who get it and share a similar goal.

If doing sprints in community doesn't appeal to you, you can also do them on your own. When I'm doing something like that, I use the Pomodoro technique. The suggestion is to work for 25 minutes (again, using a timer), and then take a five-minute break before starting again. This technique isn't generally associated with word count, as it wasn't designed specifically for writing, but you could use it that way if you wished.

Co-writing sessions are also a valuable way to get some writing done with encouragement built in. Virtual coworking sessions have become more popular in recent years, as more people work from home. It's as simple as setting up a Zoom call and working together in the same virtual space. My Parallel PlayDates are a bit more elaborate. They include a guided meditation, writing prompts, and quests, along with plenty of play time. In co-writing sessions there are different levels of guidance or DIY based on the facilitator. The support that writers find by writing in community shouldn't be underestimated.

As you get used to writing regularly and gauging your progress, notice how the process feels to you. It's time to lean on your customized writing habit and your rituals. If they don't feel solid enough, you can experiment with refining them. These containers are meant to provide plenty of space in which to write your book. If they're not working for you, try something new!

Get out your writing journal and let's take a look at how things are going for you. Yes, right now! Answer the following prompts:

> ❖ *How do you feel like you're doing in terms of making progress with your book? Are you feeling on-track? Why or why not?*
> ❖ *What tools work best for you in tracking your progress?*
> ❖ *What do you need in order to take your writing project forward to the next level?*

Don't know the answers yet? That's okay. Just keep writing. Practice makes perfect, and you're in the thick of practicing not only your writing, but your entire creative process. If you've never done anything like this before, it's natural to feel at a loss sometimes. Your sails might feel a little wobbly, but hold steady, and let Air help you move forward.

Self-Doubt: Ingrained Resistance

Just as with the element of Earth, when you find yourself in the realm of Air, resistance might begin to creep in. As I alluded to in the *Are You Sure I Don't Need a Degree?* section, the most common form of resistance in this part of your project is self-doubt.

I want to reassure you that self-doubt is extremely common among both writers (professional or otherwise) and those who want to write a book but don't yet consider themselves writers. It's almost like it's baked into us, and if you look at our culture, especially in academic settings, you can see that it is. It's especially prevalent among women and others with lots of that yin, feminine energy.

Thanks to the way the publishing industry was run until quite recently, only a fraction of those with a book idea or a manuscript could ever actually see their book in print. Most of us were assured that our writing or ideas were just "not good enough" to make the cut. Who was making that determination? For the most part, straight white men whose motivation was to make money for their company. Yeah. Far from ideal. Not very encouraging to revolutionary new ideas and fascinating uncommon stories. Right?

Most of us still have this kind of measuring stick ingrained within us, no matter where we were on the spectrum between straight-A students and rebellious dropouts. We question whether our ideas are unique enough, our writing skills strong enough, our perspective valid, our authentic truths, well, true. This doubt holds us back.

It doesn't help that in high school and college we were taught to write generically, aiming for a writing style that sounds like everyone else – or like a textbook. Those of us who were on the honor roll every quarter are perhaps the most hobbled by this early training. We try to write and edit at the same time, making everything sound perfect. We painstakingly correct our grammar and follow all the rules. Then we wonder why our writing is about as appealing and inspiring as Wonder Bread (™). If I sound like I know this one inside out, yes, this was me. It still is, sometimes.

Lucky for us, self-doubt around our writing abilities is best countered with playfulness. Uh-huh – we just need to play more!

I talked earlier in this chapter about "writing something wild every day." Remember where that idea came from? In a guided meditation during a retreat, I met a version of me from the future. I asked her what advice she had for me, in terms of being successful in my chosen career. That's exactly what she told me: *"Write something wild every day."*

"Writing something wild" can mean different things to different people, but the essence is to be playful and uncensored with your use of words. It could mean writing a poem, talking about your deepest, most uncomfortable feelings in your journal, or crafting an angry letter that you'll never actually send. Or who knows, maybe you will? Using words in crazy, free-form ways can break you out of the rut of caution. Break the rules. Make up your own words or spellings of existing ones. Capitalize those Things That Feel Important. Write dialogue that is fresh and raw and impossible.

We'll talk about this more when we enter the realm of Fire, but what makes your writing sing is your unique way of stringing words together.

Here's another well-kept secret that you won't learn in mainstream society. It'll help you counter those doubts. Ready?

There is not a limited number of good writers out there. We can *all* evoke feelings with the written language.

During the virtual (and sometimes in-person) retreats that I've been running quarterly for a couple of years, we often use part of the afternoon to showcase pieces of our work. I ask each writer to choose something to share. It doesn't have to be something they've just written that weekend. The exercise is to get used to sharing our writing with others, and to learn to give and receive useful feedback.

The magickal thing is, each piece shared evokes emotion and response. Sometimes everyone is crying because they're so touched by the piece. Other times, multiple people are laughing out loud and shaking their heads. This is just a small sampling of people, most of whom didn't consider themselves writers until recently, whose work is powerful enough to receive applause. Not just polite applause, but enthusiastic cheers!

Are these pieces of writing perfect? Often, no. Do the writers pick their best stuff to share? Of course! That's what you'll be doing when you get to the editing part of your book project. You want to share your best stuff with the readers. Duh.

But quality writing isn't rare or achieved only after a lifetime. You have it in you to do this. You know how I know? You care enough about it to read a whole book on creativity –

a magickal one, at that! Let those self-doubts have their say, then toss them (gently) in the backseat with your other shadows. You've got this.

Spirit in Air

The main thing that Air and Spirit have in common, besides being (mostly) invisible to the naked eye, is breath. Breath, as I mentioned in the description of Air, is the element that we can't do without for long. If you're breathing, you're still alive. If your body ceases breathing for a relatively short period of time, your Spirit will cross over to the non-physical realms.

The word "inspiration" comes from the act of breathing in fresh air. When you're powered by the Air element, and your brain is flushed with oxygen, chances are that new ideas will begin flowing through your mind.

Most forms of meditation, and certainly the practice of hatha yoga, ask the practitioner to connect consciously with the breath. By centering your awareness on your breathing, you're not only giving your body more of the nutrients it needs, you're also training your mind to focus. You're less scattered. When you're able to concentrate, then you're fully present to receive the ideas that enter your mental realm.

When I run the Parallel PlayDates, we begin with a guided meditation. Each one starts with taking three conscious breaths. We intentionally breathe in fresh air and exhale any stress or tension. In through the nose, out through the mouth. By taking just three conscious breaths together, each participant is better able to focus on the meditation. I then lead them to a particular scene or experience and let each person's imagination fill in the details. It's fascinating how often people on the call describe similar elements that they encounter in their meditation, even though I didn't specifically mention the creature or type of landscape they collectively came up with. The breath, the Air we take in, can lead us into the realms of Spirit, where magickal, mysterious things can happen.

Like the creatives attending the PlayDates, we can then use those mystical experiences to learn something about ourselves or our process, and to inspire the art that we create. The breath, the element of Air, is a gateway into those imaginal realms that lie within each of us.

CHAPTER 7:
THE BORDERLANDS: MAKING IT YOURS
(AIR TO FIRE)

About This Transition

It's time to take the solid skills and useful tools you've learned in the realm of Air and make them your own. Before you arrive in the lands of Fire and discover your unique voice, you'll pass through another borderland realm. As you continue to walk the spiral path of the elements, moving deosil (clockwise), you now reach the transition point between Air and Fire. As you've seen, these transition points, also known as The Borderlands, are full of possibilities. We can use their unique energy to support us as we work our magick and walk this creative, spiritual path.

The transition between Air and Fire is particularly dynamic. We move from brainstorming new ideas and analyzing their usefulness, to putting them into direct action in our lives, then to writing them into our manuscript. Thought and expression are combined in unique ways. Our creative ideas are fueled by a drive to take action, to bring them forth in the world of energy and motion. Our enthusiasm rises and we find ourselves in the midst of full, busy days. Yet our energies remain high and we revel in the variety of activities we're pursuing.

The intersection of Air and Fire lies in the southeast. The weather is hot and steamy. The jungle-like terrain is teeming with plants and animals. We hear a cacophony of sounds – bird calls, frogs, and the buzzing of insects. A riot of colorful flowers blooms everywhere. A breezy morning soon turns humid as the sun rises and the ground begins to steam. Resting at the ocean's edge on a tropical afternoon, we see the beauty of the landscape and our passions rise to meet it. The wind is hot and the sun feels delightful on our skin as we walk the beach. This is the energy of the holiday of Beltane, also known as May Day, when the fertile spring days melt into the promise of a long and luxurious summer.

Looking at the realm of time, this particular transition point represents the morning, the part of the day between dawn and noon. We rise from slumber and begin our day, stirring from our homes and emerging into the wider world around us. Our energies rise as we dive into our daily work, putting our thoughts and ideas into motion. We are busy, buzzing like the bees as they visit flower after flower. The moon cycle as we turn from Air to Fire is the waxing gibbous moon. That which we put into motion is becoming manifest. The energies hum as our powers increase, moving toward the actualization of our goals at the full moon. It is easy to find zeal for our projects and we enjoy the process of working on the ideas we've created.

The stage of life represented by the intersection of Air and Fire is adolescence. One is no longer a child, yet not quite an adult. In this chaotic time of hormonal changes to our bodies, we seek our soul's purpose in this life. "Who am I?" asks the teenager passionately, testing their mettle in various areas, comparing themself to friends and family members. In the garden, the plants have grown strong and now bear fruit, yet there are still many days until it will be time for harvest. Like human teens, they are ready for action and yet they must be patient with their growing bodies, taking in the nutrients they need in order to reach their full potential.

Some of the resources we can use to explore the Air to Fire transition include the following spiritual practices, tools, and symbols:

❖ Music and dancing are natural activities for working with the Air to Fire transition. Listening to music (Air) inspires us to move our bodies in the dance (Fire). We intuitively match our physical movements to the melodies and rhythms of the music, connecting the contemplative and active parts of ourselves.

❖ In the Tarot, the card that represents "Air of Fire" is the Knight of Wands. This card signifies the focused, purposeful aspect of the element of Fire. The Knight of Wands brings a sense of adventure and opportunity. It is time to take calculated risks and use your enthusiastic energies for self-growth and creative pursuits.

❖ The mythical creature related to this transition is the Phoenix – a fiery bird of rebirth, dying in flames and yet rising again from the ashes. The Phoenix embodies qualities of both Air and Fire. It demonstrates how we continuously recreate ourselves, moving from concept to action to concept again in an ongoing upward spiral.

❖ A sample of an affirmation to use when working with this transition is: "I merge my intelligence with my passion in order to take inspired action."

As you think about the transition from Air to Fire, observe how these two elements interact in your own life. Contemplate how you can integrate this dynamic energy into your experience – and specifically, in your writing process.

This borderland is full of creative fertility. This is where you receive the momentum you need to put your ideas into action, on the page as well as in your life as a whole. You'll find yourself filled with enthusiasm — although if you're not, be patient for a moment and read on, as we'll deal with that in the next section.

Your writing habit is now pretty well established, and you're using your tools from the realm of Air to refine your writing. Hopefully you're beginning to have fun with the process of creating your book. New ideas arrive daily, and your Flexible Outline reflects the changes you've made as you do the work of writing your book.

When we reach the realms of Fire, you'll learn some additional tools that will allow your true genius to emerge. Your playfulness will expand, and in the process, you'll discover your book's authentic voice. For now, it is enough to keep going.

Harness the energy that flows through you as you explore your passions and stories in the form of writing. Embrace the free flow of letting your writing emerge, not worrying about grammar or continuity. Trust that you'll be able to catch anything that doesn't work when you do your first rounds of edits. Focus on what *does* work, and on letting your ideas flow onto the page.

Let this place between Air and Fire be playful and experimental. You're still in the early stages of your book draft. There's plenty of room for exploration. Maybe you had a certain concept of how the book would unfold, and now you want to mix it up and make some changes in the structure. Go for it! If you're writing fiction, perhaps a minor character has decided that she wants her voice to be heard, and a subplot has begun to unfold in your mind's eye. Follow that trail!

If the process of writing your book were actually a pregnancy, this is that second-trimester burst of energy, when you stop feeling tired all the time and begin designing the nursery. You might worry that you'll burn yourself out or use up all this abundant energy. Let those concerns go. Embrace your enthusiasm and momentum and write your heart out!

If, as I said above, you haven't found that energy yet and you're still slogging through your writing sessions, or if you've fallen away from writing altogether, the next section is just for you.

Popular culture might say you have writer's block – but we're going to bust that myth and get you back on track in a jiffy.

There's No Such Thing as Writer's Block

Listen up, writer. I want to talk to you about an experience you've probably had, either during your current writing project or in the past. If you haven't had it happen to you, which is fairly unlikely, you've no doubt heard stories about it. What is this strange occurrence?

It's the myth of "writer's block." I realize it's somewhat controversial to say that there's no such thing as writer's block. It's an affliction that has been known to stop even (perhaps especially?) successful writers in their path. The two examples that come to mind immediately are both fantasy writers.

Fans of George R.R. Martin's *Game of Thrones* series – the books, not the TV shows – have been waiting for years for the final volumes to be published. Author Patrick Rothfuss released two volumes in a trilogy which are highly acclaimed and brilliantly written. Those of us who loved them have been waiting ten years for his final book.

Neither of these authors are just sitting around lamenting. Martin has gotten involved in the very successful TV series based on his books, and Rothfuss runs an amazing annual fundraiser to help feed the hungry, among other things. Each author has released other books in the interim. But I suspect that, in a sense, the success their earlier books had has contributed to them getting stalled on their big multi-book projects.

How does this mythical blockage affect those of us who aren't yet best-selling authors? Let's say that you've had an inspiration about something you'd like to write. It might be a section or chapter for your book, or it could be a blog post, a short story, or even an email.

You've thought about your idea for a while, and maybe even made some notes. You carve out some time to write, sit down in front of that blank page, and...

Nothing. Not even crickets.

The temptation is to throw up your hands and say, "Well, that's it, I've got writer's block. This just isn't working."

We often believe that "writer's block" is something that's out there floating around, like a virus, and that it can strike any writer at any time. I don't agree. I don't really believe in writer's block as such.

As with many things in life, the easiest thing for us to do is to play the blame game. If we can point to "writer's block" as the obvious problem that's holding us back, it takes the responsibility away from us. We don't have to deal with it, because it's like a big solid stone wall that we can't get beyond even if we wanted to.

When you find yourself staring at that blank page, what if instead of a stone wall, you saw it as a door? What if your lack of words was a portal which you could choose to walk through? What if this were actually an invitation?

The thing is, there is a natural ebb and flow to the creative process. There are going to be times when you sit down to write and you're just not feeling it. It might be centered around this particular project, chapter, or section, or it could be that the timing is just off. If you see it as an invitation, then there's no need for blame. There's no problem. It's simply time to switch gears.

Still, you've set aside the time to write, and hopefully by now it has become a habit. You want to do something with that time. When the words don't come, there are several useful things you can do instead. None of them involves giving up completely or feeling like you're blocked until further notice, with no choice in the matter.

Here are a few of my favorite steps to take when the words aren't flowing:

❖ **Ask yourself if there's any inner resistance** to the writing you're doing — or perhaps writing as a whole. This can show up as perfectionism, self-doubt, or feeling like you "should" write about a particular subject or in a particular way. If there is resistance, start writing about it! Journaling is one of the best ways to get past the inner resistance that pops up when you want to be creative.

❖ **Go play for a few minutes.** No, really! Playfulness taps into your Younger Self, which in turn connects you with your Deep Self and your wellspring of creativity. Play in a way that feels light and fun for you: dance around the kitchen, try a new recipe, dig in the dirt, make a faerie altar, or whatever appeals most to your inner child. Play can loosen up even the most solid resistance.

❖ **Do some chores.** When the block seems to be about how to approach a particular piece of writing, I go and clean something. As my body performs the routine task — like washing dishes or folding laundry — my mind is free to wander. I toss around my ideas like a hacky-sack (remember those?!) and often new inspirations pop up.

❖ **Shelve it for now.** No, not forever. But maybe you need to wait for a time when you're more rested, or have had a snack, or are just in a better mood. It's okay. It's not writer's block, it's just that the timing is a little off. Reschedule your writing time — without guilt or self-recrimination. The writing process involves a lot more than just the act of sitting down to put words to paper or screen. Give yourself the freedom to play, ponder, nurture yourself, and then to take action when you feel aligned.

That said, you don't want to keep rescheduling every writing session on your calendar, and never making any progress at all. If you take one or more of the above steps and you're still having trouble getting any words onto the page, it might be time to dive deeper into what's going on. Try a "drill down" about whatever feels blocked.

Drill Down — here's how: If it's a particular section or piece of writing that has you stymied, ask "Why don't I want to write this chapter?" If it's happening with any type of writing that you attempt, you might ask "Why am I choosing not to write?" or "Why isn't my creativity flowing?" Using stream-of-consciousness writing, answer the question. Then ask "Why?" about your answer and write down what comes up for that. Continue to question each "why" answer for at least three minutes — set a timer to keep yourself focused — or until you have an insight or "aha" moment.

Remember, the thing about shadow work – and this technique definitely comes under that heading – is that once you can see what has previously been hidden, it begins to lose its power. The charge diminishes. Give yourself some time to process what you've discovered, then try again. Get back on the horse right away or try some playfulness or housework therapy first.

These techniques are useful for any type of creative project, not just writing. Wherever it is that you feel blocked, try it and see what you discover. Writer's block has no power over you, because it's just a mental construct. We human beings are mutable and flexible. By dancing with that stone wall, you'll discover that it's an illusion, and will move through the portal and onward to the creative flow that is your birthright.

You're the Boss – Uniting Your Divided Will

You're in the middle of your book manuscript now – right? If not, don't get down on yourself. I mean, you're somewhere in the process, because you've started writing. I just know you have. I believe in you.

I digress.

Here in the borderlands between Air and Fire, it's time to burn some shit down. What am I talking about? Well, as promised earlier, this is the next phase of the process of Shadow Work. You're going to begin the process of uniting your will. Let me explain.

United will is a concept that is part of Western occult tradition and is also included in the teachings of Carl Jung. I learned of it from Carolyn Elliott (Lovewell), who is a powerful witch, author, and Hermetic alchemist. The basic idea is that most of us say we want certain things, yet we don't have them. "Having is evidence of wanting" is one of Carolyn's maxims. In other words, there's the conscious part of you that wants the thing you say you want – let's go with the obvious example, to write your book. There's also an unconscious part that

144

wants, well, *not* having the thing. *Not* writing the book, in our example. Your will is divided.

My biz coach, Britt Bolnick, author of *The Magick of Bending Time in Your Sacred Business*, has a great metaphor for this. She says that having a divided will is like trying to drive a car while pressing both the gas pedal and the brake pedal at the same time. Your engine revs, but you don't get very far.

Magick is the art of using one's will to change energy and consciousness, which in turn creates change in the physical realm. If your will, your most powerful magickal tool, is divided, well, you're just spinning those wheels.

We'll use a process of alchemy called solve, (pronounced SOL-vey), or burning away the impurities that get in the way. We need to do this before we begin to create the magickal elixir that will enable you to live forever – this is a metaphor, witches, or at least it is as far as I've gotten in my alchemical studies. Besides, your spirit is already immortal, so don't worry. We need to stop letting our shadow selves plant their feet on that brake pedal, and instead send them to the backseat.

You've done the work of identifying the hidden core beliefs that no longer serve you. If you haven't yet, turn back to the *Rewriting Old Core Beliefs* section in Chapter 5 before pursuing the work I'm going to suggest here.

Next you need to recognize and integrate the shadowy parts of you that still believe those old things and are trying to run your life according to them. Why would your shadow self ever do such a thing? Believe it or not, she's trying to keep you safe.

These old beliefs, patterns, and shadow habits arose when something traumatic happened in your childhood or adolescence, and sometimes later — but most commonly in your younger years. Their reason for existence is to ensure your survival. If you've endured some things that are abusive and life-threatening, this will make sense.

But even if the trauma you endured seems relatively tame from your adult vantage point, when a crisis point happened, your younger self decided that they needed to find some way to protect you. In my case, for example, a harsh critique by a creative writing professor in college meant that "I suck at writing fiction" – so my shadow self put a stop to any fiction writing, for about fifteen years. That way I wouldn't get critiqued, be embarrassed, cry, and feel like I was going to die of shame. Because to the shadow self, dying of shame is totally a thing, and obviously one to avoid at all costs. See what I mean?

There are several techniques you can do to begin the process of uniting your will on a particular topic. Carolyn Elliott (Lovewell) wrote a book all about it called *Existential Kink*, which I highly recommend. I'll let you explore that on your own time, but I will just say that the goal of the process is to figure out what your shadow self loves about *not* having what you say you want. Once you can see that, you've already begun to shift it.

As I've said before, the very process of shining the light on the shadow and its priorities will help you to gain awareness of when this shadow is holding you back. With that wider awareness, you've removed some of your attachment to it. You've stepped into the role of the observer self. In my experience, awareness is the most powerful tool you have in terms of Shadow Work.

You can train yourself to become aware of your shadows through mindfulness, journaling, and other techniques (again, I urge you to check out *Existential Kink* for some terrific ones). Basically, when you're frustrated because you're not getting what you want even though you're trying really hard, that's a sign that your will is divided on that subject. If you're not writing your book, and you notice resistance that you can't seem to get past, your shadow probably wants the exact opposite. She wants you to *not* write your book because then you'll stay safely hidden from the haters – or whatever your particular trigger point is.

Here's an example from my own life. When I sit down to work on my fiction, and I start to fret and think, "This sucks and I still have no idea what I'm doing," my awareness kicks in. "Oh, right, that's the shadow and her belief that writing fiction is dangerous and will get us shamed to death." Funny, right? When you can laugh at yourself – with compassion –

you're no longer in the thick of the fear and shame. You've removed yourself from the trauma. You can see that shadow, listen to her perspective, and then gently ask her to sit in the backseat and let you drive. You're the boss – "you" in this case being your whole self, aligned and connected.

There are deeper ways to work with the shadow and I recommend these if your own traumatic experiences feel too big to handle on your own. Working with a Jungian therapist is one way. I also recommend seeking out some type of somatic therapy. Trauma is stored in the body, and if you've been abused or bullied, or lived in life-threatening situations, then working with a somatic professional who's trained in freeing the physical body from trauma is a good way to go.

Like the core belief work we talked about before, the process of uniting your will isn't something that happens overnight. It will take some time to become aware of your shadows and how they're holding you back. When an emotional crisis has you firmly in its grip, at first you probably won't be able to see it for what it is. But later, when you're processing it either in your journal, with a trusted loved one, or in your mind, you might be removed enough to remember to do the Shadow Work and gain a new perspective. That's perfectly okay. You're doing the work! It takes some practice to gain enough awareness to see it when the moment arises.

How will you know when you've successfully begun to unite your will? Things that were previously hard for you suddenly seem easy. Yes, there are probably multiple factors that contribute to things becoming easier. If you've been practicing your writing regularly and can lean on your habits and rituals, sitting down to write will be easier than when you started. But if you were still struggling despite having had your habits in place for a while, and then you did some Shadow Work, and now it's much easier – voila! You've united your will around writing your book.

The amount of time and energy you'll need to put into this will largely depend on how traumatic the original experience was for you. If it was a fairly minor thing, like my shame around sucking at fiction, then it might only take a few weeks to integrate. If you lived with a narcissist who messed with your life to a major degree, then the beliefs you developed to stay safe will probably be a bit harder to untangle. Again, that's when it's useful to get some professional help. Also, your shadow selves might come down to you through generational trauma or even things that happened to you in past lives. One of my beloved mentors (who is also a friend and client) is Jennifer Elizabeth Moore, who leads her clients in Emotional Freedom Technique (EFT), also known as tapping. She helped me to release some generational shadows around poverty and prosperity, and it's made a huge difference in my career and personal life. If you feel like you need some support, you're probably right. Get help. There's no shame in that, and no, you surely won't die of embarrassment from admitting that you can't do it alone. Learn more about EFT and other tools in the Resources section I've shared in the back of the book.

One further word about the title of this section: You're the Boss. Not just in the sense of driving the car, with your shadow selves lined up in the backseat, although I love that picture – road trip! Snacks for everyone! Awesome tunes on the stereo!

"You're the boss" also means that you're in charge of your creativity and your experience. If you'd rather not delve into Shadow Work, because you're not ready or you've already done years of therapy or it's just not up your alley – that's great! If any of the things I suggest in this book don't resonate with you, then feel free to skip them. My aim is to provide you with a full toolbox to take on your Thriving Artist journey. The tools that work best for you will be different from those of your friend down the street. Try things, experiment, and make these techniques yours. A customized writer's toolbox is the best. You're in charge here.

Does Journaling Count?

As you might imagine, I talk about writing with a lot of people. Most of the time, people who have a book idea they haven't started yet still do some kind of writing in their daily life, but often feel like it doesn't "count" because they haven't written a book yet, or had anything published, or another similar reason. Or maybe they used to write, but no longer make the time.

See if this sounds like you: Do you write newsletters, blog posts, or social media promos regularly? Make up stories for your kids? Keep a journal? Do you have stacks of old journals stashed somewhere – or did you burn them in that one Solstice fire after a major life transition?

I've had multiple people in my group writing program, when checking in for accountability, admit somewhat guiltily that they haven't been doing any writing, except journaling. Sure, they're not adding words to their manuscript when confiding in a personal journal. However, writing is writing.

As far as I'm concerned, journal keeping is a valid form of writing practice. I'm quite the journal-holic, myself. Looking back, I credit journal keeping for allowing me to stay sane during those years when it was pretty much the only type of writing I did. I was denying my calling, but my creative spirit snuck in some writing in a way that didn't feel so threatening to me or my shadow selves.

Journaling can be useful to you as you begin to build your writing practice and hone your craft. There are many benefits to keeping a journal, and lots of different types of journals that you can choose from. It's not just a place to record your daily activities, or process difficult feelings – although those are both useful things.

First, journal keeping allows you to explore your writing style with complete freedom. Your journal is just for you. You're free to "write something wild," without anyone else ever seeing it. You can do stream of consciousness writing without having to be particularly coherent. Your process is your own. It's an ideal place to play with words and concepts.

Second, journaling can help you capture your ideas so you can use them later. In the final chapter on Spirit, I suggest that it's okay to trust your creativity, and let ideas flow without attaching yourself to them. However, that's usually something that creatives build up to over time. When you first prime the pump of your creative wellspring, you're likely to be gifted with more ideas than you can handle. Noting them in your journal helps clear more space in your mind — because you're not trying to hold them in your short-term memory — and makes you feel like you're not losing valuable concepts to the ether.

Journaling is also an ideal way to keep track of your spiritual growth. Since spirituality and creativity are so intertwined, the chances are that as you expand your creativity, you'll also integrate plenty of new lessons that will help you with your life as a whole. Reflecting on the process in your personal journal will help you see how things are changing and shifting. This means you need to take time to read your old journals and reflect on what you've written. I like to do this at the end of each calendar year.

Finally, as I noted above, writing is writing. No matter what type of writing you're doing, you're practicing your writing craft. Playing with words and using them to express your thoughts, feelings, and ideas is writing. A writer writes. So, even if you're "only" writing in your private journal, it does count. It's helping you to find your voice and become an author.

Let's talk about the types of journals that you might choose to keep. I'll run you through some of the types that I use currently or have used in the past.

As I mentioned in the introduction, one of the things that helped me to free up my creativity was doing Morning Pages, a concept shared by Julia Cameron in her wonderful book *The Artist's Way*. The idea is to write three pages in your journal each morning, sharing whatever comes to mind first. This helps you to clear your surface thoughts and feelings so that you can then focus on more creative projects. Cameron instructs those doing this technique to then dispose of those pages without reading them. That's the part I do differently. I archive my journals, and have learned from them, even when re-reading a morning venting session or a list of things I wanted to accomplish that day. That said, I also cringe when people talk about burning old notebooks, so your mileage may vary. I'm a chronicler at heart.

These days, I no longer do Morning Pages in my personal journal. Instead I keep an "alchemical journal," something I learned from Carolyn Elliott (Lovewell). I've adapted her suggestions for my own use. In the morning, I record any dreams that I remember, the Tarot card I draw for the day, any interesting astrological weather happening, and my main objectives. In the evening, I make notes of how I felt during the day, interesting synchronicities, and other significant ideas or notable experiences. In the past I've kept a separate dream journal, but now it's included as part of the alchemical journal process.

I also keep a Bullet Journal, in lieu of a paper planner. In conjunction with my Google calendar, this allows me to keep track of activities, to-do lists, and other things like budgets and projects. Each morning, I add three things I'm thankful for from the previous day, and a brief summary of the past day's activities, which is something I do because I tend to have a poor memory of past events. It's a good reference for future me. If you want to learn more about bullet journals, I recommend that you read *The Bullet Journal Method*, by the technique's inventor, Ryder Carroll. It's a highly adaptable method of organizing your life. As a Virgo, I've tried many planners and systems, and this is the one I've settled upon, in part because of its flexibility and customization.

The third main type of journal that I keep these days is a Moleskine notebook where I make notes on classes I take, brainstorm about various projects, draft shorter pieces of writing like blog posts, and record other notes and ideas that I want to save. I realize that I could do all of this digitally. For me, the act of actually writing on paper with a pen helps me to integrate and recall information. This is another type of journal that deserves to be reviewed regularly, so you can move ideas forward as desired.

If this sounds like a lot, know that I've been refining my process over the past three decades. When I first started, I wrote in my journal only intermittently, often when I was having a problem or challenge that I wanted to process. This is a perfect way to start. Over time, you'll come to find the systems that work best for you – and you'll continue to refine them to meet your changing needs.

One last type of journal that I'd like to mention comes from a suggestion by my friend and colleague Michelle Thompson, who coaches lawyers and academics, and is the founder of Resistant Vision. It sounded a bit meta when she first mentioned it to me, but it has been useful to her in her process, and she recommends it to her clients, which is why I've added it to this book. Michelle keeps a writing journal, with notes on the writing process itself. The idea is to make an entry each time you've completed a writing session. You can include the date and time you wrote, for how long, your word or page count, how it felt doing the writing, and any notes on content or inspiration that you want to capture. Over time, a writing journal will help you to further refine your writing habit and keep track of your ideas.

Still not ready to jump on the journaling bandwagon? Here are some further tips to inspire you to explore this alternate form of writing.

Here are the only two journaling rules you'll ever need:

1. **Date each entry,**
2. **Make no other rules!**

That's it! The use of a journal is completely up to you.

Here are a few creative ideas to get you started:

❖ **Start a gratitude journal.** Every day, write down three things you're thankful for. Soon it will become hard to limit yourself to just three, so go ahead and expand your list. Get creative with your thankfulness. "I'm thankful for chocolate chip cookies, freckled noses, owls, the kid on the bus this morning with that friendly smile, and pillow fights."

❖ **Ask yourself interesting questions, then answer them.** "What will I be doing on my 80th birthday? If benevolent aliens came to visit me, what would they be like? How am I like my mom or dad?" If you run out of questions, look for some new ones in self-help books or workbooks.

❖ **Keep a dream journal.** When you wake up, write down the dreams you recall, giving each one a title. Then explore them, looking at each character as an aspect of yourself or finding analogies to situations in your daily life. Have fun with the process, noticing the themes that keep popping up in your dream world.

❖ **Draw, sketch, or doodle your entries.** If writing in a journal on top of working on your manuscript seems like a lot to you, try an art journal. You might create a comic book based on your life or draw scenes from your day. Or augment your written entries with doodles in vibrant colors.

❖ **Write letters that you don't intend to send.** When you're going through a challenging situation, open your journal and write a letter to the person or people involved. It can help you release negative emotions harmlessly and even find new solutions. Or spark your inner growth by addressing a letter to your soul or higher self. "Dear Guardian Angel..."

❖ **Make a collection of fun lists.** The lists can be about anything you can think of, from your favorite things to books you want to read to names for future or imagined children or book characters. "Things I Wish I Collected, Alternative Superheroes and their Super Powers, Movie Star Crushes." As you add items to your lists, you'll learn more about yourself and your desires.

❖ **Create a scrapbook-style journal.** Gather up the souvenirs of your life: ticket stubs, photos, postcards, receipts from a fun night out, gift tags. Print out your favorite text messages or social media comments. Get some stickers, stamps and ink, a glue stick, and a sharp pair of scissors. Make your journal a creation of mementos – or perhaps cut out pictures from magazines to illustrate the life you want to lead, making a scrapbook of your future.

Lastly, I want to add this suggestion: keep all your old journals in a safe and private place and periodically review them. It's a terrific way to get an idea of how you're evolving. We're often so busy living our lives that we can't see how much we've grown or the patterns we tend to fall into. Rereading your old journals can help you gain valuable perspective. I like to do this at the end of each calendar year.

Keeping a journal gives you a safe space in which to experiment with the art of writing. It will help you practice those solid skills that are associated with the element of Air, and also to discover your unique voice, which is something we'll explore more in the realm of elemental Fire. Unless you're using your journaling practice as an escape from working on your book, which isn't the case for most journal-keepers I've worked with, it definitely counts, and contributes to your eventual publication as an author.

The "I'm Not Ready!" Resistance

In the lands of Air, you've learned – or at the very least, learned about – the solid skills that you need to write your book draft. We talked about the self-doubt that all writers have in common, particularly the vast majority of us who were taught to write generically, under tight constraints, in public school.

Now it's time to let the tools of writing be in service to your authentic voice. "Wait!" you might say, "I'm not ready!" As you walk the borderlands between Air and Fire, you may be doubting your ability to pull this off. "Authentic voice? What does that mean? Do I even have one?" You do – or you soon will.

When you first set out on the journey of writing your book, your nervousness was that of a beginner. But you've been doing this for a while now. You can trust that your habit of showing up for your writing is helping you to develop your skills. Remember, practice is really where it's at. The only thing that makes you a writer is doing the act of writing.

When one of my clients finished her manuscript and began the process of reading back through what she'd written, she was surprised to notice that, when she compared the chapters she'd written as she started to the most recent ones, her skills had gotten better. Her writing had noticeably improved. She'd developed her own voice and polished her style, which stood out even in the first draft.

Sometimes this can make us *less* confident, at this point in the journey. You've moved past the "beginner's luck" stage and into a phase where you know how much more you have yet to learn about the writing craft. This can stop you in your tracks, if you let it. You might be tempted to edit as you write, in order to polish your words and get them to sound like you dreamed they would. Resist the temptation!

That's the beautiful thing about a rough draft. It's supposed to be rough! Dear one, you're not just writing a book, you know. You're becoming an author. You're learning as you go, which is how it works with the writing craft.

The only way out is through. At this point in your journey, your responsibility is to continue to show up – and to enjoy the process! That's right. It's time to have some fun while you write your manuscript. You might think that's an impossible goal. Trust me, it's not. You know why? You're in charge of the journey. That's right. This is your book, and you get to write it the way you wish. So why wouldn't you have some fun with it? This isn't Freshman Composition 101. You're not going to be graded. In fact, if your book sounds just like everyone else's, well, that's not what you're going for. Your book is a representation of *you* and your creative magick. So let's have some fun.

Spirit Walks from Air to Fire

The transition from Air to Fire often comes swiftly, like the whoosh of a campfire when the wind gusts through, stirring the embers and sending sparks up into the night sky. Have you noticed this energy yet? Your passions are stirred, your ideas multiply, and you're eager to capture all of the magick in words.

Now that you've been practicing your writing craft for a while, and your writing habit is solidly anchored, it's time to let that fire flare up! As always, Spirit is there for you throughout your journey of becoming an author. Perhaps it's easier for you now to hear the whispers of Spirit, and to receive those inspired actions, implementing them in your writing or your life. Passion and desire are part of your spiritual journey, too – without them, you wouldn't bother to try to write your Heartfelt Book! Contrary to what some organized religions teach, having passions and preferences allows your soul to evolve. The idea is not to eliminate desire, but to follow where it leads. The passion of Fire is part of your spiritual calling.

In this Air to Fire borderland, you've learned about the myth of writer's block, and how to get past any stuck places that rear their heads. You've explored the balance between the tools of the writing craft and the creative chaos that the jungle landscape of this borderland brings forth. Finally, you've discovered that no matter what writing advice or instruction you receive, you're the boss who's in charge of your book and your experience in creating it.

It's time to jump into the realm of Fire. It can be intense, but it's rewarding, and the fiery energies will support you as you continue to write the words that form your first draft. You'll uncover the voice of your book. You'll populate it with characters and anecdotes that bring your book's essence to life. You might even connect more deeply with Deep Self, and channel your writing from your creative wellspring, that place where your self in the physical realm touches your soul beyond this realm, in the heart of the Mysteries.

No pressure, though. Your work at this point in the journey is to surrender to the passion and enjoy the wild ride. Believe me – this is the fun part! You've got this.

Delia's World

Delia could hear the snowplow edging its way along the curb outside her house. The snow fell steadily outside her office window. The girls would probably be home from

THE ELEMENTS OF CREATIVITY

school tomorrow, which meant she'd have to finagle her work schedule around a bit.

Focus! *she told herself sternly.* It's writing time, not Momma time.

She turned back to her manuscript, but soon her thoughts drifted again. Writing the ending of her novel was turning out to be the hardest part yet. She wanted it to have a "happily ever after" ending, of course, but Delia was adamant that it wouldn't be cliche. She'd been disappointed by too many wonderful, luscious books with sappy, fake endings.

It didn't help that she hadn't written in more than a month, up until this week anyway. NaNoWriMo had been a triumph, with Delia "winning" the challenge of writing 50,000 words. But then the holiday season had kicked in, and Delia had set her book aside. Now it's January. Gina reassured her that it was common to take some time away from a manuscript after such an intense focus. But Delia was worried about the ending.

Maybe she was procrastinating because she didn't know how to wrap up her beloved story. Shit, maybe she didn't even want it to end. That meant more querying, more agent events, more putting herself and her book baby under scrutiny. What was her problem? Working at an ad agency meant she was always promoting and marketing for the firm's clients. But for some reason, putting her own stuff out there was completely different.

Ugh! More procrastinating. Delia turned back to her screen, looking at the last few lines of dialogue she'd just written. Hitting the backspace key, she erased them, feeling a twinge of guilt. Gina had taught them to save everything, and to not edit while trying to write. But this was Delia's book, and she'd been trying to write this final chapter for three days. It just wasn't coming together.

She sat there for a few more minutes, trying to put herself in her heroine's sexy boots, but it wasn't working. She got up and paced the length of her office, then wandered out into the hallway. Delia tried to think of some of the tools Gina had taught them for when they felt stuck. Oh, right! Trying another form of creativity. That was one that Delia hadn't really test driven. She had enough to do in her daily life, already. Writing was her creative outlet.

But still, she had that old upright piano in the living room. Neither of the girls seemed interested in piano lessons. Shauna's passion was dance, and Zen copied her sister in most things. Delia had taken piano lessons as a girl, and had played off and on over the years, more often before she'd had kids. When they'd been splitting up possessions during the divorce, Delia had taken the opportunity to declutter, with her Virgo sister's help. She hadn't been able to part with the piano, though, even though she hardly played anymore.

She wandered downstairs, not bothering to turn on any lights. There were still faery lights hung around the ceiling from Christmas, and she could see fine. Delia sat down at the piano, wondering if it was even in tune. She put her hands on the keys and softly ran some scales. It was definitely not in tune, but she didn't care. She chose a quiet lullaby, not wanting to wake the girls. It felt good to play again.

Delia ran through a few old ballads from the 40s, the type of thing her father had loved. Nat King Cole, Sam Cooke, Eartha Kitt. It reminded her of her Dad, who had passed on several years ago. He wasn't a musician himself, but he'd loved to listen to records every evening, and he and her mother used to go to dances, back in the day. Delia still had his stereo components and some of his old records, something else she'd refused to part with when she redecorated. A tear ran down Delia's face, but she kept playing.

After her hands got tired, she closed the piano's cover and wandered into the living room. She dug out a record with Louis and Ella that was one of her Dad's favorites, and put it on. It was scratchy with use, but sounded divine to her ears. Delia sat and looked out at the snow as the album played.

***

Delia looked groggily at the laptop's clock as she saved and closed her documents. 3:13am. Ugh. Tomorrow morning would be painful. But she'd done it!

She'd finished the first draft. Completely. Now she was too exhausted to celebrate. She'd do it tomorrow; she promised to the image of Gina in her mind's eye. After she got the girls to school.

Delia zombie-walked to the bathroom and brushed her teeth. As she washed her face, she thought about what it would mean to her to be the author of this book.

The biggest thing was to have brought the story to completion. Well, she still had the editing process, and plenty of revisions ahead of her. And then there was the whole publishing process, which was still mostly a mystery. But she'd Done The Thing. She'd written a whole novel, and she actually, surprisingly, thought it was pretty good!

She found her way to the bedroom and peeled off her sweat pants and t-shirt. Delia thought this might be one of those times when she fell asleep as soon as her head hit the pillow. They were rare, but sometimes happened when she was up late and had a sense of accomplishing something.

But no. Her brain kept on churning up thoughts - not worries, at least, but plenty of busy thoughts. Delia pictured herself holding her book in her hands, which led to a series of speculations about what the cover might look like. She'd show the girls first - another part of her success that she valued was being a role model for her daughters. She couldn't resist indulging in a bit of an "I told you so" vibe to the doubters in her extended family, the ones who thought she was little more than a hot mess. This book would show them that she was also a creative, empowered woman.

Delia realized that her career, once the goal she'd aspired to, was now little more than a day job. Writing was what held the most value in her heart, after the girls, of course.

Huh. That was new. What did it mean?

Delia lay awake for another hour, thinking about how her nearly random decision to write this book had changed her, deeply. She finally drifted off with images of book signings and best-seller lists, her name in lights, floating through her head.

***

"I hate revisions with a passion," Delia confessed to her writing coach and fellow writers. "I don't know why. I can't seem to make myself work on them for more than a few minutes at a time. At this rate, I'll never be done!"

Gina smiled kindly. "Who else feels this way?" she asked the group as a whole. Nearly everyone raised their hand, even Gina herself. "You're not alone," the coach continued. "But I can give you some ideas on how to make it a bit easier."

Delia took notes as Gina offered her own tips, then opened the floor for the other participants to chime in. There were some good ideas, a couple of which she underlined in her notebook. She'd try them, but right now she was feeling frustrated. It wasn't fair. Just when she'd gotten the hang of writing consistently, she was done, and editing was a slog. There was nothing fun about it.

She'd always been able to spot mistakes in anything she read, and Delia had thought that would make editing a breeze. Somehow this weird skill didn't translate into her own work. Too bad. Maybe she just needed another set of eyes on her book manuscript. One of the other group members had already hired a developmental editor. It might help things along. Delia didn't know if she could afford it, but then again, she'd be investing in what she now thought of as her new, secret dream career.

What she really wanted to do was to start another book. But she felt guilty when she thought about writing something new when she hadn't really completed this first book. That was what she should have asked Gina about.

Toward the end of the call, when everyone had had a chance to ask their questions, Delia raised her hand. Gina called on her right away.

"I have a follow up question, if that's okay?" she asked tentatively.

"Go right ahead," Gina said with a smile.

"What if I really just want to start writing another book?" Delia asked. *"But I feel guilty about actually doing it, since this one still needs so much attention."*

"Do it!" Gina said with enthusiasm. *"I do this myself, all the time. It really helps me to have multiple projects going. For most of us, writing is the fun part. You can set up a schedule so you don't ignore the edits, but I think you should go for it."*

"Okay…" Delia said slowly. She mentally rolled her eyes about the schedule idea, which never seemed to work for her. But she could run it by her therapist, who specialized in ADHD stuff and seemed to have an infinite supply of ideas for translating productivity hacks so they'd actually be helpful.

"Is it a sequel?" Gina asked.

"No," Delia answered. *"It's actually a whole different genre."*

"Even better!" Gina said. *"Remember how I said to try another form of creativity when you're feeling stuck? This is similar. Writing something new, something you're excited about, will help your creativity flow in other areas, like the revisions."*

Delia nodded, but still felt a bit doubtful. Gina, as always, picked up on it.

"Delia, you're a good writer, and getting better all the time. There's no reason in the world to hold yourself back from writing. Especially now, when you've found your rhythm."

Delia smiled, and her eyes actually teared up. *"Really?"*

"Absolutely," Gina said. *"Consider this your permission slip. Start that new book today."*

Gina wrapped up the call, and Delia was left with a warm glow. She loved her coach and the community she'd found in the writing program. And now she could start the sci-fi novel that had been slipping through her thoughts for a couple of weeks. Delia knew she didn't need permission from anyone to do what she wanted. She was the new version of herself, after all, Give No Fucks Delia, the one who'd let go of the BS of perfectionism and external validation. But it felt good just *the same, to have received the stamp of approval from an author and mentor she respected. She'd start that new book tonight, after she got a few things done around the house.*

CHAPTER 8:
FIRE: REFINING YOUR VOICE

About Fire

As the hot Sun beats down on us, we follow our circular trail to a landing place in the South, the ancestral home of Fire. The element of Fire is about passion and creative expression. It's the spark of new ideas. We are driven by our yearning to create, to bring to life something unique.

The element of Fire lights the darkness of our outer and inner landscapes. It is in the faraway light of the stars, the life-giving warmth of our Sun, the Moon's mystical reflection, the sudden flash of lightning, the friction of flint on steel, and the spark of passion in the belly. Fire's time is associated with summer at high noon. The colors of Fire are bright and vibrant: red, orange, yellow, gold.

We wouldn't be here without Fire. The Sun brings us the warmth our bodies need. It feeds the plants that provide us with air to breathe and food to eat. The inner Fires of our amazing bodies allow us to digest and metabolize our food so we can fuel our physical existence. Since ancient times, Fire has been acknowledged in our myths as a sacred gift.

Fire is spiritual energy. Its heat brings us the things that fill our lives with joy. We feel desire for a beloved, expressing our love with passionate acts and sexual ardor. We take pride in our creations, our contributions. We reach out for connection with All-That-Is, thrilling to our part in the divine dance of life. We smile and laugh, taking pleasure in the pure fiery energy of living.

When mishandled, Fire reminds us to respect its gifts. As individuals, we may fall into rage or obsession, burning with energies out of control. Those among us with fiery tempers are both admired and feared, sought out and avoided. Walking the hot coals of our inner Fire can require delicate balance. Around the globe, we feel the effects of our quest to harness Fire in the form of electricity and transportation without regard for the messes we leave behind. At the same time, we reap the benefits of technology, sharing new ideas and delivering humanitarian aid. Humanity is still in the early stages of learning to balance our use of Fire.

The tools of Fire are the fire-starters, that which we use to light a physical flame. This might be matches or a lighter, flint and steel, a magnifying glass to capture the Sun's rays, or simpler tools like sticks and string. We use our skill and will to spark the blaze that will keep us warm, light our way, and remind us of the potent powers of Fire.

When we explored Air, we looked at inspiration and all the ideas that one's mind can come up with in a relatively short period of time. Yet even if you have the best ideas in the multiverse, unless you do something with them, either the Muses will move on to someone else, or the ideas will languish at the bottom of your mental closet. Fire provides the passion and momentum to express our creative inspirations.

Not just any been-there-done-that expression, either. When you're in harmony with the element of Fire, you're able to express your unique take on your artform. You find your voice. You pour your passion into your writing – or your dancing, or parenting, or whatever medium you choose.

That's why Fire is where you'll explore finding your voice, your expression. Using the tools and momentum of Fire, you'll begin to work on your unique voice as a writer. Continuing our home-building metaphor from earlier, voice is the interior design of your writing project. It's what makes your home — or book — uniquely your own.

The writer's voice can be kind of an abstract concept, especially as you first start writing. What makes up your writer's voice? The concept encompasses the words you choose, the rhythm of your sentences, and the way you use metaphor and simile. It's that intangible feeling that you invoke in your writing. The simplest way to see what I mean by "voice" is to think about your favorite authors. Is there an author whose writing you'd know anywhere? That's because you're familiar with their overall voice. You know their style. You may notice prolific authors' voices change over time.

In the realm of Fire, we'll take a look at how to find your voice as a writer, and for particular projects. This will involve freeing yourself from the ways you've been taught to write.

Remember the street musician from earlier? The one who could keep up with the person who studied at Julliard? Chances are that besides the many hours of practice, our street musician also took the time to develop a unique voice, a style that is all their own. Those are the things that will make you memorable.

That's not to say that your writing should be avant-garde and different from the usual voices in your genre – not necessarily, anyway. What it needs to be is authentic. In the realm of Fire, you'll burn away not only the ways you've been taught to conform, but also old beliefs that are holding you back from the full expression of your creative magick.

Along with its passion, elemental Fire also brings a playful quality to your creative work. You realize that when you're not trying to write perfectly, you can experiment. Once you've established a regular writing habit, practiced some of the skills we talked about earlier, and accepted that you shouldn't try to edit as you write, things get a lot more fun. Fire is joyfully there for that kind of creative play time.

There's an additional way in which Fire helps us to express our unique creativity. Fire is the element that has the most in common with Spirit. Many of the world's spiritual traditions use symbolism that equates Fire with the Divine: the sacred flame, twin flame souls, and the like. Fire is energy, like the chi or energy that courses through our bodies, animating us.

When you practice getting and staying aligned in your Triple Self, your energy will flow more smoothly through your entire being. You are plugged into Deep Self, and thus in contact with a source of energy that is connected with the entire cosmos. Believe it or not, that energy is full of joy and loves to play. I love the saying "never trust a spiritual leader who doesn't dance." Not necessarily literally, but dancing through the world is easier when you're in deep connection with the Source.

Some of the most delightful writing sessions I've had were when I was fully connected with my inner wellspring, my Deep Self. It's akin to channeling wisdom from another realm. We'll talk more later in this chapter about what it means to channel your creativity. But for now, know that the element of Fire is the realm where you have full reign to experiment with your energy and how it supports you in sharing your most inspired wisdom and powerful stories with your readers. In exploring this, you're finding your voice and becoming willing to express it.

Finding Your Voice

How do you find your voice as a writer? Is it something that already exists, that you're hunting for as you practice the writing craft? Maybe. It depends on how much writing, or perhaps public speaking or other word-related arts, you've done. It's also important to note that your voice for each particular book that you write can be unique. It's not like you have just one writer's voice and that's the end. Like the writing process as a whole, it's something you can playfully experiment with. In this chapter, I'll share some ways to begin cultivating your voice.

What exactly do I mean by your book's "voice?" As I mentioned earlier, the concept of voice can be kind of abstract. What makes up your writer's voice encompasses the words you choose, the rhythm of your sentences, the way you use metaphor and simile. It's that intangible feeling that you invoke in your writing.

For me, intuition plays a large part in refining your writer's voice. I'm sure some writers craft it very deliberately, but in my experience it's been more important to let it be playful and inspired — like dancing flames!

This is why it's so crucial to free-write your first drafts and not try to edit at the same time. When you edit as you go, you're often toning down your actual voice. You're making it more mainstream and vanilla — as most of us were taught to do in school. That might work for English Comp 101, but it's not the way to cultivate passionate readers who love your stuff.

I suggest that you start by writing the way you speak. If you haven't already experimented with voice-to-text writing, this is a good time to try it. Alternatively, you can imagine that you're writing directly to one person. Say the words aloud as you type them. Are they similar to what you might say if the person you're addressing was here in the room with you? If you worry that this sort of writing will sound dumb, remember that we're experimenting. Anything you write now is going to go through the editing process. If you don't like it, it won't end up in the book. Hopefully this gives you permission to be a bit more playful in your approach.

Use the heat of Fire to help you express yourself authentically. Sometimes when we write, we tend to tone down our passion. This is a leftover from writing for someone who was going to give you a grade. This isn't that type of writing. It's *your* book. Write about the things that light you up, or ones that drive you absolutely crazy. Swear if you want to or call your readers "honey." Be unapologetically *you*. As you practice, you'll begin to develop the first glimmerings of your unique writer's voice.

When I say "your voice," it's not to imply that you have just one, either. My clients are often surprised to hear me say that each book you create might have its own unique voice. Don't worry if that doesn't make any sense yet. By attuning yourself to the energy of your creation, you'll give life to your book or other work of art. If you have more than one kid, you'll get it.

Even if they're created and raised by you and the same co-parent, your kids have different personalities. Books babies are like that, too.

I mentioned in the previous section that you already know what voice sounds like, in terms of authors you've read. Think for a moment of your favorite books and authors. If you read something new by that person, or a new volume in a series you're very familiar with, you could probably identify it. You're used to the way she uses language, the rhythm of the sentences, or the way his writing consists mostly of sharp, witty dialogue.

I'm going to give some examples of well-known authors with unique voices, because it makes it easier to understand the concept — and I get to geek out as my bookwyrm self.

We'll start with fiction, because the writer's voice is easier to see there sometimes. Have you read anything by fantasy author Neil Gaiman? His books *American Gods* and *Anansi Boys* both have a sort of sassy, practical yet mysterious tone. *Stardust*, which was one of his earlier novels, and *The Ocean at the End of the Lane*, a more recent book of short stories, have a more lyrical, fae tone to them. There are things in common with all of his writings, so you can recognize his overall style, but the separate books each have their own feel.

Let's take a look at a nonfiction example. The late author and poet Maya Angelou wrote a series of autobiographies, and she employed a distinct voice for each. *I Know Why the Caged Bird Sings* tells the story of her early years and is very raw and powerful. *All God's Children Need Traveling Shoes* is about her time in Ghana, and to me it felt very musical, like a symphony that returns to the theme or reprise.

Then there's Elizabeth Gilbert. Her book *Eat, Pray, Love* was very much in the voice of a spiritual seeker, with many more questions than answers. *Big Magic*, on the other hand, was spoken with the voice of wisdom, of having figured some stuff out that she wanted to share with other creatives.

A few other examples: Brené Brown's straightforward research-based talk is backed with vulnerable stories from her own life - and her writing reads like her TED talks, in her particular style. Jen Sincero's sassy, fun, wise big sister tone in her *You Are a Badass...* books makes them relatable. The late Irish fiction author Maeve Binchy's quick yet deep personality sketches made her ordinary-seeming characters loveable. Are you getting the picture? Your book's voice is what makes it unique and memorable.

Yes, some of the differences you can see between books by the same author are probably the result of the author refining their writer's voice over time. I can see that in both Maya Angelou and Elizabeth Gilbert. I've also experienced that with my own books — *The Heart of the Goddess* is definitely more "me" than some of my earlier ones. But it can also vary by book, or even by shorter pieces of writing. Those of you who write blog posts or newsletters may be able to see how that work is distinct from what you write for your book project.

I suspect you've already been developing your distinct voice as you're writing your book manuscript. It's something that naturally happens as you move along the journey. Can you see your voice unfolding?

Your writer's voice is entwined with your authentic self. This is why it's key to get your Triple Self aligned before beginning to write, so you can access your Deep Self and the creative wellspring at the core of your being. Remember, you wouldn't be writing this book at all if you didn't have some passion for the topic or the story. Going back to your Deep Why can provide some clues about the best voice to use as you write your heartfelt manuscript.

Your voice contains an essential piece of *you* — your authentic self, the lens through which your deep creativity comes forth into the world. That means it can be challenging to share. In order to discover your book's voice, it's imperative to ease up on self-censorship.

I'll say it again: ***don't try to edit as you write***. Don't squash your unique way of engaging with the written word. Contrary to what we were taught in school, don't try to make your writing bland, acceptable, and mainstream. Do give yourself permission to play and experiment with words. Do set up boundaries about what you'll choose to share, so you feel safe in expressing your deep truths. Do have fun with it!

Try out different voices and genres as you practice finding the voice you truly wish to write in. Don't be too quick to judge your first drafts. Do let yourself enjoy the process of mining for your book's authentic voice!

Get out your writing journal and let's go a little deeper into our exploration of voice. Here are some prompts to answer that will get you closer to discovering the voice of your book.

- ❖ *What are three things you feel so strongly about that you'd gladly stand on a soapbox on a busy street corner and pontificate about?*
- ❖ *How would you describe your book's ideal voice, in five to seven words?*
- ❖ *What do you feel that you need as you continue to develop a strong voice for your project?*
- ❖ *What are three inspired actions you can take to refine your book's voice?*

Over the course of the next couple of weeks, focus on your book's voice when you sit down for your writing sessions. How will you bring it to life? What words, phrases, or expressions will give your writing a unique flavor? Have fun with this. As always, it's an experiment, so you don't need to take it super seriously.

Your Characters and Their Impact

If you're writing a work of fiction, your book will obviously have characters. But even if you're writing nonfiction, you'll populate your book with characters of some sort – the most important of whom is probably you! Let's take a look at the role of people, whether historically true or fantastically imagined, in your book.

Nonfiction writers, please indulge me and read this, even if you have no plans to ever write a story or a novel. Trust me, it will be relevant to you, even if only to spark your imagination or make you a more curious reader of other people's novels.

Characters form the basis of your story. It's important that they be believable. This is the case whether you made them up entirely or they're based on someone you know in "real life." For a character to be believable, the reader has to see their flaws. The character must, like all of us, show that they're only human.

It's tempting, especially when you first begin to write, to create heroes and heroines who are idealized and practically perfect. Don't do that. Along the same line, don't create villains who are purely evil. Neither of these types of characters are believable, and in fact they're pretty boring to the reader.

A strong protagonist, or main character, is one of the most vital ingredients in a compelling work of fiction. This invented person must be unique, fallible, and intriguing. They must, indeed, have their own voice, one that is often set apart from the voice of the writer as narrator.

The point of view you choose to write from does play into this. I'm not going to go into detail about point of view here, but I recommend studying up on it, especially if this is your first foray into fiction. Actually, if you're new to fiction writing, please do yourself the favor of picking up a writing craft book or two and taking a deep dive. There is much to learn that's beyond the scope of this book, which is more about freeing up your creativity. I've recommended some of my favorites in the Resources section.

The best way I've found to make characters who truly shine is to create a comprehensive backstory for them. You want to know your character's personality inside out before you begin writing. Write up a background sketch that includes details that may never find their way into the book itself. Include things like where they grew up, what their siblings (if any) were like, their favorite foods – any detail that occurs to you. Get to know them as you would a new best friend.

The cool thing about your characters is that they will grow and evolve in the process of living the story you're telling. While you're familiar with your character's personality and background as the book begins, you most likely won't know exactly how they'll change. Ideally, your main character will surprise you with their choices and the way they step up to the challenges you set for them. This is a good thing.

Characters who appeal most strongly to readers are dynamic. They make bad choices but have a good heart. They care – maybe too much. They are sometimes flippant or greedy, but when the shit hits the fan, they are loyal and dedicated friends. You get the idea. Like we talked about earlier, human beings live in a world where polarity is part of the package. We are a bundle of contradictions, and that's what makes us human – and lovable. When you create characters who contain both "bad" and "good" traits, your readers won't be able to put down the book. That's what you want.

In works of fiction, characters are the messengers, the individual voices which create the choir, delivering the overall message of your book. They need to feel authentic, even when they're completely imaginary. Take some time outside your usual writing times to draw up comprehensive character sketches. Make your characters complicated. Then unleash them on the page, put challenges in front of them, and see how they evolve.

If you're writing nonfiction and you've been patient enough to read through this entire section, first of all, thanks! I also want you to know that, in your how-to, memoir, or self-help book, you are the primary character. Reflect on some of the advice about fictional characters, and see how you might apply it to your own work. Here's a hint: readers will resonate with you more strongly if you share your own flaws, mistakes, and lessons learned. Be authentic and open as you tell your own story.

The Power of Anecdotes in Nonfiction

By definition, works of nonfiction aren't made up of invented stories, the way novels are. However, the best works of nonfiction do contain plenty of stories.

Think about your own favorite works of nonfiction. Even in a book that has the goal of teaching you a technique, like how to market your business, the best authors use anecdotes to make their points. Otherwise, the book is dry and boring. You're most likely not writing a textbook here. You want your book to captivate your readers' attention.

Your nonfiction book, no matter what it's about, should include stories. If you're writing a memoir or autobiography, this will be easy for you. You're telling the story of your own life. You get to tell it from your perspective, according to the way you remember it, and that will certainly differ from the way the other people in your tale recall the events. That's perfectly fine. It's up to you how you present things, but remember, the most fascinating characters have many facets. Take care not to make yourself, or the people in your story, all good or all bad. You'll probably have to make some decisions about the other people who populate your story. You might decide to change names and identifying details in order to protect their privacy.

Even when you're writing an instructional or self-help book, stories comprise a crucial part of the narrative. You'll no doubt want to share anecdotes from your own life, as I've done in this book. This shows your reader that you faced some of the same challenges that they now face. It will illustrate how you used the techniques you're sharing to overcome those problems. You can also include anecdotes and case studies from others who have used your methods. Again, feel free to change names and other details in order to protect others' privacy. If you're sharing a client's story or a quote from a mentor, you can ask their permission to include it.

As I've told my clients, it's even acceptable to make up a case study, as long as you're basing it on factual experience. For example, if several clients have shared similar feedback and experiences about a particular tool you've shared with them, you might pull the details together to create an invented client whose story you'll include in your book. This isn't lying. It's a way of illustrating a point about a truth you've experienced while preserving privacy. Again, as long as you make sure it's based on actual people's feedback, which they've shared with you, making it into a story of one particular person can be a powerful way of sharing it with your reader.

If you're completely making up an anecdote or story in order to illustrate a point, make it clear that this is what you're doing. For example, you could say something like, "Imagine a person named Sue, who has decided that she wants to learn to knit." It's fine to use your imagination when you're writing nonfiction, as long as you tell the reader that's what you're doing. Most readers are pretty savvy and will follow along with you as you get fanciful to make a point. Bringing fun stories into your narrative will capture and keep the reader's attention. It will engage their Younger Self, and thus allow you to reach them on a deeper level.

What about research and footnotes in nonfiction? Chances are that your ideal reader is already open to what you have to share. I would venture to guess that most readers find footnotes or detailed statistics to be a bit dull. They interrupt the narrative. At least, I find that to be the case. When I read a self-help book or instructive text, I want to hear about the actual tools the writer is offering, and some stories about how they work for the author and others. I'm going to try the tools on for myself and evaluate them on their merits. I don't especially care if there was a double-blind study at Yale with particular parameters. If I do care – or another reader does – citing your references in an endnotes section will make it simple for those curious readers to find. I wouldn't suggest interrupting the flow of the text with those kinds of stats. That said, you can certainly refer to studies or other works, like I've done in this book. Readers who want more can follow the trail for themselves via the breadcrumbs you provide in endnotes or your Resources section. The rest of us can read on. Unless you're writing a textbook or other academic work, keep it simple and readable.

There are other imaginative elements you might want to include in your nonfiction book, to make it more lively and fun for the reader. Some of these include quotes, illustrations, charts, graphs, poems, and channeled writing. We'll talk about channeled writing in the next section. As you write your book, chances are you'll start noticing lots of related gems of wisdom in the world around you. Your attention is focused on this particular topic, so the Universe will bring you more –

that's known as synchronicity, and is part of sympathetic magick, also known as the Law of Attraction. Capture those quotes, tidbits of information, and other treasures related to your book. Keep them in a separate document. Weave them into your manuscript if and when it feels right. Save them for the editing phase, when you might want to add quotes at the beginning of each chapter or embellish your text with illustrations.

Channeled Writing and Intuition

Writing is like channeling. No, not always. But it sure seems like it when you get into the zone — that state where it feels like no time has passed and the words are flowing forth nearly faster than you can transfer them to the page. This passionate mode of creating makes sense here in the home of elemental Fire.

What do I mean by "channeling," anyway? The most basic definition of a channel is a human being who serves as a medium for a non-physical spirit or being. The person speaks – or writes – the information that is coming through to them from the non-physical realms. Sound kind of New Agey? That's okay.

There are many beneficial practices that were once dismissed as overly woo-woo that are now proven scientifically to exist and to work. Hello, meditation, mindfulness, and the existence of the aura — my thanks to the HeartMath Institute for that last one.

But I digress (again).

I personally don't think that channeling has to involve an outside spirit, although it certainly can. When you get yourself in the groove of creativity, you can channel your own inner wisdom. The wellspring of your creativity comes from something greater than your waking mind. That connection to the non-physical realms is there already, under the surface. We're all innately creative.

If the notion of channeling feels unfamiliar to you, think about what happens when you sleep. You might have experienced this if you remember your dreams when you wake up. Have you ever woken from a particularly vivid dream and asked yourself "where did *that* come from?!" It came from *you*. Your subconscious self is continually gathering observations and information about the world around you. In dreams, you experience the creation of worlds and stories that might seem wildly fanciful.

You can do the same when you tap into a deep state of creativity. You can enter that dreaming mode, even while awake and writing. To bring science back into the picture, during sessions like this, your brain waves go into an alpha or even theta state. This is often when you come up with your most powerful, creative, and inspirational works. By cultivating a regular practice of writing, you're setting the stage for channeling your deepest creativity.

It's not going to happen every day, or even every week, but when it does — wow! Showing up regularly and making space for deep connection will allow you to tap into that wellspring of creativity within your imagination.

Have you ever experienced that flow state while writing or creating? What does it feel like to you?

If you're curious to try channeled writing, here's how to get started. First, make sure you're fully aligned in your Triple Self. Meditate silently or play a recorded guided meditation. Or do it after yoga or a workout. Sit at your keyboard and imagine yourself surrounded by a sphere of bright light. Reach out with your awareness and make it known that you'd like to channel some wisdom. Ask that whatever you receive be for the highest good of all, or something similar. This will keep you protected from non-physical beings with questionable motives. It's unlikely that anything negative will happen when channeling, but setting that intention both protects you and helps reassure your shadow selves that what you're doing is safe.

When you first begin experimenting with channeling, it helps to ask a question. Type the question on the page. Then listen for answers. It's best to start writing whatever first comes to mind. Don't second-guess it. It's tempting to begin wondering whether the channeled answers are coming from you or another source. For now, it doesn't matter. Just practice typing in a stream of consciousness style. If you know how to touch-type, you can close your eyes and just allow your fingers to type whatever answers you're receiving. If typing is a slow process for you, you might try writing longhand when you channel. I find that I can't keep up with the pace of the answers when I write by hand, but I'm a pretty fast typist, so it makes sense for me to use that skill.

Like most of the techniques I'm offering, channeling isn't something that you'll either succeed or fail at the first time you try it. It requires some practice. If you'd like to develop this skill, I'd suggest trying channeled writing once or twice a month at first, as part of one of your regular writing sessions. When I was writing my book *The Heart of the Goddess*, I blended channeling with my writing process. I would write about a particular topic from my own point of view, then do some channeled writing on the same topic afterwards, in another writing session. It was interesting to see the similarities and differences between the two sessions.

Let's talk about intuition for a moment. How does using your intuition in your work as a writer differ from doing channeled writing?

In my experience, intuition is the voice of your Deep Self. Once you've practiced being aligned in your Triple Self, you'll begin to hear it more clearly, on a regular basis. You might "hear" your intuition in the form of words spoken aloud in your head, but there are certainly many other ways to receive it. Sometimes it will feel like a nudge in a certain direction, especially if you're trying to make a decision. It might show up as signs and synchronicities in your daily life. Maybe you get that "gut feeling" and you suddenly "just know" what will work best for you.

Your intuition will help you on your creative journey by inspiring you with ideas – especially when you ask for them. Develop a relationship with your Deep Self. Make it clear that you're open to insights. Remember, Younger Self is the universal translator, so appeal to her through ritual and playfulness. When she's engaged and having fun, she'll be happy to help you stay connected with the wellspring of creativity that Deep Self inhabits.

When you do channeled writing, as described earlier, you might indeed be channeling the words from your Deep Self. You might also be gathering them from some other non-physical entity, like an ancestor or spirit guide. I don't think it necessarily matters where exactly the material is coming from. If you're curious, just ask. Again, there's no real way to prove whether you're talking to your great-grandmother, a star guide from the Pleiades, or yourself. The best thing to do is judge the material on its own merits and have fun with it. If your book is about life on other planets, then having a Pleiadian guide is perfect. If you're channeling a new healing technique and don't need to specify in the book where the information comes from, evaluate it on its own merits and keep on keepin' on!

You Can't Make Me: Rebellious Resistance

Ah, beloved Thriving Artist. Here we are, looking at resistance once again. How does resistance show up in the realm of elemental Fire? It often manifests as having trouble with consistency and follow-through. What do I mean?

Let's ease in by taking a look at how people with a lot of Fire in their astrological charts tend to show up in the world. Perhaps this describes you, or someone you know well. First, they are passionate people who come up with some amazing, inspired ideas. They are often adventurous. They love to be spontaneous. One of my best friends is an Aries, and we've had to figure out how to best spend time together. She'll call or text me, wanting to get together that day to do some amazingly cool thing she's freshly dreamed up. As a Virgo, my schedule is tidily full of already-planned-in-advance commitments, so often even when it sounds great, I have to take a rain check. These days I tend to create some space for her in my week, and then let her know the day before or even that morning. I also lean into my Cancer rising side, to leave spaces for free flow in my week. My friend has compromised by picking some choice activities that do need to be planned ahead of time and letting me know in advance.

In general, though, fiery people dislike planning ahead. They want to do the fun part of the project, and not so much the cleanup or finishing touches. When they feel complete with the energy of an endeavor, they're on to the next inspiration.

As you might imagine, this can be an asset as a creative person – they find new ideas everywhere and are often inspired. But it can also be a challenge.

Just so you know, it's not only the Fire signs who have this form of resistance arise. Resistance in the realm of Fire might look like: getting bored with a project before it's complete, having a bunch of different creative activities underway at once, getting so many ideas that you're overwhelmed, multitasking, or making sudden and significant changes in your manuscript.

As mentioned earlier, Fire is the element that's most closely related to Spirit. There's a kinship between the resistance that comes up in the realm of Fire and the tools available to us in Spirit. When we get to the section on Spirit, we'll delve deeper into how to use inspired persistence to finish your book and other creative projects.

In the meantime, please know that the flighty resistance you'll experience in Fire is natural. In fact, some of the clues I listed above are not negatives, when used deliberately. I often recommend to my clients that they have more than one writing project underway, because there are times when you just won't feel like working on your book. I do this myself. I often have a nonfiction manuscript, some fiction, and writing for my business all underway, and I move from one to another based on what inspires me and which writing voice I want to play with that day.

What we want to avoid is when you get frustrated – another trait of fiery people is their quick temper – and "rage quit" your book. Learning to move between projects without burning bridges is key to managing your resistance. It can also help the fiery types among us learn to value those writing habits we established back in the land of Earth — see, I told you all the elements touch and affect one another!

What's behind the inconsistency and lack of follow-through? As I've hinted above, it might just be part of your nature. When you're not accomplishing what you set out to do, despite having a focused intention, there could be more to it than your fae tendencies.

Using some of the tools you've been learning, take time to dig into your resistance like we've done for the other elements. Fire loves to be free and doesn't appreciate being contained. Is there a place in your past where your creativity or your authentic expression was smothered? Has someone in authority directed your talents in ways that are inappropriate or unkind? Those voices in your mind that you're rebelling against – "You can't make me do this!" – whose are they, really? How is that conformity we talked about in the chapter on Air still really pissing you off?

The Shadows we encounter in the element of Fire probably won't hesitate to make themselves known. They throw temper tantrums, storm off, and express their righteous indignation. Even though they might seem scary, ultimately they just want to be heard and witnessed. Make some time to hear their concerns before you tuck them into the backseat with some paper and crayons.

You don't want to banish your wild fiery shadows from the realm, because they are often the channel for some amazing ideas. All the same, you need to let them know that there are boundaries. Your scheduled writing session for your book is not the time to get a download of a whole new course or screenplay. If that happens, you can make some notes, hear what they have to say, and then gently move on to your writing session. When you understand and accept the resistance that arises in Fire, you can harness its useful qualities while soothing the part of you that wants to bounce around from project to project, never finishing anything. When you allow yourself multiple vehicles for expression, cultivating a voice for each, they'll feed each other in a way that's sustainable and warming. Like a hearth fire, instead of a forest fire.

Spirit in Fire

You already know that the Element of Fire is the most closely associated with that of Spirit. Prometheus was punished for gifting Fire to humanity. The gods were worried that it would give us too much power. Looking at the way we've managed our insatiable desire to consume resources, they may have been right. But that's a discussion for another time...

Fire is not just used to cook our food or power our vehicles. It's not only the massive combustion that powers our Sun and other stars. It's not just the powerful zap of a lightning strike. It's also the very energy that powers everything in our multiverse. It is chi, the life force that flows through space and time. Fire has some powerful creative magick.

Spirit is also what that energy of life is made of – it's the consciousness that makes life meaningful. We have a lot of theories about Spirit, but we don't really know what it is, because it's beyond our perception and understanding, at least most of the time.

When we look at Fire, though, we can get a sense of what it's like to exist in the realm of Spirit. Residing in Spirit, even for short bursts of awareness, often involves embracing paradox. As creatives, we use the realm of Fire to discover our unique creative voice. When we dance with Spirit, we can connect with a unity that enfolds us into the greater whole. How can we be unique individuals and while also one with the vast consciousness that pervades All-That-Is? Doesn't this perspective of vast unity make you feel insignificant?

Again, paradoxically, no. In my own experience, it has actually filled me with the passion to live more fully and to bring my very best creative work to life. The creation myths of many cultures on Earth speak of the creator as growing bored with being one with itself. The very creation of our multiverse was quite likely a grand experiment, set up to explore what it might be like to exist in many different forms. By allowing yourself to *be* your unique self, and to share your experiences with others, you're doing your part to fill the Akashic records with fascinating stories that fuel our collective existence.

Why wouldn't you want to play in the realm of creativity? It's so much fun! Standing in the flame of your passion, you're connected with the non-physical realm, the Divine, the Mysteries, that which is beyond your ego's understanding. As a co-creator, you can bring forth words that will uplift, inspire, engage, and entertain your fellow beings. You can follow your passion wherever it goes, guided by your Deep Self's wisdom.

CHAPTER 9:
THE BORDERLANDS: FROM PASSION TO FLOW (FIRE TO WATER)

About This Transition

Moving deosil around the circle once more, we now come to the transition between Fire and Water. Everyone knows that fire and water don't mix. Or do they? At this corner of The Borderlands, they have made an uneasy truce. The passionate action of Fire begins to die down a bit, and we explore the emotional inner landscapes that Water brings to bear. We wish to finish our creative projects, bringing them to fruition and enjoying the feeling of deep sighing release at their completion. Once we set them free, we can turn to dreams of what comes next, letting our intuition mingle with our desires and point the way. We find time to rest and heal from the busiest part of the cycle.

The intersection of Fire and Water lies in the southwest. The weather features long hot dry spells and sudden downpours. In the desert, water is hidden, but it's there. As in the southwestern United States, great rushing rivers have carved and sculpted beautiful dreamlike canyons. The animals we encounter are tough and mystical: snake, coyote, hawk, desert fox, wild horses. At night, a myriad of stars fills the wide-open sky. We dream of our heart's desires, and in our imagination the dry gullies fill with life-giving water once again. The transition between Fire and Water is full of the energy of Lammas, when the first harvest is safely in and we revel in the long hot summer days, yet sunset comes earlier each day and we begin to feel a hint of fall.

Looking at the realm of time, this particular transition point represents the afternoon, stretching out from noon to sunset. Our energies begin to flag a bit, and we may sneak away for a brief catnap or siesta. As we quiet toward dusk, we wrap up the tasks of the day, beginning the transition into evening time. Our activity begins to slow, and we turn inward, exploring our inner landscape. The moon, which was so recently full, now begins to wane. We are able to banish the energies which no longer serve us, using our creative powers for healing and renewal.

The stage of life represented by the intersection of Fire and Water is that of later adulthood, as we approach the passage to crone or sage. We make peace with what we have or haven't accomplished in our lives and seek to share our wisdom with our communities. Feelings which may have been hidden come to the surface. Sometimes the passage can be challenging, as our passionate feelings find expression and we search for our new role. Perhaps we are ready for a quieter lifestyle, yet the demands of family and career still jostle for our attention. Or maybe we seek to keep up the fiery pace we're used to, only to find our aging bodies unable to sustain our earlier speed. The early-autumn plants are in full harvest mode, with fruits and vegetables ready to be gathered. Yet at the same time, the leaves are beginning to turn toward fall colors, and the Earth and her creatures prepare for the colder weather soon to come.

Some of the resources we can use to explore the Fire to Water transition include the following spiritual practices, tools, and symbols:

- ❖ Fire and Water combine to form steam. This transition is the perfect time for a healing sauna or sweat lodge, perhaps followed by a massage or Reiki session. Approach your cleansing in a ritualistic way by setting intentions for healing and self-exploration. If you don't have access to a sauna, a

184

hot tub or bathtub surrounded by candles is a delightful alternative. Sip some hot tea or perhaps a bit of cider and let yourself drift into daydreams.

❖ In the Tarot, the card that represents "Fire of Water" is the King of Cups. This King is the wounded healer, bringing his power to bear in a gentle and imaginative manner. He is a caregiver who uses his intuition to serve, yet he has hidden depths of passion. When this card appears, you are advised to wield your creativity and intuition with calm confidence no matter the situation.

❖ The mythical creatures related to this transition are selkies. Also known as silkies or selchies, they have both a seal form and a human form. As seals, they live in the ocean, yet they can remove their seal skins and live with humans on land. Selkies are attractive and seductive, often taking human lovers. Yet they cannot stay on land for long without pining for the sea. Selkies show us how to balance our passion with the need for introspection and solitude.

❖ A sample affirmation to use when working with this transition is: "I passionately embrace my dreams and discover creative ways to heal myself."

Take some time to observe how Fire and Water interact with one another in your experience. Find new ways to integrate this dynamic energy into your daily life.

It makes sense that this borderland feels a bit chaotic. Fire and Water are said not to mix – though as a beloved of mine says, they can make for a lovely hot tub experience.

At this point in the journey of writing your book, you're likely more than halfway finished with the first draft, or maybe even further. The passion of Fire and finding your book's voice has been carrying you along as you've done the work of writing. Hopefully you've been following the weekly and monthly ebb and flow of your creativity. In a bigger-picture look at this cycle, this is often the portion of the arc of writing your manuscript when some weariness sets in. Don't worry about it. This is a natural part of the process.

The borderland between Fire and Water allows you the space and ease to move from passion to flow. You begin to wonder what will happen when you *do* finish the manuscript. How will your book be published? What about editing? Do you need to start thinking about a cover?

When these questions begin to arise before the book is complete, I offer my clients ideas for beginning to gradually work toward publication. This helps you get prepared for that part of the book's birth, but it also provides something useful to focus on when you begin to need a break from the actual writing. When we enter the realm of Water, you'll learn how to nurture your community and to be nurtured by it.

Here at the borderland, though, the notion of sharing yourself and your book with others – even those close to you — might sound scary. You worry that you don't have the stamina to finish the book. You wonder if writing it was a good idea, if you're going to have to put yourself in the spotlight in order to promote it. You even might reach a crisis point where you question nearly everything in your creative process!

This is the perfect time for what I call some exquisite self-care. I first originated that phrase during the month of March, which for various reasons I often find personally challenging. After noticing this pattern of either illness or some kind of emotional crisis each year in the early spring, I decided a few years ago to head it off at the pass. I devoted myself to nurturing myself so thoroughly that there was less chance of burnout, and it has worked.

I find that it's best to be proactive with your exquisite self-care, but it will also help if you already find yourself in crisis mode. I'll share some ways to implement it in the next section.

Exquisite Self-Care for Creative Crises

When you're walking the borderlands between Fire and Water and you hit a point of existential creative crisis, or if you feel one lurking in the wings, it's time for implementing exquisite self-care.

Let's start by defining what it is I'm talking about. What do I mean by an existential creative crisis? It's when you reach a point of resistance that seems to block any further progress, like hiking in a canyon and reaching the back wall unexpectedly, with no trails that continue. It feels like you either have to go back the way you came, or just sit there for a while.

It's not exactly like the feelings of blockage or procrastination we've dealt with earlier. It tends to manifest more like a feeling of emotional exhaustion, overwhelm, or burnout. You've been walking in the realms of Fire, letting the momentum of passion and exploration carry you forward. But now, as you begin to transition into the more touchy-feely realms of Water, you feel like the Fire has died. Your book draft might lose its shiny glow. You feel kind of "meh" about what you've written, or even actively hate it, wondering how you ever thought it would make a good book.

Sometimes this crisis manifests when your life suddenly gets overly busy. When you start to work with your creativity, you become more strongly connected with Deep Self, and your own *power-from-within*. This can ripple outward into many areas of your life – perhaps you've caught glimpses of it by now. These changes, while positive in nature, can seem threatening. You're getting lots of new offers and opportunities. Your work, particularly if it's related to the book you're writing, will gain a wider following, and new clients will flood in. Part of you loves this, but remember those shadow selves? They can tend to feel frightened when things shift and change a bit *too* much. You get busy, you aren't sure how you'll get to your writing amidst all the other stuff you have going on, and suddenly it's all just too much for your emotional – and perhaps physical – body.

What about *exquisite* self-care? How is that different from the everyday variety? Throughout this book, I've encouraged you to support your writing practice by also taking good care of yourself. Rest, water, healthy food, movement, body care, time to be alone and to be with those you love – all of these things are essential to a balanced life. They make a deep-dive into creativity, like writing an entire book, possible. That is self-care in the everyday realm.

Here in the borderland between Fire and Water, the exquisite self-care I'm suggesting is even *more* nurturing. How do you implement it? By treating your existential creative crisis, or feelings that indicate one might be on the way, as a true health crisis.

When you get sick, you take certain actions: consult a healer, cancel or postpone events in your schedule, stock up on food and drink that support good health, and make a quiet spot for recovery. Exquisite self-care looks like that.

First, reach out for help. Talk with your writing coach or accountability partner and let them know that you're in a place where you need extra support. Do the same with the people you live with, or your closest friends. If they'll think "an existential creative crisis" or "exquisite self-care" is a bit weird, phrase it in your own way. Tell them you're exhausted and you're going to need some extra help for a while so you don't get sick. They'll get it.

Next, go through your calendar and cancel or postpone everything that isn't essential or truly nurturing. Start with a two-week period. Don't feel guilty about doing this. This is your health that you're talking about, just as if you'd caught the flu or broken a bone. Don't feel like you have to offer an explanation for changing your plans, either. Everyone does it when it becomes necessary. Now, add in some things that feel truly nourishing to you. This could mean a hike in the woods, a massage, an afternoon in a museum, or a visit to a sensory-deprivation float tank — those are so awesome! Feel into what your creative soul truly craves, and do your best to make it happen, within that same two-week period.

If you have work responsibilities that make it impossible for you to take actual time-off, you can build your exquisite self-care around it. Remove any commitments that are not work-related. When you get done with your work for the day, immediately move into time-off mode. Go full force with your exquisite self-care on your days off. Eliminate or restrict the social activities you agree to, unless they are ones that will truly feed and nourish you.

Whether or not you're able to be in full time-off mode, stock up on food, drink, and other supplies that will nourish your physical and emotional well-being. This can be tricky, because sometimes when we're suffering emotionally, we crave foods that make our bodies feel worse, which perpetuates the suffering. What things nourish you on multiple levels? Maybe it's hot tea, small amounts of high-quality dark chocolate, or sushi. Be sure you're hydrating and getting regular showers or baths. Water is healing. Other supplies might include magazines, books, shows, art supplies, a weighted blanket, your journal, or whatever makes you feel comforted.

Build a creative nest for yourself. Think of it as your blanket fort, where you'll retreat to recover. Banish electronics from your sleeping area, so you'll be sure to get plenty of deep rest. Make a comfy spot on the couch or in your favorite chair, with easy access to your nourishing supplies. Ask a friend or family member to bring you a meal or two.

Exquisite self-care means treating yourself as you would a beloved child who didn't feel well. Don't pressure yourself to hurry up and heal. Take full advantage of this down time and follow your impulses. You might do absolutely no writing for two entire weeks, and that's totally fine. You may feel called to the page on the second day, and if it's an inspired action, not a guilty forcing of your own hand, then indulge it. It might not truly be your creativity that's keeping you down, but some other aspect of your life that's no longer serving you. If that rings true, you can explore it in your journal or with a therapist, but again, not in a way that feels like pressure. This is your time to fully relax. By removing yourself from your daily routine, you're allowing yourself the space to heal.

When you feel ready to emerge from your creative cave or blanket fort, take it slowly. Tap into the energy of Water to help you flow gently back to your routines. If a particular activity or person feels scary or wrong, perhaps it's time to make a change. If you're still not sure about the quality of your book, take some time to read what you've previously written, or seek feedback from a trusted friend or your coach. Slowly ease back in, keeping any of your exquisite self-care that feels particularly nourishing right now. Make a list of what helped most, so you can have it on hand if and when another crisis looms. Continue to build your self-care toolbox, and thus your confidence that you can handle the ebb times as well as you do those of creative flow.

Chosen Community: A Guide for Introverts

As you've probably gathered by now, the work we'll be doing in the next chapter is in the realm of Water, associated with community. I want to acknowledge here that many creative people like us are introverted, empathic, highly sensitive, neurodiverse unicorns. Despite mainstream society's opinions to the contrary, this is not a bad thing. In fact, these qualities are part of what makes our creations so powerful.

Yet the mainstream community has failed us. We've been bullied, shamed, forced into boxes that stifle our creative spirit, made to comply, asked to change, and sometimes abused. That totally sucks. Because of your experience – often in the crucible that is public school, or if you're young enough, on social media – you may have a completely understandable aversion to community settings.

Before you skip ahead or shut the book with a decisive, "No way," I want to show you how we'll be focusing on the concept of community in a way that's different from what you might think.

Actually, it's not just my definition of community that's different. You, too, are evolving past the version of yourself that suffered when you showed up authentically. Remember the visibility work we've been doing? The shadow selves you've brought forward into the light? Doing the work of uniting your will around showing up in the world helps change the frequency you bring as you walk into communal spaces. That's the first component of navigating community settings in a healthy way.

Now onward to the new definition. The access that we have to the entire world, thanks to the internet, means that interests and topics once considered weird or niche now have entire virtual spaces dedicated to them. Being able to talk to groups consisting solely of people who share your unusual interests is sometimes disparaged – but it's actually a gift for creatives like us. There's absolutely no rule that says you have to go out there and talk about your book to the entire world, or your judgmental extended family, or the people in your local community. You can find where your ideal readers like to hang out, and craft relationships with them there.

Virtual communities also allow you to protect your privacy to the level you desire. You don't have to use your legal or given name. You can craft an entire author persona, if that feels safer to you.

In fact, the key when we're talking about community is choice. You get to choose who to share your creative work with. Sure, when your book is published, whether by a publisher or on Amazon or other platforms, it'll be out there in the world for everyone to access. But you get to decide exactly how your readers are (or aren't) able to reach you. Your website, your email list, your author bio – all of these things are designed according to your needs and desires.

Isn't that good news? Now, this isn't to say that you'll never have critical reviews or even haters. The more widely your creative work becomes known, the more chances there are that some people won't like it. Some people will even be triggered by your words. But that's okay. They are not your ideal readers. By focusing on the effect you want to have on your aligned readers – remember your intention for your book? – you'll be able to shake off those who criticize. If this is a big concern, you can hire a virtual assistant who will read reviews and reader mail for you and screen them so you receive only the positive ones. Yes, some authors actually do this. See? You have options, and you're going to be safe from the bullies of the world.

The community that we'll be carefully crafting together in the next chapter will be designed by and for you. Unlike mainstream communities, it will support and celebrate you and your unique creations. In fact, I'd like to offer you a place to start.

I've been cultivating a community of Thriving Artists for several years now. In my Facebook group, the Book Birthing Center, you'll discover a curated gathering of writers and other creatives who support, inspire, and uplift one another. It's not that we don't share real talk about important subjects, but kindness and compassion are at the center of our communications. Authenticity is essential for creative people, but it's impossible to be authentic when you're constantly worried about being shot down. I want to invite you to a space where collaboration, compassion, and love are core values. Join us. I hope it will inspire you to discover and create your own dream communities, as we enter the realm of Water.

I Still Don't Trust It: The Resistance

Here we are, Thriving Artist, almost all the way around the circle of elements. Can you believe it? It's time to take all the amazing things you've been learning and implementing and share them with a community of colleagues and supporters.

Wait, where did you go? Is that you hiding under that fuzzy blanket? What did I say?

Oh, I know... It's that whole notion of sharing your ideas and your newfound writing skills that has you running away. But it's okay. I understand that you might not want to put yourself and your writing out there just yet. The world as a whole – and especially the internet – isn't always the friendly, welcoming space we wish it could be.

As we talked about before, it's normal not to trust in community, especially if you've been burned in the past. Most of us have. We're creative people, visionaries, and freethinkers. We're not here to conform. But most of us have been hurt by trying to be our true selves, and many of us have learned to hide in one way or another.

Don't worry, though. In our chapter on Water, I'm going to show you in more detail how to create a community that will serve you and your book, even as you serve it in return by sharing your wisdom. This isn't just a fanciful daydream.

Community is what you make it. You can still have privacy, boundaries, and even safety.

We'll get into the details later, but for now, just know that the ideal community you wish for *is* within reach. After all, that's part of why you're writing your book. You want to reach people who resonate with what you have to say. Your ideal readers are actual people, ones who share at least some of your values and goals. Don't try to trust everyone in the whole world. But consider trusting that your readers are out there, and that they want to find your book.

Your responsibility at this point on the path – along with continuing to show up, write your book, and refine your voice – is to let yourself imagine that you have a supportive and enthusiastic community to help you spread the word about your book. You're not even taking the actions steps to get there, yet. Just envisioning that it's actually possible is where we're at, and it's not really all that hard for an imaginative person like you. Right?

Spirit Walks from Fire to Water

The borderland from Fire to Water is like that afternoon lull in your workday. You've been powering along, getting things done. You might have had lunch or taken a break for a walk out in nature. You dive back in, doing your thing, and then it happens. You slip into a trancelike state, perhaps discovering yourself daydreaming or just staring off into inner space.

Don't freak out. This kind of ebb happens in any long-form creative project. It's the transition from the full-on passion of Fire to the quieter, burbling flow of Water. It's a natural part of the journey.

Spirit is there with you, in the wild enthusiasm of finding the true voice of your project, as well as in the soft release of gathering in support and nurturing yourself. This ebb and flow allows your creative work to be sustainable. Spirit is also there in the community you're building. There's a spark of the

Divine in each of us. Ultimately, we're all part of the greater whole that forms the unity of All-That-Is. Spirit lurks there, in your soul, in your colleagues, in your readers and collaborators, and in the form of your non-physical guides.

During one of my virtual retreats, I led a guided meditation where the writers were surrounded by concentric rings of support. It started with their close family and friends, then outward to acquaintances and colleagues, to readers, to the world as a whole, and then I included their non-physical guides and support team. During the shares afterward, I got scolded by the lifelong guides of one of the participants! She told me that her two main spirit guides were adamant that *they* were the inner circle, always right there by her side. I loved that! This voice of Spirit was exactly right. I adjusted the meditation so that in future versions, each writer's guardians were in that very inner circle.

As you've walked the borderland of Fire to Water, you've discovered how essential self-care is to the process of writing a book. You're in this for the long haul. In order for you to complete your project, you need to support yourself on all levels: physical, mental, emotional, and spiritual. A hefty dose of exquisite self-care is just what the healer ordered. Spirit agrees. You've also learned about the value of a curated community, and how it's different from the dysfunctional ones we've been part of in the past. As with refining your voice in the realm of Fire, community in this context means your Dream Team, your ideal readers, your way.

As we make our full transition into Water, you'll begin to build your Dream Team and ready yourself for the completion of your manuscript. We'll do this in the full flow of Water energies. Your writing during this phase will most likely be less fiery, but more fully in the groove, which resonates with the spiritual dimension and realms as well. Before we go swimming, meet Alex.

This is Alex 2.0

Hey there. I'm Alex. I'm supposed to write a bio for my book project - among a million other things - and it's freaking me right the fuck out. I mean, I have bios out there for lots of other stuff. It's not like I'm not the poster child for activism. You'd know if you saw me. But this book thing is bigger than I'd planned to go, at least right now.

Okay, okay, gotta focus. What is it that I'd want my hypothetical-soon-to-be-actual readers to know about me? That's the hardest part. My brain goes to what I want them to know about themselves. You know, the pep talk stuff: you're not alone, you deserve to be your authentic self, even in a world that doesn't want to hear about it, especially my fellow queers and BIPOC and wild feral rebels. We are the leading edge of humanity. Our differences make a difference. Blah, blah, blah.

Not that I don't believe it. I've staked my career, my life, really, on it. I've been out for a long time, and have had it backfire on me, for sure. Not from my family. They're the absolute best. Maybe I should say that in the bio. But then what about the folx who've been thrown out, just for being who they are? I definitely don't want to alienate them.

I'm a sexual abuse survivor. That's a solid truth about me. But it also sounds like a cliche. Like, why else would I be doing this work?

Damn it. That's why this particular bio is so hard. First, I'm writing it on my own. Second, it feels like there's a lot more at stake now. I've wanted this forever, this widening of my reach, this expansion. But it feels like it's, I don't know, too fast, or something. I've gotta go clear my head. Time for a walk.

***

Alright. The bio ought to have something about my educational background. I mean, I don't want to discourage anyone who hasn't had my educational privilege. But, yeah,

I went to a good college. I've got the academic creds to back up what I'm offering in the book.

I went to NYU on a full scholarship for my undergrad - I know, right?! A freakin' unicorn, that's me. Loved living in the Big Apple, for the most part. So many weirdos there that you can't feel too lonely - though there are always dangers when you're an enby, and multiracial to boot. I was at NYU when the assault happened. But that's not relevant to the bio. I got my graduate degree right here in Cambridge, at MIT. I thought I wanted to be a game designer, but ended up doing PolySci. It was okay. The people were great, and I'm still in touch with a lot of them.

I feel like I've been an activist since I was a little kid. Uncle J. always teased me for being such a chatterbox, with strong opinions. Save the whales, stop buying blood diamonds, all that stuff. I know it drove my Mom crazy that I wouldn't eat meat, but she was cool about it. I've never "fit in" or "gone along to get along," and I don't want to. There's way too much of that already.

I even know about some of my past lives, though I don't think the publisher wants me to put that in an official bio. But let's just say that I've always been a revolutionary. Died for it, too. I don't wanna do that this time. Though I will, if it's asked of me. Of course I will. And who knows? With the way things are going in this country, it might be.

***

I shouldn't write when I'm hung over. But I've gotta do something or I'll jump out of my skin. I can't sleep since the meeting with the publisher. I mean, worse than usual. I know better than to use alcohol for sleeping, I really do. But still.

I wish I had someone to talk to about this. I mean, my besties are always here for me - but they're more excited than I am about the book offer! It's what I've been wanting for so freakin' long. I feel like if I share my fears I'll be letting them down, or something. Colleagues? Same story.

I'm not dating anyone right now, or not seriously. There's Helena, but, well, I don't exactly know her well enough yet to get this deep. Bryce is always willing to listen, but he's got a little baby to focus on.

None of my usual coping skills are handling these nerves. What's that book with the stuff about "reaching your upper limits" or something like that? Gay Hendricks, I think? Well, I'm there.

The insomnia is really getting to me. Xanax doesn't even seem to touch it. I need to go see a therapist again, but Sherry moved to the west coast, and I literally can't do one more thing on Zoom. Maybe I need a life coach? Ugh.

CHAPTER 10:
WATER: COMMUNITY NURTURING

About Water

The element of Water nourishes us, body and soul. Life on this planet began in and emerged from the deep, mysterious waters of Mother Ocean. The never-ending cycle of water is visible to us as lakes and rivers, clouds and raindrops, sweat and tears. Water resides in the West, and its time is autumn and twilight. The colors of Water are soothing blues and greens.

Our bodies are made up largely of Water, and our consciousness flows like a stream. Our emotions ebb and flow each day like the ever-changing waves. Yet we also can plumb the depths of our souls, the place where our dreams connect us to the collective unconscious. When we dive deep into those mysterious waters, we receive messages from our intuition, from our divine connection to the source of life. We see the moonlight sparkling on the water, hear the ethereal singing of the whales deep beneath, swim with the dolphins as they dance above and below the waves.

Water is healing. We use its loving energies to nurture ourselves, to fill ourselves up, to rock ourselves gently to sleep. In sleep, we dream and heal. When we visit the healing springs, we wish for cleansing and wholeness. Romantic love is another aspect of Water's joy. When we open our hearts with love and trust to another, we join our spirits together and become more than we were before. Held and buoyed up by Water, we navigate life's path as partners.

The tool of Water is the chalice. We are each searching for our own Holy Grail, the container for that which we are, deep in our subconscious, where our waking consciousness touches our eternal spirit. When we realize that we are part of the great ocean of life, we can craft our own chalice and learn to fill and refill our cup. We flow with the sacred Waters of life, returning to rest in Mother Ocean's loving embrace and dreaming ourselves into being.

Ah, Water...so deeply nourishing. This is the element of the dreamers and creatives, those who crave freedom and live in the lands of imagination. Those who feel deeply and love freely.

Does that sound like you? You're not alone. It's like the bumper sticker says, "There are more of us than you think." This is why I've chosen Water as the place of community nurturing.

You might think of writing as a solo activity, but that's not the whole picture. My clients and I find that doing our creative work in a community of Thriving Artists is much more productive — and fun. Being part of a community of writers and other creatives is endlessly inspiring. Your circle will motivate you to keep going, give you insightful feedback, and comfort you with empathy when you're struggling.

At this point, I find hanging out with other Thriving Artists to be essential to my writing process.

In addition to that, unless it's a personal journal that you plan to destroy, your writing is meant to be shared. This means that you'll need readers. The best time to begin building a community of readers, fans, peers, and supporters is now — yes, even if you haven't started writing your book yet!

In our house-building metaphor, your community includes the electricians, contractors, plumbers, and painters who help put your new house together, as well as the family, friends, and neighbors you'll welcome through the door when it's complete.

Writing an entire book doesn't have to be a struggle, but it is a big endeavor. Surrounding yourself with supportive, understanding people during the process will help ease your journey. Pre-paving the eventual arrival of your book with an appreciative audience will help you launch your book in grand style.

You are also an essential part of your own nourishing community. Taking good care of yourself is a key part of becoming a Thriving Artist. It might sound a bit trite, in this day and age, to talk about self-care. But the reason it's such a hot topic is because we have collectively ignored taking care of ourselves for so long. In the realm of Water, we begin to relearn how to nurture ourselves and our art. Our society is set up so that having the time and resources to do so are seen as a luxury. Not everyone has the privilege to be able to devote energy to their art on a regular basis. But this is – hopefully – changing.

There is a rhythm to our creativity. One way to describe it is that it's akin to the ebb and flow of the ocean's tides. Creative people need to honor the various phases of our creative experience. Yes, there is that full flow when we are pouring forth words onto the page, and the ideas keep rushing forward. We're in the zone. Time passes quickly, and we might not feel like we can even keep up with the material that's flowing forth.

When that energy recedes, like the water, we're in the ebb time. This is when most creatives I've spoken to want to take in some kind of input, to fill the space that you've just emptied. We read, we binge an entire season of something, we scroll through Instagram, we engage in philosophical conversations with friends. Sometimes we want to go deeper, so we take a course or a certification in a subject that interests us. In the ebb phase, you might not feel like writing. This is completely natural. Even if you worry that you'll never again be in that sacred flow, be patient. Things will shift and change.

Next comes a pause. If you've watched the waves at the beach, you know the moment I mean. The water has receded as far as it's going to, and the next wave is bearing down toward you. Yet there is a moment where it's like the sea is holding its breath, and neither ebb nor flow are happening. In your life, you might suddenly grow bored with all the books on your shelf or shows in your queue. Yet you're not ready to dive back into creating. Interestingly, this creative pause often syncs up with the moon's dark phase or one's bodily cycles. It doesn't last as long as the other phases, but it can feel intense and often emotional.

Surfing the waves of our own creative ebb and flow is part of the practice we engage in here in the realm of Water. How can we best do that? By building a life where we have the freedom to follow our natural creative rhythms. This might sound like an impossible dream, or at least a tricky proposition, if you think about the way your life is currently set up.

But remember, a lot of times the constraints we find ourselves in are (at least in part) created by our beliefs. One of the most powerful things we can learn in Water is that not only is nurturing and support good for us as artists and as people, we are each deserving of receiving the support that we most desire. Read that sentence again. It might push some buttons, especially if you were raised to put others' needs before your own, be a caregiver, and diminish your own talents.

We'll talk about this further when we get to the section on resistance. But in the meantime, this is why it's when we reach the Water element that we put our focus on cultivating our community. Despite the mainstream conception of the art, writing a book is not generally a solo project. Take a look at the "acknowledgements" section of any random book you come across. I know, I'm possibly the only one who always reads those – but I find it fascinating how the more successful an author is, the more people they thank, the more team members are there helping them out behind the scenes. Human beings are not solitary creatures by nature. We thrive in community. When you set out to take on a huge project like birthing a book, I believe that you can begin cultivating your community from the start. We'll dive into some resources for doing that as this chapter unfolds. Follow the flow and see how far it can take you.

Gifting Yourself Nurturing and Support

Earlier we talked about exquisite self-care when we reach a crisis moment. But that's not the only time that self-care is key. In fact, I urge Thriving Artists to take good care of themselves, on all levels, all the time. It's an ongoing practice. This self-nurturing forms a container in which it's easier to create on a regular basis. What do I mean by self-care as a practice? Let's begin with a story.

Years ago, when my kids were little, a friend of mine who was also a Mom came to me, feeling frustrated about her home life. At the time, both of us were the breadwinners for our families, while our partners both stayed home and took care of the kids.

Her issue was that she worked outside the home full time and then found herself also doing a bunch of work in her home after hours. Her partner cooked the meals, but she planned and did the shopping, did much of the laundry, and felt like she was constantly washing dishes.

My friend was an intense person who had suffered lots of trauma in her childhood. Her kids were also intense, and their energy could be pretty wild. Her partner, in contrast, was mellow and had a calming presence about him.

Probably because of all the uncertainty she'd experienced, my friend also preferred things in her home to be done a certain way. She had very high expectations, often to the point where she was the only person who could do things the way she preferred.

Let's set aside for now the obvious societal issues between the sexes, where it is actually women who do most of the work in the household, whether or not they and/or their male partner work outside the home. In my case, my husband took care of much of the housework because I was doing the breadwinner thing. I was aware of the imbalance that the majority of households experience.

In my friend's case, though, I pointed out to her some of the intangible contributions that her male partner was making to their household. I'd seen it in action. This man could calm the chaos with a few words and a smile. He had a soothing presence that improved their family's life experience every day. He was supportive of my friend in ways that she needed, given the repercussions of trauma that haunted her – but these weren't always easy-to-see gifts. It was his presence and energy, which he tended through playing music and being in contact with nature, that were essential contributions to their home and family.

When I pointed this out to her, giving concrete examples that she could see and recall, she got it. She realized that in some ways, she'd been taking her partner for granted. Yes, she still wanted to make sure that the workload was equitable and not burning her out. But she could now take into account his intangible gifts and how they uplifted both her and their children. It wasn't something her partner had been able to see or articulate for himself, but he acknowledged that sometimes maintaining the energy of their space was hard work and meant that perhaps he didn't get to the laundry in what she felt was a timely manner. They were both grateful to me for pointing out the value of his calming presence.

This story came back to mind recently when an acquaintance was talking about how historically, artists in some societies were funded by wealthy patrons of the arts. Their work was valued. A patron would pay the artist's expenses so that they could focus on their art, rather than having to struggle for daily necessities.

The system was by no means perfect. Gender equity was not even on the radar in most of the societies that had patrons, and often there were strings attached to the patronage.

But the concept... I recently told Quester that I wanted that. I could easily fill my days with my artistic process. Imagine having all the time you wished to read, learn, travel, get inspired, nurture yourself, do spiritual practice, meditate, and then write or create based on those inspirations!

Indeed, we creative people tend to be the ones who become overwhelmed by the setup of modern society. "Adulting" is especially draining for us. We're the highly sensitive, empathic, often neurodiverse people who find ourselves on the fringes of the mainstream. We need more time in nature, more quiet, more down time than appears "normal" to the majority. I know you understand what I mean!

What if we had someone (or several someones) to take care of those things for us? What if, like my friend's partner, we used our gifts in ways that were perhaps not so tangible, but were still valuable to others? Doesn't this sound amazing?

This might sound like a utopian dream, but it's not necessarily so. You can start today, where you are. Cultivate friendships with people who see you for who you are and value your gifts. Avoid those who judge you by mainstream society's ridiculous standards. Find your people. Remember, you're setting up this whole community thing in a way that makes the most sense to you.

If you have a partner or partners, talk to them about your household and its workload, and who does what. Include the intangibles. Bring your writing project into the mix. Sure, it's not making you money (yet) – but money is only one measure of many. Have multiple conversations. You might be surprised. The fact that you've started to work toward a big dream of yours might be inspiring to them. Maybe they have a heartfelt project they'd like to make space for, too. Perhaps it makes sense to hire a housecleaner, and you can collectively devote some of your income to getting support in that way and creating more time for your passions.

If finances are an issue, maybe you can barter with someone to do stuff that's hard for you, while doing something for them that they need but don't want to do themselves. There are so many options when you start to think outside the box. You've been opening up your creative powers through writing your book – tap into that energy to brainstorm ways to nurture yourself, your household, and your creative dreams in new ways.

In the following sections, we'll go more deeply into ways to support yourself and your writing. Right now, though, let's focus on nurturing in the personal realm.

You've already begun the process of nurturing your creative spirit, by creating a regular writing habit and the rituals associated with it. Most of my clients find that, as they write their book, their nurturing rituals also expand outward into other parts of their lives. I've shared some of my own spiritual practices with them, and they've adopted and customized them to their own needs.

Your needs for nurturing will vary according to your personality and situation. They will change as you evolve. Here are a few ideas to spark your imagination. Remember, even if *all* of these sound great, you don't have to take them all on at once. Begin where you are, with the resources you have available, then dream it forward.

We'll start with the physical realm. Which of these would help you along the way?

If you have kids, a regular babysitter, a mother's helper, or a nanny can assist with the many tasks parenting brings. With older kids, setting up a car-pooling group can help with driving them around. For pet parents, getting a dog-walker or pet-sitter can help.

We all have household chores that can take up hours of time we'd rather use to create or to relax. Get a house-cleaning service, which is often more affordable than you'd think, or hire a teenager to help with needed tasks on the weekend. Maybe a meal preparation service makes sense, if you don't like to cook or it takes up too much time. Or one of those meal subscription services where all the ingredients and recipes are provided might be more your speed.

Nurturing your physical body can be overwhelming sometimes, too. How about getting a regular massage or chiropractic care? Getting a membership to something that makes physical exercise easier and more convenient for you to move your body makes a huge difference: a gym, a yoga studio, dance or martial arts classes, or a pool membership are just a few examples. Make it super easy to incorporate exercise into your week.

How about the mental and emotional realm? Would having a therapist or life coach make a huge difference for you? Maybe it's having a weekly coffee chat with a like-minded friend or setting aside time each week to write in your journal. Taking time-off is important for your mental and emotional well-being, but we sometimes neglect to do that. We fill our weekends and days off with family time and social events and forget that we need down time. As creatives, we probably need more of it than the people around us. Build it into your calendar. I have the last Friday of each month set aside as an Artist Date, which is another wonderful concept from Julia Cameron's *The Artist's Way*.

When you plan your vacation time and days off, remember to not fill each moment with activities. You need time to daydream, rest, and process. This will feed not just your writing, but your productivity across all parts of your life. You need to feed your soul. Getting out into nature, in whatever ways appeal most to you, will also help with that.

Speaking of the soul, what is your ideal level of spiritual practice? I don't start my workday until at least two hours after I wake up. I've designed it that way on purpose. Along with the usual body-care things that need to be done in the morning, I have time for writing down my dreams, meditation, journaling, and just plain pondering, along with my daily yoga asanas. At night, I head up to bed an hour or more before I want to fall asleep, making space for reading, more journaling, and connecting with my partner. What practices would you most like to include in your daily routines?

Other ways to fill your cup might include going on regular retreats, getting readings from a psychic or Tarot card reader, going dancing, getting together with friends, doing crafts, attending concerts or plays, taking classes or learning a new skill from YouTube videos, or whatever else you love to do.

You'll notice that while some of these ideas cost money, many of them only require your time. It's a myth that you have to "pay your dues" and struggle along until some imaginary day when you'll be able to afford to live a life of leisure or retire to a warm place. Fill your life with as much ease and enjoyment as possible, starting today. Decide which things are important to you, and which simply aren't, and focus more on the former. If you start today, you'll soon discover a whole new level of joy and creativity. Your Younger Self approves this message.

The Inner Circle

Here in the realm of Water, we're focused on community nurturing. You'll be both giving and receiving. You want to begin crafting and nourishing a community which will eventually receive your book. You'll also learn to receive support from your existing network, and expand your reach, so you can achieve your goals as an author. The emphasis here is on collaboration and co-creation. You'll discover the power of a writer's circle to support you in writing your best work. We'll focus on building a resilient circle of colleagues and readers who will guide you through the creation of this book...and the ones to come.

Let's start where you are. Earlier, I asked you to identify encouraging people with whom to share your creative process. Have you reached out to anyone yet? If not, don't worry. We'll get there. If you did reach out to tell someone that you're writing a book and would like their support, what kind of reaction did you receive? Have you accepted their encouragement?

We begin by cultivating your inner circle of supporters. This might include family members, your partner(s), kids, friends, acquaintances, mentors, beloved pets, and even people you don't know personally who nevertheless inspire you – like favorite authors. I humbly submit that I, through this book that you're now reading, am part of your support network. Your non-physical guides — like ancestors, guardian spirits, angels, etc. — are also part of your inner circle. We'll talk more about them in a bit. Who else would you include? Think outside the box.

As we proceed through this chapter, the circle will expand to include beta readers, your audience, your author platform, professionals who might help you, publishing platforms, and your street team. I'll explain as we go along.

For now, let's look at your circles of support in a big-picture sort of way. If you were in my group writing program, this process would start with a guided meditation.

That's a bit challenging to do in text format, but let's try it. At the very least, do this as a visualization that stimulates your creative imagination. Begin by breathing deeply and getting aligned. Once you feel centered, imagine that you are a star in the night sky. You see a myriad of other stars around you, appearing as points of light. Each star represents a person or being. All the people and beings in your inner circle, the ones you were thinking of before, surround you. Beyond them are stars that represent the people and beings *they* know and trust. This network of connections, these sparkling lights, expand outward into infinity. Imagine that from your own bright point of light comes a new star — the birth of your book! Observe how its light touches your inner circle and spreads from there outward. Can you see how your work will make an impact in ways unknown and unexpected?

Grab your writing journal and make some notes on any insights you've received from doing this visualization exercise. Then answer the following prompts.

With the starry sky visualization in mind, write down the top five to seven people in your life who are most nurturing to you and your creative projects.

❖ *Who supports you unconditionally, or could, given the chance?*

Next, write down three needs that you have for your writing project. This could be anything: someone to watch the kids while you write, an infusion of cash so you can take time away from your day job, a connection to someone with a huge audience relevant to your topic, a rush of followers for your blog or social media. Think big and blue sky here.

❖ *What would best help you write your book and get it out into the world?*

Finally, think about the big impact you want your book to have in the world. This harkens back to your intention, so read that to yourself again, allowing it to inspire new ideas for support.

❖ *What community elements would you love to have in place for your intentions to come true?*

Write them down freely. Again, let yourself dwell in the blue-sky, ideal results mode, not worrying about how to get there. If you want to be featured in Oprah's book club, or you'd like a personal secretary, write that down!

- ❖ *What forms of community would you most love?*
- ❖ *Who's on your team?*

We've gotten a blue-sky overview in this section, and now we'll begin to dive deeper into the various aspects of your ideal nurturing community. When you have a solid goal or dream in mind, it's easier to get there. You can take inspired actions toward your goal, showing up consistently, rather than just vaguely wishing to be a best-selling author.

Dream Team

Your book is part of your mission here on the Earth plane. You wouldn't have been called to write it otherwise. Your Muses are cheering for you. You might have already reached out, sharing about your project and getting support you didn't even realize you could receive.

In the previous section, you started the process of tapping into your biggest dreams around having a supportive community. Before we get to the practical steps, let's flesh out that vision a bit more.

I want you to imagine for a moment that *all* of your wildest dreams have come true. You are successful in all the ways you dreamed of, as well as some you didn't, and your book is a best-seller. You are, in fact, a wealthy celebrity – on your own terms, of course. You have the time, money, and other resources to do whatever you most want to do. You're following your callings and changing the world in powerful ways.

When you're operating on that level of impact, you're no longer doing it alone. You're fully supported by a Dream Team of people who help you do this powerful work in the world. The people who work for you are following their own callings, and they too enjoy what they do.

Given those parameters, again, on your own terms, who do you have on your Dream Team?

Here are some examples you might wish to include: editor, writing coach, writing group, publicist, beta readers, healer, cover designer, virtual assistant, project manager, agent, house cleaner, massage therapist, website designer, personal psychic, stylist, nutritionist, personal shopper, babysitter, dog walker. You won't necessarily need all of these – or maybe you will! After all, this is a blue-sky visioning exercise. The sky's the limit.

Get your writing journal and answer the following prompts:

❖ *Who in your life is already helping you make your writing dreams happen?*

❖ *Make your own blue-sky list of the Dream Team that would best support your writing & creative work. Draw from the list above and add your own ideas as they occur to you.*

Envision your life now, and then picture adding in one or two of your Dream Team members. Visualize how that might look, and how it will feel. Don't try to figure out how you'll get there, not yet. Just free-write about what the results will be like for you.

Non-Physical Helpers (Tough Love from the Muses)

Remember how I got scolded by the two spirit guides of one of my clients during a retreat? They were adamant that they belonged in the very inner circle of their charge's support network and insisted that I hadn't included them soon enough during the guided meditation I led. They were right, of course. Your spirit guides are here to help you to live a better life, in all ways. They've been with you since your birth and will remain with you after the death of your physical body.

Yet we live on the physical plane, which can take up a lot of our attention. It's a complete-immersion experience. You have a full, busy life, with its joys and challenges, to which you've added your book project. It's a lot. I get that. It's completely normal to forget that you have access to non-physical guidance and help.

From the perspective of your guides, though, chances are that you aren't fully availing yourself of the nourishing support they're here to provide. The best way I've found to access this support on a regular basis is to include it in regular rituals. This makes it a habit.

It took me a while to get in the groove of this, but now it's part of my daily life. Each morning in my daily spiritual practice, I draw a Tarot card for the day. Before drawing it, I ask my guardian angel, "What do you want me to know today?" I also include my guides' input in my other rituals, such as my weekly Sacred Strategy Ritual that I'll talk about later.

I've created personal symbols and touchstones that remind me of my guides and their input. Some are tattooed on my body, others are placed around my home, and yet others are triggered by a feeling or by seeing a natural object (like the moon) or particular animals and birds. That way, when I get too immersed in the physical world, forgetting about the magick, these symbols will pop up and remind me to tap in.

I wrote about non-physical helpers in much more detail in my book *The Heart of the Goddess*. Find more about it if you're drawn to learn more, in my book and/or in one of the other books on spirituality in the Resources section.

For now, simply begin to cultivate awareness about your own spiritual guides. Tuning in to the possibility of their presence gives them more leeway to help you.

Your Street Team

The idea of a Street Team started out in the music world, back before social media was a thing. A Street Team is a group of fans who volunteer to help promote an album or musician on a grassroots level. The musician Amanda Palmer is one of the people who used a Street Team in a big way. She wrote about it in her book *The Art of Asking*. The Street Team has been fairly recently adopted by authors, too, especially as self-publishing has risen to new heights.

From an artist perspective, Street Teams offer free promotion and a wider audience for your creations. For fans, working on a Street Team gives them a chance to connect with their idols and get hands-on experience promoting their favorite artists. Often they also receive free stuff or early access to books, manuscripts, signed copies, etc.

Creating a Street Team means that you need to have faith in the value of what you're offering, and you also need to be willing to ask for help. This can take some inner work around visibility, which we'll talk about in more detail later in this chapter.

In the meantime, here are some tips for developing your Street Team. First, you need to talk about your project. Yes, this means talking publicly about your book, even before your first draft is done. You might do this on your blog, a social media account, your YouTube channel, or elsewhere. Have fun with this process. You're at the starting point, which means your goal is to generate interest in what you're doing.

Many, many people have an idea for a book they'd like to write. In comparison, relatively few of us actually write the book. You might be surprised by how excited people get on your behalf! Just by taking the step of writing your book manuscript, there are people in your community right now who will be super impressed. I know, that seemed weird to me, too. I still get surprised when I post about completing National Novel Writing Month at the end of each November and I get all kinds of congratulatory messages. Writing books has become normal to me now, but believe me, in many peoples' eyes it's a Big Deal.

After you've started sharing your process a bit, and have gotten some attention, it's time to start your Street Team. Create a spot somewhere (on your website, in a private Facebook group, etc.) where people can apply to be part of your team. Remember, you get to choose who you're letting in! This is your book baby and you get to decide which people and energies are best for her.

Create an application that gets to the heart of the qualities you want in your street team. You'll want them to be readers of your genre and interested in your topic or type of story. You may want them to be LGBTQ+ allies, or witchy people, or members of another community that's connected with your book and/or your personal values. Think about related communities. For example, when one of my clients was writing a book about her work as an animal communicator, I suggested that she reach out to people who are environmentalists or connected strongly with nature. For my partner BlackLion, who's the author of a science fiction series and loves games, his Street Team includes video gamers and role-playing gamers as well as sci-fi readers. Look for your Street Team members in places where your potential readers hang out. Invite them to complete the application.

Prepare a virtual space for your Street Team. This could be a separate email list, a Facebook group, or as part of a Patreon account. This is where you'll communicate with them and receive their feedback, questions, etc.

Come up with a rewards system. You'll want to give your Street Team valuable rewards for helping spread the word about your book, without exhausting your own resources. An obvious reward is a free copy of the e-book version, which won't cost you anything. For those dedicated fans who bring in a lot of new readers, you might add prizes like a signed hard copy of the book, a group call with you where they can ask questions, VIP seating at a book signing or other event, behind-the-scenes looks at your writing process, early copies of future books, etc.

Even if you're not quite ready to officially create your Street Team, you can start the process now by thinking of friends, family, or colleagues who are genuine encouragers. Think about people who are really great at shouting out others and sharing their work, or encouraging artists to share it in their spaces. If you get stuck, look around your virtual networks, such as social media, professional organizations, etc.

Make a list in your writing journal of the people already in your life who would be perfect for your Street Team.

Beta Readers

Advance readers, also known as beta readers, are people you invite to read through your drafted manuscript and give you feedback. I realize that you might not yet be close to needing them. That's fine. You're building the foundation.

Don't freak out on me, now... Feedback on your writing, even at an early stage, is invaluable. But yes, it can also potentially be quite scary. I've been there and done that, so I get it. It might help to remember that *you* are the one in charge of your book manuscript. You get to choose who gets to see it, at each stage.

You can carefully curate your beta readers, choosing people who will give you honest feedback, constructive criticism, gentle suggestions, or whatever you most need. Starting this process before your manuscript is done will allow you to have a seamless process once your draft is ready. It can also give you some extra accountability. Knowing that there are people waiting to read what you've written can provide momentum that keeps you on track with your writing sessions.

To find my beta readers for the first book in my contemporary fantasy series, I made a Facebook post on my personal page, telling people about my book and seeking those who enjoy the genre and had the reading time available. Out of the people who responded, I chose the ones I felt would be best for my project. For the others who had replied, I responded and told them that I now had enough beta readers. I then took the post down. Easy-peasy.

Here are a few tips for choosing your beta readers:

Pick people who actually read and enjoy your genre and have an interest in the topic matter. They'll be the most familiar with this type of writing, and thus able to give you valuable feedback.

Unless they have particular experience that will be invaluable, don't choose your best friend or sister just because they want to help out. You want people in your life who are cheerleaders for whatever you do, but they aren't the best beta readers for you. They can still read your book manuscript and give you those good-feeling comments. Just don't rely on them exclusively.

Get *more* beta readers than you think you'll need, because inevitably life will happen and a couple of people won't be able to follow through. I like to start with a dozen people.

Create a list of written questions that you want your beta readers to answer about your book. Make sure they're not just "yes or no" questions. You want to encourage them to write more than "I liked it." That's nice, but not helpful in making your book even better.

When your book draft is ready, plan to send it to them as a pdf. It's a format that most people can easily access. It's also not super easy to mess with.

Set a timeline by which you'd like to receive your readers' feedback. Get their agreement on this timeline ahead of time, so you can reach out and remind them if you haven't received it by the mutually agreed-upon date.

Be brave enough to actually follow through with getting and using your beta readers. It will help improve your book. Feel the fear, if it's there, but then do it anyway!

You'll have to share your book with your audience eventually. Beta readers are, when you choose them carefully, an easy trial run. You've got this!

Building Your Author Platform

Pretty much all forms of publishing require you to have an author platform in place. What is an author platform? It's a term that simply means a ready-made audience for your books. Your platform consists of the people who are interested in what you do, and the ways in which you communicate with them. As with your Street Team, if you start working on your author platform now, it will help give you a head start when you complete your book.

Chances are that you already have the start of your author platform. If you're an entrepreneur, or if the work that you do involves marketing yourself – such as a massage therapist or other type of healer – your clients and communities are a natural audience for your book. Or you may have a hobby that lends itself well to becoming an author platform. For example, if you belong to a historical reenactors group like the Society for Creative Anachronism (SCA), the other members would be a terrific audience for your historical romance novel. Get creative as you think about existing communities and groups you can tap into as you generate interest about your forthcoming book.

It's never too soon to start telling the world that you're writing a book. If you lead workshops, write articles, or have other venues where you provide a bio, include that you're "author of the forthcoming book XYZ." Even if you only have a working title for your book so far, put it out there. As I mentioned earlier in this chapter, just the notion that you're writing your book will impress people – and the more often you say it, the more likely they are to remember.

Whether or not you have any type of author platform, here are some things you can do to begin creating one or to cultivate the ones you have in place.

Start an email list if you don't have one already. I recommend you begin with a free service. I use MailChimp, and it's pretty simple and user friendly. Start by inviting people you know, your beta readers if you have them, and acquaintances with similar interests. When you first start your email newsletter, you can just do a post once a month, or even once a quarter. What should you talk about? You can discuss the process of writing, offer interesting tidbits of research you've discovered as you write your book, and share excerpts from your book draft. This is a bit easier for nonfiction authors, but even with fiction, you can share the behind-the-scenes pieces of your writing process.

Blog about your process. Again, this can be as frequent or infrequent as you wish. Share book excerpts. Show behind-the-scenes glimpses of your writing space. Do some vulnerable shares about the ups and downs of your creative process. Readers love to see how a book comes together and to learn more about you.

Create an audio or video podcast where you share your writing journey. This is potentially a bit more time intensive, so only do it if it feels fun and easy. Some people love this medium, while others would find it draining. Listen to your Younger Self and choose methods of sharing that light you up.

Be present on social media, on your own terms. Pick one or two platforms that feel fun and easy for you. You don't have to do All The Things, truly. You can do written or video posts, whatever feels best to you. I started building my author platform on Facebook, but lately I've been having much more fun with Instagram. I leverage the ability to make an Instagram post and have it automatically copy onto my Facebook business page. As of this writing, there is a thriving "bookstagram" community of readers and writers sharing all kinds of cool stuff about books. A good friend who is a writing coach for academics loves Twitter and has built a thriving community there. Since Twitter never really appealed to me much, I haven't given it much attention. Each author's experience will be unique. There's no need to force it. You don't have to get sucked into comparison and doom scrolling. Find your peeps where they hang out. Post interesting things. Interact with those who like what you're doing. It can be that simple.

Leverage others' spaces to grow your audience – with their permission, of course. There are many ways to do this. Try guest blogging for a website with similar topics to yours. Most blogs accepting submissions will have their submission guidelines on their website. Take a look and make sure the post you send falls within these guidelines.

If that sounds like too much work, maybe you'd like to be a guest speaker on an aligned podcast. You can start by reaching out to podcasts you enjoy. There are also several free services that connect subscribers to podcasts looking for guests. At the time of this writing, I've been using podcastguests.com with good results. It's easy – you sign up for their email list, and each week they send lists of podcasts looking for speakers. When you find one that's in your zone of genius, you submit a simple form to the podcast host.

You could also do a Facebook or Instagram Live with someone else on their page, to get in front of their community. Make sure when you set up the gig that your two audiences have shared interests. Another option is showing up in Facebook groups related to your topics. Be a good community member. Make sure you participate in conversations, rather than just spamming everyone about your book. Building an author platform is about building a community of people who are interested in what you do. As a bonus, you'll discover other fascinating folks doing cool stuff in the world.

Depending on where you live, there may also be in person gatherings where you can make connections and build your audience. These might consist of networking groups, book clubs, library events, free workshops, readings at bookstores, conventions, or hobby groups. Again, bring along your genuine interest in others and their creations. This isn't a one-way street. The connections you build on mutual respect and sharing will become those who most enthusiastically shout out your book and other creations when the time comes.

As you build your author platform, you should know that consistent and persistent actions are best. This is tough to hear, especially as a creative person whose energies ebb and flow. There are, however, plenty of workarounds for those times when you'd rather avoid social media altogether – whether it's because you're deeply immersed in your writing, or you're resting in the creative cave. You can plan and schedule your posts on your calendar, giving yourself a few days in advance to write or craft something to share. Batching your content ahead of time works great. When you're feeling inspired, you can write several social media posts or blog entries and then publish them slowly over the next few days or weeks. Figuring this out has certainly changed my work life for the better.

If you're able to do so, hire a virtual assistant to help with your social media and other communication. I hired a social media manager about a year ago, and it made a world of difference. She tells me that authors are among her favorite clients, because we already have plenty of words to share!

Think of shortcuts you can use to make things easier. Perhaps the most valuable thing I've learned about creating an author platform is that it's okay to repurpose your writing. You don't have to find fresh ways to say the same thing again and again – although that can be a fun challenge. Take old blog posts and make them into shorter social media shares. Post excerpts from your work-in-progress. Make some funny memes. Take pictures or videos of your messy desk or share about what you're reading lately. Your ideal readers won't care about perfection. They want to see you and what you're up to – and again, just the fact that you're writing a book will be inspiring to many people.

Other examples of shortcuts might include using tools like Canva to quickly create images to go with your posts, and setting up a scheduling tool like Later.com, Loomly, or HootSuite (or one of the many others available) to schedule posts in advance. Again, hiring some help with this is fantastic if you're able to do so. If you're an entrepreneur who already has a virtual assistant, you might add social media posts for your author platform to the things they do on your behalf. Or maybe you have a teen in your life who would have fun helping out for some extra spending money.

It's important to note that in the realm of building community, less is more. You don't want to use up all your energy creating a platform and have nothing left for your book project. Do you hate social media? Don't use it. Love podcasts? Maybe that's where you'll find your people. Follow your heart and your intuition. Taking inspired actions will bring you a long way toward your goal and is far better than forcing yourself to do it and quickly getting burned out. Remember, leading with an aligned mindset is key.

Answer these questions in your writing notebook:

- ❖ *What is one place online where you can show up regularly, with joy and lightness?*
- ❖ *Which people or groups can help you with spreading the word? (This might also be the start of your Street Team).*

❖ *List 1-3 "baby steps" (i.e. they take less than 30 minutes each to do) that you'll take to begin (or continue) building your author platform.*

Visibility Fears

Dear writer, as you now know, you don't have to do things alone. At the same time, you are the starting point, the spark for this "movement" of yours. Writing a book involves being visible, in a way you may not have been before.

I mean, yeah, you could theoretically do your actual writing in secret, without even telling your besties, but at some point the idea is to share what you've written. Your book needs readers.

Visibility can be super scary.

That's especially true when you're an introvert, an empath, sensitive, shy, or otherwise a private, "fly under the radar" type of person. I feel you. So how can you be visible as an author and expert *and* stay safe?

Part of the answer involves common sense factors like not giving out your home address, making sure you have strong passwords and computer security measures, and so forth. Those are the practical steps involved in protecting your safety and privacy. Don't skip them.

But what I'm talking about here is *feeling* safe and secure while stepping into the limelight. That involves mindset and inner work. Yep, that shadow work thing again.

Here are some ways to get started on clearing your fears of being visible:

    ❖ Listen to the part of you that's afraid. Acknowledge your fears. Don't repress them, and don't let them make the decisions — but do hear them. Writing them out in your journal can help that frightened part of you feel heard and held.

    ❖ Try tapping, aka EFT, on those fears to loosen their hold. There are many great resources for EFT online. My favorites are Jennifer Elizabeth Moore and Brad Yates. Find them on YouTube.

❖ Get some support. Take a workshop or class, explore shadow work with a coach, or find a book that can help you begin to release old beliefs and patterns. I highly recommend Carolyn Elliott (Lovewell)'s book *Existential Kink*.

No matter how you choose to take action on making visibility less scary, it's key that you do something. Hiding yourself (and your book) isn't the best option. The world needs your wisdom and your stories!

From my own experience and that of my clients, I can tell you that one of the most common fears around being visible relates to worthiness. This is a form of imposter syndrome, where that inner voice is constantly asking you "Who do you think you are? Who are you to write a whole book? Are you really an expert?" It's completely normal if you're feeling this! You're not alone. Many of us, especially when first getting started, struggle with self-identifying as an author. Hear those voices but don't let them lead.

Let's take a bit of time to examine your inner resistance. It probably won't be solved in one go, but the more you can see these pieces and become aware of them, the less they are able to derail you.

Write out your answers to these questions in your writing notebook or journal.

❖ *What comes to mind when I tell you: you are worthy of telling your stories, being an author, and having raving fans of your work?*

❖ *What old stories about yourself are surfacing for you, whether from parents, siblings, teachers, schoolmates, partners, or your own inner critic?*

❖ *What do you need right now that will help you take that first step into greater feelings of worth?*

It's time to take off that invisibility cloak and learn to shine.

Wait, you might be saying, but I already dealt with this shadow. Why does it keep coming back and stopping me in my tracks? Perhaps you're getting stuck in the swamp.

Stuck in the Swamp: The Resistance

You know how I said that there's no such thing as writer's block? I told you how those times when you can't find anything new to say are really just part of the "ebb" side of the ebb and flow of creativity. You now have some tools and techniques for getting yourself out of that stuck-feeling place.

But what happens when this "feeling stuck" pattern repeats itself over and over again? In the realm of elemental Water, your creative flow might have gone stagnant. This is the energy of resistance as it shows up in the realm of Water.

Resistance in this realm might look like:

❖ not knowing where to go next with your story or narrative
❖ lack of clarity
❖ getting creative ideas while you're otherwise occupied but having them vanish when you sit down to write them out
❖ allowing distractions to pull you away from the blank page

You'll know you're immersed in this kind of resistance when you feel awful about not making progress on your project.

Where does this form of resistance come from?

I have a theory.

Resistance in the realm of Water feels to me like it comes from underlying issues of insecurity and self-worth. This is a deeper version of the imposter syndrome we talked about earlier. Because of these old beliefs, we distrust the flow of our creativity. We don't believe that our process deserves nurturing. Because of that distrust, we start to force things.

During those ebb times when it might be best to take a guilt-free break, we force ourselves to continue. We value output over process. We don't seek out support, because we don't think we're living up to our end of the bargain. We base our own worth on what we *do* more than who we *are*.

Paradoxically, not allowing yourself time to rest and be nurtured makes you less productive, not more. Creativity isn't a machine. Nor are you.

Much like some of the other forms of resistance we've explored, feeling blocked and stuck comes from things we were taught as a child or young person. This culture has a whole trainload of baggage around the areas of self-worth and productivity. From Puritan beliefs about idle hands being tools of the devil, all the way to the modern cult of hustle, we're brainwashed into believing that we should always be on and going. I call B.S.

Thinking that you're lazy because you like to take naps and daydream is ridiculous. You're a creative person. Your process must include three essential components: time to receive input, time to process your experiences, and time to create. Our culture emphasizes and rewards the latter. This is "work" as we understand it. We can usually rationalize the input piece – reading, learning, and watching are acceptable forms of entertainment and leisure. But it's that processing time that gets vilified. That's because it looks like "doing nothing." It's immediately labeled as lazy and worthless.

When we don't take time to honor this part of the process, or we hide it and diminish its value in our creative life, our shadow self gets resentful. If you find yourself in this mode of being blocked and unclear, your shadow is asserting a boundary. "No way," she says. "You're not going to write another word until you go lie in the hammock and look at the clouds." This makes our Talking Self feel bad. "How awful am I, that I just want to lie in the hammock when there's all this Important Work to Do?"

One of the keys to recognizing and overcoming resistance in the realm of Water lies in opening a dialogue between the "DOing" and "BEing" parts of your psyche. If you're unable to write, don't simply give up or feel bad about yourself. Explore the ways in which you may need time for the ebb: for lying in bed, taking a bath, daydreaming, walking in the woods, or hiding out in your blanket fort. You could even engage support in your ebb process, for the graduate level of assimilating Watery resistance. Get a massage, grab takeout, or book a retreat. Give yourself the gift of the nurturing that your shadow self is craving. Acknowledging your need for nurturing and down time will go a long way toward healing the divide between productivity and rest.

This means, ultimately, learning to unconditionally love yourself. You may not have experienced being unconditionally loved before, or you might not have had enough of it. That's okay. This is a gift that you can give to yourself. It involves listening to your inner voices and allowing them to exist without judgment. This is the ultimate in healing resistance. When you begin to understand that just by existing, you are already of value, things will shift in all areas of your life, including your creativity.

You'll now know – and believe — that when you don't want to write on a particular day, it's time to focus on self-care. Rather than evaluating your day or week based on what you completed or achieved, you'll look towards how it feels and how much fun you had. Your deepest truths will emerge and become part of the way you live your life. You'll fully believe that you're not lazy simply because part of your process involves doing nothing. You're a whole being, a Thriving Artist who dances among the currents of your unique creative process. Your stagnant pool will flow back into the stream of consciousness, becoming part of the living Waters that support you and the other beings in your life.

Spirit in Water

Don't tell the other elements, but Water is perhaps not-so-secretly my favorite. This could be because of my Cancer rising sign, or from growing up close to a lake, or maybe it's because I'm one-quarter mermaid. But the connection that Water has to Spirit seems especially strong and powerful to me.

Think about the energies of Water: flowing, soothing, buoyant... The calm joy you feel when you're listening to waves crash on the shore. The smell of the Earth after the rain. The deep relaxation that comes from a soak in the bathtub.

Water relaxes and comforts us. Perhaps this is because we grew in the waters of the womb. It was our first environment when we arrived on the Earth plane.

Many of our myths and origin stories talk about life emerging from the sacred waters. We were created there in the realm of Water, and when we connect with this element, we drift into a different type of awareness. Time seems to slow down. We're immersed in a mysterious, yet somehow friendly, consciousness.

Water is also associated with the land of dreams. When you're in a dream, events seem to flow in a way that's almost alien to your waking consciousness, the Talking Self. This flow is often experienced when you're deep into creating something new. You might describe a writing session where you were in the groove, saying, "The words just flowed out of me onto the page."

In this book, I've often talked about the ebb and flow of one's creativity. Our creativity itself, which as we've seen is strongly connected to spirituality, moves like Water. When we immerse ourselves in those sacred waters, we're bringing our creations forth from the wellspring of creativity. This is the part of us that is connected with the non-physical realms, where all is Spirit, as yet unmanifested.

By flowing with the sacred waters of your imagination, you're allowing your true essence free reign. You're not just making up stories with your ego-brain, although that can be fun. You're infusing your writing with something more universal. The energy consciousness that flows through everything is accessible to you. You'll have new insights, discover deeper wisdom, and be able to evoke a response from your readers. You'll also see firsthand how we're all connected by the ocean of consciousness that underlies our surface understanding of reality.

CHAPTER 11:
THE BORDERLANDS: BRINGING IT IN
(WATER TO EARTH)

About This Transition

As we conclude our trip around the circle, we reach the transition between Water and Earth.

Water's dreamy fluidity gradually gives way to the more solid reality of Earth. Our dreams and passions will soon manifest themselves in our lives and we must be patient and positive as the often-slow transformation unfolds. We dive deeply into ourselves, discovering our most cherished dreams. From there, we can rest assured that our intentions are being knit together and will be born into our daily reality. We weave our spells, drop our wishes into the still pool of intention, and then wait for the right time to take action.

Water and Earth intersect in the northwest. Rain prevails, yet the climate here is still mild. As we move from fall to the onset of winter, the rains may turn to snow, particularly in the mountains, where Water touches the solid rock of Earth. There is a gentle quality in the relationship between the rains and the forests. At the rocky shoreline, you can feel the ocean spray. The misty landscape feels dreamy, yet safe and protected. The animal guides who make themselves known are bear and eagle, owl and salmon, sea otter and bobcat. These figures move through our dreams, protecting us and guiding our way through our inner terrain. The transition between Water and Earth peaks at Samhain, also called Halloween, when we allow our deep inward movement to carry us into the darkest part of the year, dreaming like the trees as the Earth goes to sleep. Fall moves into winter, and we let our souls rest and hibernate.

Looking at this transition in terms of time, the combination of Water and Earth represents evening, the time from sunset to midnight. We settle into our nightly routine, which means some of us head off to bed, while the night owls among us enjoy the quiet of evening to create or relax. It is a time for peace and calm, for reflection and winding down towards sleep. The moon's light is mostly hidden from us now, as the waning crescent thins. The dark of the moon allows us to rest in the deep silence of the night. We are held gently in the womb of the darkest time of the year.

At the stage of life represented by the intersection of Water and Earth, we move from elderhood towards our death. We don't know exactly when we'll make the transition to the other side, but we can begin to prepare ourselves emotionally. We may be inspired to give away our treasured possessions to our loved ones, complete our autobiography, and wrap up creative projects. We explore our faith, thinking about our passage through the veil and our return to the Earth. As autumn turns to winter, the frosts come and the plants die away. The leaves have dropped from the trees and the Earth sleeps.

There are resources available to help us in exploring the Water to Earth transition, such as spiritual practices, tools, and symbols.

Here are some ideas:

- ❖ Meditation is a fitting practice for the Water to Earth transition. There are many types of meditation to explore. Mindfulness meditation works particularly well with Water and Earth. As you move through your day, stay grounded in the present moment, letting your thoughts and feelings flow through you freely, letting go of any attachment to them. Come back again and again to the present moment, without judging it, but simply letting your experience be fluid and natural.

❖ In the Tarot, the card that represents "Water of Earth" is the Queen of Pentacles. She is a down-to-earth, grounded woman who enjoys the sensual pleasures of the body. She receives her dreams and feelings, transforming them into creations that delight the senses. It is time to put your full effort into a task, yet remember to allow yourself to go with the flow and take time to play and relax.

❖ The mythical creatures related to this transition are dryads. These fae creatures live in the trees and are closely connected to the cycles of nature. They are protectors of the forest, guarding it from those who intend harm. When winter comes, they dream with the trees. We can learn from them by taking the time to nurture our dreams and giving them space to grow slowly into a beautiful grove.

❖ An affirmation for use during this transition might be: "I empower my most cherished dreams to become manifest in my life."

Emerging from the waters of self-nourishment and building your dream community, you suddenly find yourself on the shore, grounding yourself once more in the realm of Earth. This borderland, like the liminal space of an actual beach, feels mystical and fae.

Now you can see your writing habits and rituals with a new eye. You have some experience under your belt. You've had time to experiment with your personal creative flow. What have you learned?

This particular borderland is a delightful place to pause and reflect. Sit with your journal and write about how your book project is going.

❖ *What have you discovered about your process?*
❖ *What resistance have you uncovered – and overcome?*
❖ *What blockages still seem to stand in your way?*
❖ *What questions do you have?*

❖ *How could you further refine your writing habit to best serve you and your book?*

❖ *How close are you to the end of your first draft?*

❖ *How has your focus on creativity rippled outward to touch on other aspects of your life?*

Let the words flow onto the page, making sure that you're checking in with your Deep Self for some intuitive answers. Be as objective as you can, but also kind. You're doing deep work here.

As we discussed earlier, in the section on keeping a journal, taking stock is an essential part of the creative process. The borderland between Water and Earth provides the perfect vibe in which to slow down and assess your progress.

Some of my clients, as they near the end of their first draft, have enjoyed printing out a physical copy of what they've written so far. This allows you to see and feel the words on the page in a whole new way. Take some time to read over your manuscript as it stands now. Get a bird's eye view. Don't try to do a full edit yet, but make some notes on what is missing, out of order, or whatever comes to mind as you read.

If you've been keeping a writing journal or a document with notes on the process, look at those notes, too. See what has shifted and changed since you first began your book draft. Reflect on the wisdom you've gained and the skills you've been building.

As you near the completion of your first draft, doing a reflection session will help you to see what is still left to do. You might want to make a list for yourself and update your Flexible Outline. You may now be able to estimate how much longer the draft will take.

Be sure to take time to celebrate your progress so far! Looking at how much you've actually written, congratulate yourself. Even if it still feels like there's a long way to go before your book is complete, you've done a lot. You're taking an ethereal idea that you had and manifesting it into the physical world in the form of a book. You have words on the page. Lots of them!

As we walk the borderland between Water and Earth, you'll learn to maintain your creative wellspring and refine the rituals that keep your Triple Self aligned. Before you dive into the rest of the chapter, though, find some kind of gift or reward to give yourself, to honor all the work you've done so far. Celebrating your progress will help you stay committed to your project during the final stage. Don't skip this step!

Learning to Clear Your Creative Wellspring

As I shared earlier, I have wanted to be a writer since I was a little girl. I was pretty much born with a love of stories — thanks Mom, for reading to me! I started devouring books quite early, and then began creating my own tales.

Somewhere along the way, though, as so many of us do, I succumbed to the idea of conformity. *Sigh*

I ended up setting aside my writing dreams for a *long* time. Like decades, literally. Rediscovering my natural creativity and relearning to believe in my powers of creation has been the best thing I've done for myself as an adult.

Once I began writing and publishing books and blogs, while still journaling and playing with words in other ways, I wanted that for *you*, too.

It feels amazing and joyful to be a Thriving Artist!

The thing is, we are all naturally creative. Yet there are so many layers of conditioning, old beliefs, fears, scars, patriarchal bullshit, all the stupid "isms" we're taught, etc. covering up our creative wellspring. It can take time and attention — and courage — to uncover it.

I love helping others to clean out that well inside and drink deeply of those icy refreshing waters.

By now you understand the value of aligning your Triple Self before you sit down to write or create. That solid connection with your Deep Self allows for the free flow of your creativity. It makes writing your book easier.

As you progress through your journey, you might have noticed that your rituals are starting to really work their magick. As you first began your writing habit, you might have taken several minutes to really settle in, and you had to set up your space just so. Now, some of your rituals have become shortcuts. When you hear the opening chords of your writing playlist or smell the scented candle that you light at your desk, you can already feel yourself drop into the creative space. The words begin to flow almost before you put fingers to keyboard or pen to paper.

No, this won't be the case every day or in every session. But it's beginning to get easier. If this feels true to you, then this section will help you to further expand your creative connection. You'll learn some additional ways to tend your wellspring of creativity.

If not, don't despair. This section will help you take your Writing Ritual to a new level. It will also guide you to expand your creative connection into other areas of your life.

Here at the borderland between Water and Earth, you're invited to become even more familiar with your unique inner landscape.

Remember how I mentioned that your connection to Deep Self is located in your abdomen? For some people it's centered around the solar plexus, or hara. For others, it feels rooted just above or below your navel, in the sacral chakra.

Take a moment now to explore where *your* Deep Self resides:

Close your eyes and breathe deeply. Imagine that your thoughts are gathering into a little ball of glowing energy behind your eyebrows. Now let this ball of energy, which represents your attention, drop down along your spine. Notice when it lands in your heart center. Let the little glowing ball gather up any emotions that are flowing through you. Attune yourself to your Younger Self for a moment. When you can feel her energy, let the ball float downward once again. Let it settle gently somewhere in your abdomen. See where the ball feels most comfortable, then locate it within your body. Where has the ball of energy and awareness landed? Take a few deep breaths here, focusing on that glowing ball of energy. What does it feel like? Is this where your Deep Self lives? Listen carefully and see if you receive any messages or inspiration. When you feel complete, let your eyes open. Make some notes for yourself in your writing notebook about what you experienced.

If you struggled with connecting to your Deep Self or receiving any messages, you probably need to clear your creative wellspring. What do I mean by that? Imagine a well, dug deep into the ground. On the surface, you have perhaps a simple circle of rocks around the opening, with a bucket that can be lowered down on a rope. If you come to this spring each day to dip out some fresh water, chances are that the well's water will stay clear. If a long time goes by without use, the well might gather fallen leaves, branches, dirt, and other debris. If it's abandoned for a long time, the well may run dry, or become filled in with so much detritus that it's hard to access the water at all.

By tending to your creative wellspring regularly, you become a caretaker of that fresh, inspiring source. When you began creating your writing habit at the start of this book, I advised you not to try and schedule writing times on too many days, or to have sessions that run several hours. That was so that you didn't quickly become overwhelmed and feel like you were failing.

Now that we've circled back around to Earth, or nearly so, I want you to reevaluate how much time you spend on your creative projects. This time, don't include just your book writing. Think of the other creative things you do: journal writing, crafts, making music, doing magick, art projects, baking, doing the creative parts of your paid work. Include anything that feels like it taps into your creative energy. You'll know the feeling, now, from doing your regular writing practice.

Think about the energy with which you approach these creative endeavors. Do you enjoy yourself? Do you come to them with a joyful attitude? How much time do you spend on these things in a given week? Are you doing something creative each day?

Harnessing and using your creative energy is a delightful way to tend your creative wellspring. But it's not the only way. Next, take a look at the things in your life that inspire you. Your answers will be unique to you. Some people are inspired by hiking or camping in nature, while others love to play video games. I'm a lifelong bookwyrm who is consistently inspired by reading. You may be a movie fan or love live theater performances. Exploring a vibrant new city or neighborhood might light you up, or you may prefer a philosophical conversation with a good friend in a quiet café. Perhaps you love all of these things, and more! Make some notes on your favorite ways to take in experiences that inspire you. How often do you do these things? Do you take yourself on Artist Dates regularly?

Finally, evaluate the ways that you rest and do nothing at all. Yes, doing nothing is essential to the creative process. It helps to reset your connection with Deep Self. Do you get enough good sleep? Do you let yourself daydream? Are there times in your daily calendar where absolutely nothing is scheduled?

Maybe it's hard for you to do nothing, and you have to deliberately set aside a few minutes where you choose not to pick up a book or your phone. Having a day each week or month where you unplug from the digital world can help with this. Sometimes repetitive tasks, like doing the dishes, showering, or driving somewhere familiar, can allow for this Zen kind of mind space. Take advantage of those when you have a chance. Don't rush to fill the silence with music or TV. Let your attention drift as it wishes.

Finally, one of the ways that I love to keep my creative wellspring clear is by adding more magick to my week. Only do this if it truly appeals to you. Add little rituals to your life, ones that are just for you. Make them meaningful and fun. I like to make offerings of chocolate and other delicacies on the four main moon phases: new, first quarter, full, and last quarter. It delights me to buy flowers for the Goddess. I collect rocks and shells and use them to decorate my altars. I gather stickers and adorn my notebooks. I make Spotify playlists for the seasons, moon phases, and holidays. I cut up magazines and catalogs to make new collages in my art journal. As you may have guessed, these things appeal to my Younger Self. Because she's so strongly connected with Deep Self, keeping her happy and playful helps to keep that wellspring fresh and clean.

Tending to your wellspring takes your creative connection to a deeper level. When you do this regularly, you'll notice more inspired ideas and synchronicities appearing in your everyday life. New opportunities will present themselves. You might decide to write more often or lengthen your writing sessions. Maybe you'll be inspired to try a new form of creative expression. Your resistance, once so strong, will fade – not just around your creativity, but perhaps in connection with how you show up in the world, your style, your confidence, and your authenticity.

One of the hidden benefits to writing a book is that it changes not only your readers and the world, but it changes you, too. You're transformed from a wanna-be writer to an actual author. This transformation doesn't have to wait until you hold your published book in your hands, either. When you allow it, it will seep through your life like fresh, clear water to parched soil. In the borderland of Water and Earth, you are the caretaker, the one who allows your self-nourishment to grow and flourish.

An Unsafe Universe: The Resistance

It's the final stretch, my friend. You've soaked in the nourishing Waters, and now you're moving back around toward Earth. Your first draft is (hopefully) almost complete. What could stop you now?

Interestingly, on this stretch of the path, what sometimes comes up is a lack of trust in your body. What do I mean by that? You've been integrating lots of new tools as you walked the spiral path of writing a book. Your customized writing habits, your solid skills, your book's voice, that brand new community, your deepest self-nourishing practices – all of this adds up to a significant amount of change.

I've been teaching you ways to write a book sustainably, with ease and pleasure. Chances are that your physical body is on board for this idea. After all, you're prioritizing good rest, self-care, and not forcing your creativity to fit into a rigid box. You've learned to align your Triple Self so that the energy in your body flows smoothly. You now have a stronger relationship with the intuitive wisdom that comes from your Deep Self. But sometimes the brain, the ego self, doesn't trust that your body actually knows what she's doing.

The ego's purpose is to keep us safe, and it often uses some rather questionable methods for doing so. Doubt and worry, for example. At this point in the journey, the voices of doubt might be telling you that it's too easy. All of those old B.S. adages about something not being worthwhile if you haven't worked hard, struggled, and hustled rear their ugly heads.

Hopefully by now you can recognize them for what they are, and not let them drive the car. In fact, your responsibility at this point on the path is to let go. To surrender to the process that you've already honed, refined, and practiced. To stop trying to control the journey, and instead let it flow. It's harder than it sounds. I know. I've been there myself, many times. We all want to control our experience, but that's what keeps us from enjoying each moment. The ego has its place, but it's not the boss. Talking Self will blather on about all the things that could possibly go wrong. Listen, and then keep writing anyway. Keep taking inspired actions. Complete your draft. Finish the journey. You can do this.

Spirit Walks from Water to Earth

At the borderland of Water and Earth, you're rounding the final stretch. This is my favorite part. The book manuscript you've been working on for oh-so-long is finally, really, truly almost complete! Not only that, your writing habits are now so familiar that it feels like they're an essential part of your week. Perhaps you've even begun to find writing your book meditative and fun. That's the hope, anyway.

This could be a time when some of your shadow selves feel a bit fearful, or apprehensive, about what happens when you complete your draft. Don't worry, though. Spirit has your back. Your Deep Self has a bigger picture than your ego mind, and knows that everything really will be okay – and better than okay! Spirit sends you messages in the Watery realms of dreams, and whispers inspired ideas in your ear all day long. There's also Spirit in the realms of Earth, grounding you in the habits that provide a safe space in which to create. Remember, your spirit guides are your biggest cheerleaders! They're the innermost circle of your Dream Team.

As you've walked this borderland, emerging from the depths of Water back onto the Earth, you've learned to tend your creative wellspring. You've refined your writing process so that it works best for you – not only for this book, but for future projects.

If for some reason you're not feeling grounded in your writing habits, it's time to revisit the section on Earth and make some refinements. Evaluate what has shifted. It might be that you started a new job or changed your weekly schedule. Perhaps you've tuned in to the moon phases in a new way and want to merge your creative sessions with the times when you feel most energetic and creative. Or maybe you're just feeling "blah" and need to jazz up your Writing Ritual a bit, to recapture your Younger Self's attention.

Lastly, we're going to revisit the realm of Spirit. We'll be talking about cultivating a state of inspired persistence. We'll cover what to do when things seem to fall apart – which they sometimes do at the end of a project (thanks, shadow selves!). We'll also learn about trusting your own creative process and adding even more creative magick to your week. It'll be fun! Let's go - after we check in with Alex.

This is Alex 2.0

I went down a rabbit hole looking for a life coach - with nothing to show for it - and now my deadline is looming closer. I hate the bios I've written so far. All of them. They either sound too pretentious or entirely frivolous. I can't seem to strike a good balance.

And this is just the beginning. Imagine when I'm on deadline with the publisher for content? I mean, sure, a lot of it is written already, from my workshops and talks, which is a huge advantage. But there's still a lot to do, and it has to be perfect. This is more important than anything I've ever done.

I had a date with Helena last night - our third, officially. I was kind of shocked when she asked me what was wrong, what was going on. I thought I could keep it under wraps. Because how can I mention something so messed up? How dare I tell people that having one of my dreams come true is sending me over the edge?

We went back to Helena's place after the show - we're taking things slow, but she's an amazing kisser - and when I got up to leave, she handed me a book by a writer I'd never heard of: Existential Kink by Carolyn Elliott. I hadn't said much about what was getting to me, but Helena's on point. Even though I was still really buzzed by the time I got home, I stayed up super late reading it. Shadow work, kink metaphors, smart writing. Will it help? I don't know, but it's freaky enough to make sense on a deep level. Okay.

This might be one of those books where I actually do the exercises rather than just say I'll come back to them later. I'm that desperate.

***

I wrote the fucking bio, finally, after doing a bunch of the shadow work in the EK book. I haven't hit "send," though. I'm still waiting for a few peeps to get back to me with their feedback. I'm leading with that, but it's not my big news.

Nope. Here it is - I broke my fucking hand. I have to write my book and my dominant hand is busted! WTF? I'm voice dictating this now. I was barreling down the stairs like I always do, and I guess I tripped over my laces or something. When I landed I put out my arm - Tio Rafe would be so disappointed that I didn't use his falling instructions - and BOOM. I felt it crack. Gross, right?

And can I just say, how strong are these shadow demons in my psyche? Finally break through the resistance and do the thing, and then I wind up broken that same night.

What do I do now? I have a publisher, a deadline, a shit-ton to do. Maybe I can scrape enough money together to hire an assistant. I think I'm supposed to get an advance. Maybe that's what I should use it for, instead of putting it in my house fund. Wait, can you hire an assistant on a credit card? Asking for a friend.

***

Okay, I couldn't have seen this coming, but Helena's gonna be my personal assistant and all-around Goddess. I know, I know, new relationship, don't put pressure on it, blah, blah, blah. But it was her idea. And I love it. She's amazing, and it means we get to spend more time together. Plus I insisted on paying her. Keepin' it professional.

I got the feedback on the bio, and the biggest suggestion was making the pronouns more clear. Modern life, it's all about the pronouns. I did mention that before, right? I'm enby, or nonbinary, and I use they/them. Born a girl, wasn't feeling it, discovered my essence - it's not a new story. But, yeah, it can get confusing in a paragraph where I'm talking about myself and the groups I'm part of, I get that. Editing it for clarity is good practice for the book.

Helena's coming over tonight and we'll finish the edits and send off the bio - only a couple of days late. I got the whole "broke my hand" sympathy extension. Thankfully.

Next up is pulling together all the stuff I have written in various places. It sounds like a super boring chore to me, but Helena's all over it. Seriously, she's Virgo sun with Capricorn rising and she's actually excited about this job. Thank you, Goddess, for bringing her into my life. Did I tell you the story about how we met? I'll save it for another time. My hand is aching. Gotta re-ice and maybe take some more ibuprofen.

CHAPTER 12:
THE RETURN TO SPIRIT: EXPLORING INSPIRED PERSISTENCE

More About Spirit

As you've learned by now, while moving about the spiral of the writer's journey with the elements, Spirit touches on everything. The Spirit part of you, which you've gotten to know as your Deep Self, is eternal and unendingly creative. Now that you've made your way around the spiral and back to Spirit, what's in store for you and your book project?

We're going to focus on what I like to call inspired persistence. Let me ask you a question, as you've made it this far through reading this book: is your manuscript finished? Before you answer, you should know that I'm fully expecting the answer to be, "not yet." If you *are* finished and things are wrapped up, then simply use the information in this chapter for your next big creative project.

Otherwise, let's look at some of the qualities of Spirit that will help you to finish your first draft.

Spirit never gives up. Because this is the part of you that's connected with the non-physical realm, which is beyond space and time, Spirit doesn't care when, or even if, you'll finish your book. From the perspective of Spirit, you have all the time in the Universe. In a sense, this sort of laid-back attitude can be unhelpful. You're a mortal, with goals and plans and desires.

You have reasons for wanting to finish the book, although your shadow side probably has reasons to abandon it as well. But on the other hand, this lack of urgency also means that Spirit is vastly patient and won't give up. If you put your book project in a drawer or stick it on a thumb drive somewhere, then pick it up several months later, Spirit won't mind. As long as you connect with your Deep Self, you'll pick it back up again and won't have a problem connecting with the contents. It's our Talking Self, the ego, that labels our actions and non-actions. Your ego might say that it's too late for your project, that the content was once timely but is now out-of-date, or that it's time to just move on and start over. It could even be right, but what's the motivation for these opinions? Fear? Boredom? Self-criticism? Connect with your Deep Self, and you won't find any of those things in the mix. Spirit won't give up on you or your book project.

That said, Spirit is also mutable and endlessly in motion. From our limited perspective as mortal beings, it appears that Spirit is ever-changing. This is both true and false. The parts of Spirit that we encounter may certainly be different from moment to moment. Yet Spirit also contains all things and is the unity of the cosmos. In that sense, it is unchanging, as it contains everything that is and ever has been and ever will be. What changes is our perspective. We are constantly learning and growing as we move through the experience of life on the physical plane. The way we perceive Spirit changes with us.

In terms of your book project, this means that as you do the actual work of writing your draft, you may discover aspects of the book that need to change – sometimes in a major way. Spirit has your back, as does your Flexible Outline. That's why it's flexible, remember? When you need to do a major change in the structure or contents of your manuscript, Deep Self will help you make the necessary decisions. You might want to try working with a pendulum, asking yes or no questions and then following the intuitive guidance you receive.

Spirit is attuned with your Deep Why. Remember when you set an intention for why you wanted to write this book to begin with? If you haven't looked at – or updated – your intention for a while, now is the time to return to it. Does it still resonate with you? Do you feel inspired when you read it? If not, it might need to be refreshed. Tap into the connection you have to your Deep Self, your wellspring of creativity, and do some brainstorming. What would make you excited to finish this book? Write down your ideas and use them to update your intention so that it once again lights you up. If you do still feel those feelings of inspiration, desire, and momentum, breathe them in. Allow them to help motivate you to continue to write the remainder of your book.

Spirit is everywhere and anywhere you go. Since you're connected to Spirit, you can draw on inspiration from anything you encounter or experience. Here at the tail end of your book project, gathering inspiration is key to your success. Try to make time to take in experiences that feed you. When's the last time you took yourself on an Artist Date? Have you had a true day off lately? Do you have any other forms of creativity that you engage in? When was the last time you did them? Spirit might be eternal, but it's not stagnant or boring. Don't let yourself get into a pattern of activity that doesn't inspire you.

Remember, you're a Thriving Artist. You can be creative no matter the setting. Bring your creativity with you in your daily life. See what thoughts and feelings are inspired by the people you talk with, the sights you see, the objects you encounter. Even challenges can be useful in motivating you to write. If you're experiencing something new with a client, how does that fit with the content of your book? Does an amusing anecdote illustrate perfectly how a technique could work for your reader? Would someone you met in the course of daily life make a perfect character for the world you're creating in your book? Keep an eye on how the events of daily life can feed your creative projects. It's all Spirit.

Spirit is made of magick, and so are you. If you're feeling uninspired or like your book draft will never be done, it's time to return to some of the magickal practices you did before you began writing. Visualize yourself holding your completed and published book baby. See all the details of that moment in your mind's eye. Reward the work you've done so far by giving yourself one of the special treats you decided on earlier, or begin putting those plans into motion. For example, if you decided to go away on vacation once your book draft is done, you might start checking airfares and looking at hotels or Air BnBs in your chosen vacation spot. If you made a vision board based on your book project, bring it out and look at it. Update it with new images and words, if that feels good. Not sure what to do to pour magick into your book project? Check with Deep Self. Use oracle or Tarot cards, your pendulum, or other forms of divination to get some advice on next steps. If you feel blocked, return to some of the exercises and journaling prompts around resistance that were offered earlier in the book.

Finally, Spirit is ultimately quite playful. That's why Younger Self and Deep Self speak the same language. Maybe it's time to infuse a sense of playfulness into your writing. Our tendency is to get serious, especially as we approach the end of a Big Project. Perhaps you've unconsciously started wearing your editor's hat when you should be just focusing on writing. Has your Writing Ritual become rote and dull? Jazz it up a bit. Put on some lively music and move your body before you sit down to write. Find an evocative poem or chant to use when you call upon your Muses. Your Younger Self and your Deep Self are in league when it comes to having fun. Get rid of any pressure you're putting on yourself and your writing, and just write for the sheer joy of it. Do some wild writing, or bring in some channeling. Try writing in a completely different voice or from an unusual perspective. Not everything you write has to end up in your book. It's perfectly fine to experiment, particularly if it gets your creative juices flowing.

In the next section, we'll take a look at what happens if and when things start to fall apart.

When It All Falls Apart

This is the time in the process when things can seem to fall apart a bit. Your schedule gets full, you're extra busy, you begin to feel disconnected from your creativity, real-life things come up that you need to deal with and that interrupts your creative process. In fact, this is quite common: when you begin something new, your old patterns will try to pull you back into your old ways of being. When you come to the completion of a huge project like writing a book, Talking Self gets scared. Don't worry. This is natural. It's your brain trying to keep you safe and comfortable.

Now is the time when you most need to lean on the habits, tools, and intentions you've been cultivating over the course of creating your manuscript. You need to trust your creative magick, which can be hard to do when it feels like you're newly aware of it, or if you've just recently rekindled that connection.

It's also a good time to reassess. Sometimes, the act of doing a big thing like writing a book weaves itself into your life and creates change. The thing that you committed to doing has shifted the ground underneath you. Life has opened up and expanded, causing you to notice things in your life that you need to release. It's all in service to your growth. Creativity is part of your spiritual beingness. It's not linear.

Given the potential for things to move and shift around you, what's next for you and your project?

Let's explore that a bit. In this section I'm not just talking about persistence for its own sake, but rather about *inspired* persistence. That means connecting in with your Deep Self and listening for inner wisdom.

Get your writing journal and pen. Then begin by going into a meditative state. Align with your Triple Self and connect with inner wisdom in the form of Deep Self. Listen for messages about your creative projects and your life as a whole. Make a note of them. Then ask Deep Self to stay with you and help you as you delve into the following set of journaling questions.

- ❖ *Given the inner wisdom that you've just received, how would you like to adjust your goal for completing your book?*
- ❖ *Has your intention for your book changed? Make some notes on how.*
- ❖ *Are there any new inspired actions that you feel drawn to take?*

❖ *What tools, support, and rituals do you need to lean into starting now?*

Trusting Your Creativity

As we focus on how to stay motivated and persistent throughout the creation of your book, and in a broader picture, your life as an artist, I'd like to talk about *faith*. Now, if this word has negative connotations for you, as it once did for me, let's change it up. A decent synonym for *faith* is *trust*.

I want you to know that you can trust your creativity.

When you're just starting out, this statement might not seem like the truth. But think about your journey with creativity. Chances are, like me, you were full-to-bursting with creativity as a child, and then something happened. Whether this was full-on abuse and trauma, or the pressure to achieve that comes with attending school, or something else, you were led to believe that it was more important to give the "right" answers than to imagine your own. You were taught that it was better to belong than to fly your unique freak flag. Even if you resisted hard, you learned that our culture as a whole wants each of us to conform.

That can, and often does, mess up your relationship with your Deep Self and your personal wellspring of creativity.

To add insult to injury, you could see each and every day how creativity gets devalued in the mainstream realm. You're sold a bill of goods about successful creative people: they are rare, they either had such mad skills that they had to succeed, or they ran into some luck or knew the right people or were born with that mythical silver spoon. In other words, they were Not Like You. Or, more poignantly, you were Not Like Them. So, you could be creative if you want to, but keep it in a box, let it be a hobby, and find a Day Job. Or, conversely, throw all of your life's energy, time, and passion into your chosen creative pursuit, until you either "made it big," or starved (literally or metaphorically), or got so discouraged that you gave up and squished your creativity back in that box and stuck it in the back of your closet of dreams.

Not a very inspiring way to look at what is actually a completely natural part of your innate being.

If you decide that you *do* want to trust your creativity and weave it into the tapestry of your life, you'll have some healing to do. It's not like you'll just drag the box out of the back of your closet, free your creativity, and "poof!" you and your Muses live happily ever after together.

I mean, anything could happen, of course. But in my experience and that of many of my clients, crafting a trusting and loving relationship with our creativity takes time and patience.

What do I mean by trusting your creativity? Here's an example:

I wrote much of this particular book during National Novel Writing Month in 2021. I usually use NaNoWriMo to work on my fiction, but this time I wanted to finish up this book so that I could get it out there into the world. In early October, I decided on the plan. But I had a particularly busy month, filled with travel, retreats, and more. On the first day of NaNo, I went on a walk in the woods with BlackLion. I told him how, that morning as I was waking up, I'd been thinking about writing the rest of this book and wondering if I had enough to say about creativity to add 50,000 more words to a manuscript that already had nearly 30,000. I reported to him that when I thought about it, my imagination immediately shifted into gear and started pouring forth sentences and phrases, and I knew that it would be fine.

"So," he said, "then you started taking notes?"

"Nope," I replied. "I trust my creativity. I'm sure the ideas will return when I need them."

This is a different space for me to be in. I used to write down every creative idea that occurred to me, hoarding them carefully in case the wellspring ran dry. I was afraid it might, because it had before. I was saving ideas, making notes, from a place of fear and scarcity.

That's not to say that I don't take notes or capture creative ideas anymore. My memory is notably mercurial. I keep a "study notebook" (for my fellow journal and notebook geeks: a 10x7 black Moleskine lined notebook, which I immediately cover in stickers) in my messenger bag. But I'm no longer coming from a place of lack. I trust that when I need the ideas, they'll be there for me. And guess what? It's true.

The flow of creativity is like a stream of water flowing forth. We may or may not be tapped into it at any given time. But it's always there.

Perhaps my fear wasn't that I'd forget my best ideas, or that the flow would slow or trickle to a stop. Maybe I was afraid that I wouldn't be able to find my way back to the stream when I wanted to be there.

There's no need for you to fear that your creativity will cease to flow, or that you'll lose your way to the shore. You're nearly at the end of this book, and hopefully by now you've learned many new ways to access your creativity. At the very least, you have five particular points of entry – the elements – with associated tools to guide you on your creative journey.

It's time to trust your creativity.

If this still sounds impossible or very difficult to you, pull out that flashlight and let's shine some light on what's hidden in your shadow.

Why don't you trust your innate creativity? What are you afraid will happen if you release your tight grip on your ideas, your process, or your results? What's the very worst that could happen?

Yeah, we're gonna go there. Picture what life might be like if your worst fears about your creativity came true. Let the scenario play out for a moment. You sit down to write and... *nothing*. Day after day. Or your first book is a powerhouse of a success, with raving fans and zillion-star reviews, but when you start to write the next book, you get crickets. Or someone awful steals your unique idea and runs with it, and they're the one who gets all those juicy accolades, before your book manuscript is even finished.

That's pretty bad, right? Okay, take a deep breath. Now imagine what you would do if this came to pass. How would you deal with it? You now know that there are many ways to feed your creative spirit, right? You could book yourself a writing retreat. You could engage the help of a writing coach. You could throw yourself fully and wholeheartedly into playful adventures that are seemingly unrelated to writing, because you now realize that playfulness and your Younger Self are excellent at opening up your creative flow. If someone steals your big idea, you can pivot – changing it up or adding to it until it's something even better than before. There are so many options! That's the entire point of cultivating your creativity and imagination. You can imagine your way out of nearly any crappy scenario.

And although this is a book about creativity, you may have noticed by now that the creative magick detailed here seeps into all areas of your life. You have the ability to find creative solutions for your relationship with your rebellious teenager, to heal rifts between you and a loved one (or move on, if necessary, in a healthy and nurturing way), and conjure up more prosperity. In fact, your creativity is your ally. It accompanies you as you walk through your day. When you learn to tune yourself to that intuitive voice from Deep Self, you're allowing yourself to receive support from within.

Why wouldn't you choose to trust it? When you cultivate that relationship with your creative Muse, then it will trust you, too. Showing up for your creativity on a regular basis enables the process to flow more smoothly. You'll feel inspired, and it won't take you as long as it once did to get into the groove. You'll bring that spirit of creativity to all aspects of your life, and problems that might have seemed insurmountable become a fascinating puzzle to solve. Yes, of course you'll still suffer sometimes. You might even face off against the blank page and choose to walk away, but only once in a while.

Trusting your creativity allows you to focus on what you enjoy about the process, rather than fretting or resisting. That in turn will keep you returning to the page until your manuscript is finished or your series of books is complete. Your trust will bring you on new creative adventures of learning and practice. It will take you to new heights. Having faith in your creativity will expand your faith in the Universe as a whole. You'll learn ways of being in the world that serve you best. This will allow you to uplift others along the way. You'll discover that you are made of spirit, you reside in the center, and all of the elements come together to co-create the very life you're living. What could be better than that?

Sacred Strategy Ritual

As we wrap up, and in the context of letting your creativity suffuse all areas of your life, I like to offer you another tool for your toolbox. Each Sunday evening I sit down with my bullet journal, calendar, oracle cards, and my favorite rocks & crystals, to prepare myself for the coming week. If I have a busy Sunday, I do it first thing Monday morning.

Because I designed it to suit me, my Sacred Strategy Ritual is a combination of the practical and the spiritual. I look over my calendar to figure out my priorities and make sure there's time scheduled for the things that are most important to me. I also set an intention for the week and draw an oracle card. I've included some of my favorite decks in the Resources section. I have my rocks & crystals on hand because they bring me joy. I often light a candle and play some relaxing music.

Preparing for the week ahead is a deliberate choice that helps me focus on how I want to feel and the most important things to get done. It helps me to balance my work schedule, my writing time, my self-care, and my social calendar.

I find that if I *don't* approach my week with intentional focus, time slips away from me. Even though I identify as a writer, if I don't deliberately make time in my schedule to work on my creative projects, a whole week can go by without me even opening my current book manuscript. Or if I'm in a busy patch with my business, I might cram in so much work that there's no time for nature walks or hanging out with a friend.

Doing my Sunday evening planning ritual helps me to balance the various aspects of my life so that my days reflect my priorities. It's not a perfect system, but it helps me work steadily toward my goals, both personal and professional.

How do you currently set yourself up for the week ahead? Does the idea of a Sunday evening ritual appeal to you? What elements would you like to include in your own version?

Doubt, Again? The Resistance

What kind of resistance arises when we return to the elemental realms of Spirit? Quite often, it's a deeper level of doubt, and fearful beliefs that connect us to our past lives and our ancestral line.

Spiritual growth is like an upward spiral. As you move around and around, gaining ground with the lessons you learn and integrate, you might come to a point where you run up against something you thought you'd resolved. This time, though, you're encountering it from a new level of awareness.

Let me give you an example of what I mean. As we explored the element of Air, you perhaps encountered the self-doubt that came from the way you were taught to write in school, and the beliefs you bought into about starving artists and how rare it is to succeed as a writer. You've explored some of those old beliefs in your journal. You've practiced your skills, shared your writing with a few people you trust, received positive feedback, and healed some of those doubts.

Over time, you've discovered that you actually *like* the book that you're creating. You enjoy showing up to work on it, and the process of writing has become fun. You find yourself looking forward to the day when your manuscript is complete.

As you approach the end of your first draft, though, new doubts begin to creep into your consciousness. You question whether the book is good enough to establish you as an expert, or unique enough to gain you a following. Will it be a good enough calling card for your work in the world? Does writing a book even fit with what you've been called to accomplish? Is the topic matter relevant to the change you wish to create in our society? Wait – what if the book opens you up to haters? What if sharing your vulnerable truths and hard-won discoveries will actually be dangerous to your existence?

You've uncovered some new doubts, from a different vantage point on the spiral of spiritual growth. If those last two questions resonate with you, perhaps you've discovered what is called the "witch wound." The witch wound is the fear of others seeing your connection with the unseen realms. Many of us recall other lives where we were literally burned, drowned, hanged, or otherwise executed for knowing herbalism, magick, and other wisdom related to the Mysteries. Even if you don't recall these things consciously, when you begin to expand your connection with Spirit, this deep-seated fear can arise, sparking doubts about your safety.

The witch wound isn't the only way we might experience our resistance in the realm of Spirit, but it's a good example because it's fairly common among healers, witches, mystics, and creatives like us. The resistance that arises for you might be something else entirely.

The thing is, the doubts that emerge at this point in the journey are often held deep in your body and are connected to more than just your current lifetime. They might have to do with your ancestral or spiritual lineage, particularly if you identify as part of a group of people who have been oppressed. It could be that you've played a very particular set of roles in other lifetimes, and it hasn't always ended well. It might also be something deep and traumatic that you experienced in this lifetime – even if it seems unrelated to your creativity and self-expression. These traumas are stored in your body, in the memory of your very cells.

As I write this, much more research and information about the trauma we carry is emerging. Along with that information, thankfully, come therapeutic and healing practices that can help to release the trauma so that you can continue to move forward.

Somatic therapies, or practices that help to release the traumatic energies stored in your body, are becoming much more widespread. There are many different types of somatic healing, but the common thread is that they address the body, as well as the mind and emotions. One of the ones I've found most helpful in releasing both personal and ancestral traumas is EFT, which we talked about earlier. I've included some resources in the back of the book if you're called to explore it for yourself. I recommend that you start by having a session with a certified EFT practitioner, like I did, but once you've learned the basic technique, it's easy to do for yourself.

Somatic practices like EFT will help you to release the witch wound or other deeply embedded forms of resistance that emerge as you approach the completion of your book. Remember that you deserve to be supported in the process of writing your book, and that it takes a village. Just as you'll need an editor and beta readers, having healers or therapists on your side will help you to reach your goal of writing and publishing your Heartfelt Book, and lead you to fulfilling other dreams and callings that come to you as you open further to your creativity and spirituality.

This is Alex 2.0

This week is Thanksgiving and I'm heading home to Florida for a few days. I can't wait to see everyone! Helena already flew out to Seattle to see her Mom. I wish she was coming with me, but it's kinda too soon for the "meet the family" bit, anyway. Although I think I'm in love with her. I haven't told her that yet. She's so cool and centered, and I know I'm rather intense. We'll get there.

The book manuscript is coming along okay. Helena's doing amazing things with the stuff I've already got. I'm the speed bump.

See, I have to write these transitions to weave the reader in and out of the chapters, and also an introduction, which feels like it's just a bigger and more impressive version of the bio. I'm freezing up. I dictate stuff but then it sounds lame so I start over. Helena had a fit when she saw me erasing paragraphs (with my left hand, no less). Her brother's partner is a writer, and she apparently says that you should never try to write and edit at the same time. Which I'm totally guilty of - that's probably why the fucking bio took so long.

Ugh. I hate this. I just want the book to be done and submitted and to get on with the next steps.

Plus, my hand still hurts. And I still have to pack. I'm taking another gummy bear. Pain sucks.

***

The book's deadline is creeping up on me. I've gotten into a bit of a groove. Helena helped me find a process that seems to be working, at least most of the time. I have no idea if the writing is any good. I'm just baring my soul over here, hoping to inspire the next generation of activists so we can save humanity and the planet. No pressure.

I love working with Helena, though the work time might be toning down the romantic feels a bit. Not on my part, but she seems to be more interested in editing than cuddling lately, you know? I'll have to think up a fun date night to distract her - wait, what am I saying? I'm the worst at staying focused. I know this. No, that's just my shadow self shit-talking. I got my master's degree, for fuck's sake! I have a book deal as an unknown. I'm doing fine.

That's my pep talk for today. I'm dictating this journal entry instead of the book. I need to get back into my groove. I have a music playlist to write by, my favorite fuzzy blanket with Appa (from Avatar: The Last Airbender*) on it, and even a special beeswax candle to light, though that sounds New Age corny as hell. But hey, if it ain't broke...*

***

I've hit a wall. I'm trying to write about my sexual abuse and I'm just bawling. I mean, this happened years ago. I've had hours and hours of therapy, I've been open about it all along, and I've even talked about it on stage in front of a decent-sized crowd. But right now, it feels too fresh. This is a core part of my message. It's what inspired me to be brave AF in the work that I do. Why can't I write it?

I'm thinking it might be related to the shadow work I've been doing. It's supposed to help with healing, but it can also open up a deeper level of vulnerability. Sure, I often talk about the abuse and the assault, but it's like I'm telling someone else's story. The late-teens-girl version of me. In thinking about writing it for the book, it feels like it's more a part of who I actually am, here and now. Does that even make sense?

Helena's been great, but I can tell she's getting frustrated, trying to help me get past it. The folks at the publisher are awesome. My family and friends are all just so excited for me to take things to the next level with this book. I still feel sort of stranded, though.

I'm the only one who can do this part. It's all on me. What if I fuck it up? It's that damn bio all over again, in bigger form.

This is some basic shit, like "Who am I to talk about sexual abuse? My family is almost embarrassingly functional. Most of my life has been great." "Who am I to write this book? I don't know what I'm doing!" Even "Who would want to read what I have to say? It's been done way better by others." Shut up, shadows! You're pissing me off.

CHAPTER 13:
ARRIVING AT YOUR DESTINATION

What's Next?

A common question people ask when they learn I'm a writing coach is, "How," with hope in their eyes, "do I know what step to take next on my book project?"

I'm so glad you asked!

Here's a 4-step process that works well for me and my clients.

It doesn't matter whether, at this point in time, your book is just a vague idea, or a nearly-finished draft. This process draws on your inner wisdom, so it'll automatically be customized to your situation.

STEP 1: Get centered and grounded. Establish a connection to your inner wisdom.

Don't overcomplicate this step. Here are some ways to get centered and connected: take a walk outside in nature, do a guided meditation, or just take a series of deep, relaxing breaths. You might wish to light a candle or play some soothing music.

STEP 2: Bring your book project to mind. Stay centered as you do so. Breathe deeply.

STEP 3: Ask yourself this series of questions. Listen for the answers. Don't force it. Let the answers arise naturally.

You can do this mentally, or in your journal — whichever way best allows inner wisdom to flow to you. Stay relaxed and centered as you go through this process.

Here are the questions:

- ❖ *When I think about the next step to take, what scares me?*
- ❖ *When I think about the next step to take, what excites me?*
- ❖ *What do I love about my book idea or manuscript?*
- ❖ *When I think of my book project, what do I worry about?*
- ❖ *Who or what are my allies in this process? (This can be people in your life, non-physical beings like ancestors or spirit guides, and/or qualities you possess, such as a strong imagination or being good with details).*
- ❖ *What's standing in my way?*
- ❖ *What are three small inspired actions (aka baby steps) that I can take this week to forward my book project?*

Listen carefully to the answers you receive. If you're not already journaling them, make some notes for yourself.

STEP 4: Honor your inner wisdom by taking baby steps this week to act on the advice you've received.

You already have the answers you need — or the resources you need to help you discover them.

The next step in your book project doesn't have to be The Perfect Thing. Truly, just choosing to take action based on your inner wisdom is the best thing you can do.

If you're feeling overwhelmed, you might not get clear answers from your inner wisdom — and that's okay. Reach out for support.

One of the secrets of Thriving Artists is that we choose to do our sacred work in community. You don't have to go it alone.

And Then What?

If you're not as close as you thought you were to manifesting your book, be gentle with yourself. Think about the creative unfolding that you've experienced while reading this book. Chances are that you've been working quietly behind the scenes, letting these new ideas percolate in the back of your mind. Remember all the inner resistance you've had to overcome and the external tools that you needed to learn to bring you to exactly where you are today.

What's one thing that you're grateful for having learned or integrated? You must have at least one celebration. It can be anything – large or small. What's coming to mind right now?

Take a look at your Flexible Outline and the intention you set at the beginning of our time together. If you haven't created them yet, return to those sections and do so now.

Ponder how your intention and the baby steps you discovered in the last section fit together. Ask your Deep Self for more wisdom, if needed. You could ask while in a meditative state, or use your divination tools.

Keep this information in mind as you read the Epilogue. After Alex's story concludes, of course...

This is Alex 2.0

Celebration time! I got the cast off today, and I've finished the first draft of the manuscript!!! Helena's taking me out for a special dinner at The Red House. Maybe I'll even get lucky later, lol.

I wonder if the book is any good. I'm so nervous about sending it off to the publisher for edits. But as Helena pointed out, we're not quite there yet. Each of us is going to go through it once more before the deadline, which is next Friday. I can't believe I'm not doing it all at the last fucking minute, like I usually do. This woman is a good influence on me, for sure.

I should probably tell her I love her. Yikes. Maybe tonight at dinner would be a good time for that. Romantic setting and all, you know. I get the vibes that she feels the same, but then again, Helena's sort of hot and cold. Sometimes it's like the professional relationship comes first in her mind. Other times, she's way, way into me (like, tingles all over just thinking about it).

I think I'll call Mamma and talk to her about the next step with Helena. Yes, my mother is my romance guru. She and Pappa are the ultimate couple, and yet they also have their own independent lives. They're not poly, but if that had been a thing back in their day, they totally would have rocked it. Mamma's super respectful of my way of doing things, and always manages to have the best advice.

Okay, okay, here I am going all romance in my writing journal. Back to The Book. I've had to get hot and heavy with it - see what I did there? - and I'm hoping it's paid off. Some of the stuff I hardly even rewrote at all. The best of what I think of as my "pep talk speeches" seemed to fit perfectly. They're already in my voice. The workshop notes were pretty easy to expand into a coherent narrative. The exercises are fun and I hope, unlike me most of the time, folx will actually want to do them. The parts I worry about are the transitions, the anecdotes I added, and of course my nemesis, the introduction. Why is it so hard to write about my own experiences? I wonder if other writers - or whatever it is that I am - have this problem, too.

***

The. Book. Project. Is. Done!!!

Helena and I submitted the edited manuscript late last night, meeting the deadline with a couple minutes to spare. I already got the confirmation email from the editor, so I know they received it. "Acknowledged," like in Star Trek.

My brain still feels like it's packed with clouds of doubt and the fog of that last long push to finish editing. But my heart is clear. I have a strong feeling that the book is as good as it can be. Does that even make sense?!

I'm a first-time author, sure, but the material is mostly stuff I've been polishing for years. That's how I got the book deal; someone from the publisher saw one of my talks and reached out. Which is supposedly super rare. I told you I'm a unicorn.

The oddest part is that I have this craving to write more. I used to procrastinate like mad, but I'm actually missing my writing sessions. Maybe I'll start another book. Or I could revive my blog. I'm reminded of back when I did LiveJournal, in college. The writing - not just mine, but lots of it - was raw and vulnerable and somehow transcendent back then.

In a frenzied burst of celebration, I told Helena my feelings for her last night. She reciprocated!!! But she wants monogamy with me, and I'm not sure how I feel about that. Though my poly is mostly theoretical at the moment; I haven't been out with Bryce for months. So I'm definitely considering it. Hey, maybe I should write a poly book? That would piss off some conservatives, which I'm so good at anyway. Heh.

Next (for this first book) comes the revisions the publisher suggests, though I have at least a couple of weeks before those come in. I think I'll do some writing. Scratch that itch, ya know? I'm just gonna grab my tablet, head to my favorite park bench, and see what emerges. I'll see you on the other side. Adios!

EPILOGUE:
KEEP UP THE GOOD PLAY!

Dear reader, let's take a moment to assess where you are, here at the end of this book on creativity.

Let's picture this journey as a spectrum of learning and action. At the extreme edge of the spectrum – let's say it's the left, just for easy visualization – you might have used the tools in this book to their fullest. You might have been primed and ready to run with what you've learned, and now you're sitting here with a completed first draft. Go, you! It's time to celebrate!

On the far right edge of our imaginary spectrum, you might have simply read this book and done nothing else. Maybe you even skipped some sections. You know what? I'm cheering you on, too! You deserve to celebrate! So many people have book ideas, creative yearnings, and flashes of inspiration, yet they repress them. They save them for later (like, for never). They don't even read a book about creativity. You're already ahead of the pack.

I'm imagining, though, that you're somewhere in the middle. Perhaps you did some of the exercises, or even all of them. You might have written them in a notebook, made notes in the margin of the book, or just thought about your answers. Maybe you did a little bit of writing. It's likely that you made at least a small start on your book. I'm cheering you on, as well! How will you celebrate your achievements?

You see, creativity, particularly when it's tied with personal spirituality, the elements of magick, and the cosmos, is a process.

It's not like you just force yourself to sit down and write. Although many people actually do that.

You've seen the ads, I'll bet. *WRITE YOUR BOOK IN 30 DAYS! FINISH YOUR MANUSCRIPT IN ONE WEEKEND!*

When I see those kinds of ads, I'm like, "But *why*?!" What's the hurry? Do you *really* think a book that's cranked out over a long weekend is going to be unique and life-changing?

I mean, it's possible. But not very likely. It makes me think of a yoga teacher I admire, who emphasizes the transitions between the yoga poses. She says that rather than forcing yourself into the pose, or swinging your body into it using momentum, it's much better to take time to learn how to use, and build, your core strength. She encourages students to see the body as one moving piece, rather than isolated groups of muscles. This helps you to build your flexibility, strength, and grace over time. It contributes to holistic wellness.

That's what we're doing here. I want your experience of writing a book – or doing some other big creative project – to be integrated into your life as a whole. I want you to be firmly connected to your Deep Self, to that endless wellspring of creativity that lives within each of us. I want you to share your wisdom, your stories, and your life experiences in a way that feels good to you and to the readers.

I delight in that moment when one of my clients tells me that she's come up with an idea for her second book – often while she's still writing the first one. Creativity is your birthright. We all have it in abundance when we're born into this life. Then the forces surrounding us begin to shut it down, often not intentionally.

My dream is for everyone to awaken to their own unique creativity, and to connect with the energy that powers the Universe. You can't do that when you're forcing it. It happens, I've found, in moments of play, silence, introspection, inspiration, and expansion. Our creativity gets powered up when we allow space for it on a regular basis. It is enhanced with the tools of spirituality – the fun ones. Notice I didn't say religion, which is often based more on dogma and structure. Creativity needs freedom and play and exploration.

I hope that you've found those things within the pages of this book. Please continue to let these tools awaken and sustain you. Keep this book handy and open it when you need some fresh inspiration. Answer some of the questions, even if you skipped them the first time around. Don't restrict yourself to my specific suggestions, but instead let them spark new ideas and games. Play with your creativity, your way. This book is intended to support you in that journey.

If you'd like more direct support, reach out to me. I'm here for you. Sometimes you just need the handholding and accountability of working with a coach. This is normal. We're not encouraged to think that it is, in our DIY culture, but it's okay.

You may not realize it yet, but your creative soul might be longing for a community of like-minded people. I've been joyfully gathering Thriving Artists who, like me, blossom within a supportive community.

In my world, there are plenty of options to get both support and community: Parallel PlayDates, virtual and in-person retreats, 1:1 coaching, and my signature group program. Perhaps by the time you read this, some of those containers will have changed, but the offer stands. If you're ready to dive in and would like a guide, let me know. The best way to reach me is via my website, nikkistarcatshields.com. My favorite social media platform right now is Instagram, and you can find me there @nikkistarcatshields.

I also encourage you to reach out to other creative and writing coaches. I'm certainly not the only one who combines spirituality and playfulness with creativity. Thank goodness! This is a movement. We're freeing our creative minds. Let those of us who stepped onto the path a little earlier show you what we've discovered, and again, let it spark your own ideas for your journey.

You don't have to do this alone. Wherever you are on that imaginary spectrum of learning and action, you're right where you're supposed to be. Get centered, listen inward, and see what inspired actions come forward. Then take those baby steps. Play. Celebrate. Do it again.

I'm sending you so much love. You are a creative, spiritual being who is already changing worlds for the better, from the inside out. Keep up the good play!

AFTERWORD

This volume is part of a series of books, called *Inspired Living*, centering around the chakras and on using the ancient wisdom associated with them to inspire more joy and freedom in your daily life. What are the chakras? Put simply, they are the power centers of your body's energy system. The concept of the chakras originated in ancient India, as part of a spiritual tradition that includes yogic philosophy and a focus on meditation. These spinning spheres of light help you to regulate your life on all levels. In the system I use, there are seven major chakras, lined up along the spine. Each is associated with not only a particular zone of the body, but also with certain basic areas of human life.

This book, *The Elements of Creativity*, focuses on the fifth or throat chakra. The Sanskrit name for this chakra is vishuddha, which translates to "especially pure." This chakra is associated with the clear expression of your creativity. It is located at the neck, near the cervical spine. While creativity is also connected with the second chakra, near the reproductive organs, the fifth chakra allows us to share our creativity with the outer world.

The color of the throat chakra is a clear sky blue. The element is Ether, which in the system we've been using throughout this book is known as Spirit. Ether, or Spirit, is vastly expansive and could even be perceived as "empty." In the realm of the fifth chakra, this sensation of emptiness creates room for our creativity, our truths, to shine forth.

Some of the key concepts of the throat chakra include communication, sound, music, vibration, self-expression, art, and clarity. It is where we both transmit and receive communication, from within and without. The throat chakra is the home of all of the creative arts, especially those of speaking and writing.

The energy of the throat chakra manifests as sound. Sound is made up of vibration, which also includes rhythm and pattern. The sacred texts of many religions, including Hinduism and Christianity, connect sound with creation. By speaking our authentic truths, whether aloud or in writing, we are sending out a vibration that reverberates throughout the cosmos. We step forth as conscious co-creators.

The physical area of the fifth chakra is, of course, the throat. There are other, minor, chakras between this and the sixth chakra (which is also known as the third eye center). These minor chakras encompass the sinus area, the eyes, and the ears. I mentioned in the introduction that my pure creative expression was interrupted as a preteen, when I became more focused on pleasing teachers with the "right" answers than I was on my creativity. At that time, and on into my early 20s, I suffered from multiple episodes of sinusitis, strep throat, and earaches. When your energy system gets blocked, you may experience physical symptoms or ailments that are meant to alert you to what's going on deep within. As an adult, since I began to write regularly again and share my writings, I haven't had any of these illnesses.

When the energies of the throat chakra are blocked, often the emotion that you're stuck on is guilt. Given what we've learned about our resistance, that makes sense. We might feel guilty for prioritizing our creativity, for not going the traditional route, for becoming lost in the realm of people-pleasing, for *not* prioritizing our creative work for so long, for ignoring our Younger Self, and/or other reasons. Releasing this guilt through doing the Shadow Work outlined within this book (and in the recommended resources) will allow you to more fully express your unique creative visions.

By embracing the healthy expression of your throat chakra, you are on the leading edge of the expansion of consciousness. Currently, our collective consciousness is rising from a focus on the third chakra, the will center, to the fourth chakra, or the heart chakra. As a Thriving Artist (or one who yearns to become one), you are taking this expansion further. Anchoring your throat chakra work in the heart center is useful when following your creative callings. It can help you to access your deepest truths and to express them with love and compassion. My book *The Heart of the Goddess* explores how to live soulfully, from the heart chakra. If you're drawn to learn more about the heart center, it's a helpful resource.

Rest assured that your creative ambitions are vital, both to you and to the entire planet. Whether or not you write a whole book, are ever published, or reach any kind of "best seller" status, your creativity matters. Remember, the very act of writing and speaking your truth sends out ripples in the pattern of existence. As you walk the path of the elements of creativity, may you joyfully embrace your unique stories, wisdom, and visions. You are an integral part of the whole. Together we are creating powerful positive change.

RESOURCES

Books on creativity, journaling, and the writing craft:

Baldwin, Christina, *Life's Companion: Journal Writing as a Spiritual Quest* (Bantam Books, New York, NY; 1991)

Cameron, Julia, *The Artist's Way: A Spiritual Path to Higher Creativity* (Jeremy P. Tarcher/Putnam, New York, NY; 1992)

Carroll, Ryder, *The Bullet Journal Method* (Portfolio/Penguin, New York, NY; 2018)

Ferriss, Timothy, *The 4-Hour Workweek* (Crown Publishers, New York, NY; 2007)

Gilbert, Elizabeth, *Big Magic: Creative Living Beyond Fear* (Riverhead Books, New York, NY; 2015)

Goins, Jeff, *Real Artists* Don't *Starve: Timeless Strategies for Thriving in the New Creative Age* (HarperCollins Leadership, Nashville, TN; 2017)

Goldberg, Natalie, *Writing Down the Bones* (Shambhala Publications, Boulder, CO; 1986)

Greene, Robert, *Mastery* (Penguin Books, New York, NY; 2012)

Grout, Pam, *Art & Soul, Reloaded* (Hay House, Carlsbad, CA; 2017)

King, Stephen, *On Writing: A Memoir of the Craft* (Scribner, New York, NY; 2000)

Kleon, Austin, *Steal Like An Artist* (Workman Publishing Company, New York, NY; 2012)

Moss, Robert, *The Three "Only" Things: Tapping the Power of Dreams, Coincidence, and Imagination* (New World Library, San Francisco, CA; 2007)

Osho, *Creativity: Unleashing the Forces Within* (St. Martin's Publishing Group, New York, NY; 2011)

Palmer, Amanda, *The Art of Asking* (Grand Central Publishing, New York, NY; 2014)

White, E.B. and William Strunk, Jr., *The Elements of Style* (MacMillan Publishing Co., Inc., New York, NY; 1959)

Yardley, Cathy, *Rock Your Plot* (CreateSpace Independent Publishing, Scotts Valley, CA; 2012)

Books on inner (including shadow) work, the elements, and magick:

Adler, Margot, *Drawing Down the Moon* (Viking Press, New York, NY; 1979)

Bolnick, Britt, *The Magick of Bending Time in Your Sacred Business* (In Arms Coaching, Saco, ME; 2021)

Coyle, T. Thorn, *Evolutionary Witchcraft* (TarcherPerigee, London, UK; 2005)

Cunningham, Scott, *Earth, Air, Fire & Water* (Llewellyn Publications, St. Paul, MN; 1991)

Cunningham, Scott, *Wicca: A Guide for the Solitary Practitioner* (Llewellyn Publications, St. Paul, MN; 1988)

Elliott, Carolyn, PhD, *Existential Kink: Unmask Your Shadow and Embrace Your Power* (Red Wheel Weiser, Newburyport, MA; 2020)

Hendricks, Gay, *The Big Leap: Conquer Your Hidden Fear and Take Life to the Next Level* (HarperCollins, New York, NY; 2009)

Moore, Jennifer Elizabeth, *Empathic Mastery* (Modern Medicine Lady LLC, North Yarmouth, ME; 2019)

Shields, N. Starcat, *Starcat's Corner: Essays on Pagan Living* (Moon Books, Winchester, UK; 2013)

Shields, Nikki Starcat, *The Heart of the Goddess* (Tidingdale Press, Hollis Center, ME; 2016)

Shields, Nikki Starcat, *Centered In Spirit: Crafting Your Daily Practice* (Tidingdale Press, Hollis Center, ME; 2015)

Shields, Nikki Starcat, *Cultivating Self-Love: Your Path to Wholeness* (Tidingdale Press, Hollis Center, ME; 2013)

Shields, Nikki Starcat and Brent BlackLion Nelson, *Follow the Ebb & Flow: The Law of Attraction and the Tides of Life* (Tidingdale Press, Hollis Center, ME; 2020)

Starhawk, *The Spiral Dance* (HarperCollins, San Francisco, CA; 1979)

Valiente, Doreen, *Witchcraft for Tomorrow* (Phoenix Publishing, Custer, WA; 1978)

Wolfe, Amber, *In the Shadow of the Shaman: Connecting with Self, Nature, and Spirit* (Llewellyn Publications, St. Paul, MN; 1988)

Wright-Popescul, Jean, *The Twelve Winds of the Ancient Gaelic World* (CCH Canadian, Ltd., Toronto, Ontario, Canada; 1997)

Books on Tarot:

Greer, Mary K., *Tarot for Your Self* (Newcastle Publishing Company, Hollywood, CA; 1984)

Jayanti, Amber, *Living the Tarot: Applying an Ancient Oracle to the Challenges of Modern Life* (Newcastle Publishing Company, Hollywood, CA; 1988)

Jodorowsky, Alejandro, *The Way of Tarot: The Spiritual Teacher in the Cards* (Destiny Books, Rochester, VT; 2004)

Louis, Anthony, *Tarot Plain and Simple* (Llewellyn Publications, St. Paul, MN; 1996)

Ziegler, Gerdy, *Tarot: Mirror of the Soul* (Red Wheel Weiser, Newburyport, MA; 1988)

My favorite Tarot and oracle decks:

Chris-Anne, *The Muse Tarot* (Hay House, Carlsbad, CA; 2020)

Crowley, Aleister and Lady Frieda Harris, *Thoth Tarot Deck* (U.S. Game Systems, Inc., Stamford, CT; 2005)

Fairchild, Alana and Autumn Skye Morrison, *Sacred Rebels Oracle: Guidance for Living a Unique & Authentic Life* (Llewellyn Publications, St. Paul, MN; 2015)

Franklin, Anna and Paul Mason, *The Sacred Circle Tarot* (Llewellyn Publications, St. Paul, MN; 2014)

Sams, Jamie and David Carson, *Medicine Cards: The Discovery of Power Through the Ways of Animals* (St. Martins Press, New York, NY; 1999)

Sterle, Lisa and Vita Ayala, *The Modern Witch Tarot Deck* (Sterling Ethos, New York, NY; 2019)

Books on yoga and meditation:

Desikachar, T.K.V., *The Heart of Yoga: Developing a Personal Practice* (Inner Traditions/Bear & Company, Rochester, VT; 1995)

Fuerstein, Georg, ed., *Living Yoga: A Comprehensive Guide for Daily Life* (Penguin Publishing, New York, NY; 1993)

Iyengar, B.K.S., *Light on Yoga* (Schocken Books, New York, NY; 1979)

Kempton, Sally, *Meditation for the Love of It* (Sounds True Publishing, Louisville, CO; 2011)

McAfee, John, *The Secret of the Yamas: A Spiritual Guide to Yoga* (Woodland Publications, Woodland Park, CO; 2001)

Salzberg, Sharon, *Real Happiness: A 28-Day Program to Realize the Power of Meditation* (Workman Publishing Company, New York, NY; 2019)

Books to read with a curious mind:

Allende, Isabel, *The House of the Spirits* (Alfred A. Knopf, New York, NY; 1982)

Angelou, Maya, *I Know Why the Caged Bird Sings* (Random House, New York, NY; 1969)

Binchy, Maeve, *Heart and Soul* (Knopf Doubleday Publishing Group, New York, NY; 2008)

Brown, Brene, *Rising Strong* (Random House, New York, NY; 2015)

Gaiman, Neil, *Stardust* (HarperCollins, New York, NY; 2006)

Gilbert, Elizabeth, *Eat Pray Love* (Penguin Publishing Group, New York, NY; 2006)

Hoffman, Alice, *Practical Magic* (Berkley Books, New York, NY; 2003)

McKillip, Patricia, *Winter Rose* (Ace Books, New York, NY; 1996)

Morgenstern, Erin, *The Starless Sea* (Knopf Doubleday Publishing Group, New York, NY; 2019)

Rothfuss, Patrick, *The Name of the Wind* (Gollancz, London, UK; 2007)

Sincero, Jen, *You are a Badass* (Running Press, Philadelphia, PA; 2013)

Websites:

Alchemy Anytime/The Alchemy of Core Beliefs https://www.felinedreamers.com/alchemy-anytime/

EFT: Empathic Mastery with Jennifer Moore, Jennifer Elizabeth Moore's YouTube channel https://www.youtube.com/@empathicmastery

EFT: Tap With Brad, Brad Yates' YouTube channel https://www.youtube.com/@tapwithbrad

About mind mapping https://tonybuzan.com/mind-maps

National Novel-Writing Month (aka NaNoWriMo) http://nanowrimo.org/

Yoga with Adriene YouTube channel https://www.youtube.com/@yogawithadriene

ABOUT THE AUTHOR

Nikki Starcat Shields is an author, book midwife (aka writing coach), and leader of transformational writing retreats. She loves to share ways to prioritize your creativity and spirituality, rooted in reverence and joy, even in the midst of a full, busy modern life. Nikki is a licensed priestess, practical mystic, and fae scholar of the mysteries.

Nikki has been a bookwyrm since birth, which helped her navigate life around her highly sensitive Virgo nature. Never having been part of any organized religion, she grew up immersed in the world of Mother Nature and the life of the imagination. She has been an actively practicing Pagan for more than 30 years, studying Buddhism and Eastern philosophy, yoga, Earth-based religions, Tarot, quantum metaphysics, spiritual alchemy, meditation, and Reiki healing. She is a Reflector in Human Design, which explains why she is such a strange unicorn.

Nikki's passions include creativity, magick, cats, books, Nature, dancing, swimming, drumming, art, and dreaming. She is a hippie-geek hybrid who loves The Grateful Dead *and* playing Dungeons & Dragons. She believes in freedom for all beings, loves diversity, and is always learning.

Her other books include *The Heart of the Goddess, Centered In Spirit: Crafting Your Daily Practice, Cultivating Self-Love: Your Path to Wholeness*, and *Starcat's Corner: Essays on Pagan Living*. She is also the co-author, with Brent

BlackLion Nelson, of *Follow the Ebb & Flow: The Law of Attraction and the Tides of Life*. Nikki walks her spiritual path in Maine and other faerie-approved lands. She can also be found at her website, www.nikkistarcatshields.com, or on her blog, Starcat's Corner, www.starcatscorner.com. Follow her on Instagram or TikTok @nikkistarcatshields.

Like what you've read? Join Nikki's email list to learn about new releases, retreats, coaching programs, and other offerings. www.nikkistarcatshields.com/join

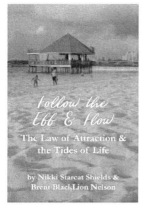

Follow the Ebb and Flow: The Law of Attraction and the Tides of Life
By Nikki Starcat Shields and Brent BlackLion Nelson

Follow the Ebb & Flow takes you through the seasonal transitions and moon phases, demonstrating how to harness natural energies to live your dreams. We've written this book to bridge the gap between neo-Pagan devotion to the natural world and Law of Attraction manifestation techniques. Learn how to use sympathetic magick to stay connected with the tides of life - the natural ebb and flow of the Universe.

https://amzn.to/3tSOP08

The Heart of the Goddess: A Handbook for Living Soulfully
By Nikki Starcat Shields

We are at the forefront of the peaceful revolution. You are part of The Heart of the Goddess, and you can learn to fully embody the qualities of the Feminine Divine in your daily life. We are the role models, teachers, wise women and men, those who will midwife the expansion of human consciousness. The Heart of the Goddess is a guidebook, a treasure map which will guide you to self-healing of old wounds and uplifting yourself and all your communities by being you fully. Will you heed your calling?

http://bit.ly/HeartoftheGoddess

Starcat's Corner: Essays on Pagan Living
By Nikki Starcat Shields

Starcat's Corner: Essays on Pagan Living by N. Starcat Shields is about walking a reverence-filled spiritual path in the midst of a hectic modern society. Rather than rehashing the basics of Paganism, Starcat shares wisdom rooted in her own experience. She answers the often-overlooked question, "How do you live your earth-based spirituality, day in and day out, particularly in a culture that doesn't share your values?" Shields offers insights to those who wish to enhance their personal spirituality, foster loving relationships, and live in harmony with the natural world.

"Starcat's Corner shows us how to bring earth-oriented spirituality to life in a very hands-on, real-world way." — L. Perry (USA)

http://bit.ly/StarcatsCornerEssays

Guided Meditations for Self-Care
By Nikki Starcat Shields and Brent BlackLion Nelson

These guided meditations are a wonderful tool to help you relax and explore your inner world. Go deeper within yourself and experience your personal divine connection. You'll bring back wisdom and energy that will help enrich your life every day.

https://www.felinedreamers.com/shop/audio/

282

Centered In Spirit: Crafting Your Daily Practice
By Nikki Starcat Shields

How do you cultivate a positive relationship with the Universe and create a life filled with more peace, joy, and meaning? The best way to begin is with a daily spiritual practice, one that fits you perfectly. Your practice might include meditation, gratitude, yoga, sacred play, or more – there are a myriad of choices.

In Centered In Spirit: Crafting Your Daily Practice, Nikki Starcat Shields offers a clear, simple method for designing a practice that fits into your lifestyle. Spirituality isn't "one size fits all." In order for it to become an essential part of your life, your daily practice needs to be tailored to your unique desires and circumstances. Starcat shows you how to create a spiritual practice that supports and delights you each day.

https://bit.ly/Centered-In-Spirit

Cultivating Self-Love: Your Path to Wholeness
By Nikki Starcat Shields

Want to live a more joyful, fulfilling life? One of the best things you can do is to learn to love yourself. Most of us have been taught to treat ourselves with disdain and criticism. Yet within you is a wellspring of love that, when you learn to tap into it, will increase your compassion, creativity, and joy. This book will lead you on a gentle journey to greater self-love and confidence.

"Once I finished it, I was excited to go back and read it again, more slowly so that I could truly absorb all of the amazing wisdom and start putting the concepts and ideas into practice." — D. Ford (USA)

"I couldn't simply skim the surface, I had to delve in, read slowly, and give each chapter time to digest and manifest. She's not preachy or complicated; to the contrary her wording is simple and clear..."
— K. Alley (USA)

http://bit.ly/CultivatingSelfLove

Made in United States
North Haven, CT
29 September 2023

42129677R00157